计算机英语实用教程

第2版

吕云翔◎编著

清华大学出版社
北京

内 容 简 介

本书是面向计算机及相关专业英语课程的教材,它全面介绍和讲解了深刻影响着我们生活的信息技术,既包括最新的科研成果、业界前沿课题和发展趋势,又有计算机文化典故和名人轶事。本书信息量大,知识性强,注重英语的听、说、读、写、译能力的全面培养和实际应用。各章内容均分为读与译、模拟写作、听与说三大部分;采用场景式教学和体验式学习相结合的方式,融合了角色扮演、多人会话和小组讨论等行之有效的训练方法。

本书适合国内各类院校计算机科学、软件工程等相关专业教学之用,也可作为其他相关专业或 IT 领域人员的自学参考用书。

本书封面贴有清华大学出版社防伪标签,无标签者不得销售。

版权所有,侵权必究。举报: 010-62782989, beiqinquan@tup.tsinghua.edu.cn。

图书在版编目(CIP)数据

计算机英语实用教程:中文、英文/吕云翔编著. —2 版. —北京:清华大学出版社,2022.4(2022.8重印)
ISBN 978-7-302-58477-3

Ⅰ.①计… Ⅱ.①吕… Ⅲ.①电子计算机－英语－教材－汉、英 Ⅳ.①H31

中国版本图书馆 CIP 数据核字(2021)第 121291 号

策划编辑:魏江江
责任编辑:王冰飞　李　晔
封面设计:刘　键
责任校对:李建庄
责任印制:朱雨萌

出版发行:清华大学出版社
　　　　网　　址:http://www.tup.com.cn, http://www.wqbook.com
　　　　地　　址:北京清华大学学研大厦 A 座　　　邮　编:100084
　　　　社 总 机:010-83470000　　　　　　　　　　邮　购:010-62786544
　　　　投稿与读者服务:010-62776969, c-service@tup.tsinghua.edu.cn
　　　　质量反馈:010-62772015, zhiliang@tup.tsinghua.edu.cn
　　　　课件下载:http://www.tup.com.cn,010-83470236
印　装　者:三河市铭诚印务有限公司
经　　销:全国新华书店
开　　本:185mm×260mm　　印　张:19.75　　字　数:478 千字
版　　次:2015 年 5 月第 1 版　2022 年 5 月第 2 版　印　次:2022 年 8 月第 2 次印刷
印　　数:1501～3500
定　　价:49.80 元

产品编号:090355-01

Preface 前言

《计算机英语实用教程》于 2015 年 5 月正式出版以来,经过了几次重印,许多高校将其作为"计算机英语"课程的教材,并深受这些学校师生的钟爱,获得了良好的社会效益。但从另外一个角度来看,作者有责任和义务维护好这本书的质量,及时更新本书的内容,做到与时俱进。

这些年来,信息技术突飞猛进,在云计算、大数据和人工智能等方面发展得越来越快。即使在前一版的文章中已经涉及的一些技术,由于有了进一步的发展,也有必要将其内容做出及时的更新。本书改动内容如下。

(1) 每一个单元"读与译"(Reading and Translating)中的文章,大部分都进行了更换。

(2) 每一个单元"模拟写作"(Simulated Writing)中的文章,几乎全部进行了更换,并且用中文来阐述。

(3) 每一个单元"听与说"(Listening and Speaking)中的文章,有一半进行了更换。

(4) 个别单元的题目略有改动。

(5) 每一个单元的练习题都有所改动。

希望通过这样的修改之后,教师和学生更喜欢本书;希望本书信息容量大,知识性强,注重英语的听、说、读、写、译能力的全面培养和实际应用的这些特点能够很好地延续下去。

资源下载提示

课件等资源:扫描封底的"课件下载"二维码,在公众号"书圈"下载。

听力原文等资源:扫描目录上方的二维码下载。

音频资源:扫描封底刮刮卡中的二维码,再扫描书中相应章节中的二维码可以在线学习。

本书的作者为吕云翔,曾洪立参与了部分内容的编写并进行了素材整理及配套资源制作等。

本书在编写的过程中得到了美国 Auburn 大学 Yvonne Williams 女士的指导,在此表示衷心的感谢。

吕云翔

2022 年 2 月于北京航空航天大学

Teaching Suggestions 教学建议

    本书共有12个单元,每个单元的训练都分为读与译、模拟写作和听与说几个部分。读与译部分包括云计算、物联网、人工智能、深度学习、机器学习、NoSQL、大数据、移动互联网、社交网络、5G等深刻影响着我们生活的信息技术的文章;模拟写作部分讲解IT常用文体写作方法,且在方法指导的基础上辅以实例;听与说部分是与各章主题相关的专题讨论,将计算机的相关知识与实际的场景对话相结合,旨在综合训练读者的听与说能力,并在对话中掌握计算机的相关知识。针对各部分的教学,教师可采用如下方式。

    读与译(Reading and Translating)部分:教师可让学生阅读文章(教师可根据文章的长短和难易程度来设定阅读的时间),并完成文章后的练习。之后教师公布练习答案,并讲解文章后的单词表、短语表和复杂句子来帮助学生进一步理解这篇文章。

    模拟写作(Simulated Writing)部分:教师可先让学生阅读写作方法指导,并配合本书的写作样例进行讲解和指导。教师还可根据实际情况设置场景,让学生根据写作指导并参照写作样例完成一篇类似的文章。如果课堂时间不够,教师可建议学生课下自学"模拟写作"部分。

    对话(Dialogue)部分:教师可先让学生听对话录音,并以提问的方式,引导学生根据所听信息概括对话的主要内容,让学生了解和学习对话中涉及的相关知识。然后,教师可将学生分成三人小组,让其中一组或两组(分别)朗读这段对话,并纠正学生的发音;或让一组或两组参照已有对话并通过替换右侧练习中的词语,组织完成一段类似的对话,并对学生完成的情况加以点评。

    短文听力理解(Listening Comprehension)部分:教师可先让学生听短文录音和短文后的问题,让学生根据所听内容选择正确的答案。若播放一遍短文学生感觉有难度,教师可酌情增加录音播放次数。教师最后公布答案,并且讲解相应的单词和短语及句子,解释这篇短文的重点和难点。另外,可让学生读一遍原文。

    听写(Dictation)部分:教师可根据实际情况播放1~3遍短文录音,让学生根据所听内容填空,将文章补充完整。文章填充完整后,教师最后公布答案,并且讲解相应的单词和短语及句子,解释这篇短文的重点和难点。另外,可让学生读一遍原文。

    本书的教学安排建议如下。

章　　节	内　　容	学　时　数
Unit 1	Introduction to Computers	3～4
Unit 2	Hardware	3～4
Unit 3	Software	3～4
Unit 4	Operating Systems	3～4
Unit 5	Computer Programming	3～4
Unit 6	Database	3～4
Unit 7	Computer Network	3～4
Unit 8	The Internet and World Wide Web	3～4
Unit 9	Ecommerce	3～4
Unit 10	Computer Security and Privacy	3～4
Unit 11	Software Engineering	1～4
Unit 12	Artificial Intelligence	1～4

建议理论教学时数：32～48 学时。

教师可以按照自己对计算机英语的理解适当地增减一些章节，也可以根据教学目标，灵活地调整章节的顺序，增减各章的学时数。

理论授课学时数 32～48 学时包含课堂讨论、练习等必要的课内教学环节。建议授课时间比例为：读与译部分 40%，模拟写作部分 20%，听与说部分 40%。

Contents 目录

随书资源

Unit 1　Introduction to Computers ········· 001

- Part 1　Reading and Translating ········· 002
  - Section A：Cloud Computing ········· 002
  - Section B：The Internet of Things ········· 008
- Part 2　Simulated Writing：Uncovering the Secrets of Clear Writing（I） ········· 014
- Part 3　Listening and Speaking ········· 018
  - Dialogue：Buying a New Notebook Computer 🎧 ········· 018
  - Listening Comprehension：Quantum Computer 🎧 ········· 021
  - Dictation：John von Neumann 🎧 ········· 022

Unit 2　Hardware for Systems ········· 024

- Part 1　Reading and Translating ········· 025
  - Section A：Random Access Memory（RAM）：The Genius of Memory ········· 025
  - Section B：Touch Screen Technology：How the Screen Is So Smart ········· 030
- Part 2　Simulated Writing：Uncovering the Secrets of Clear Writing（II） ········· 035
- Part 3　Listening and Speaking ········· 038
  - Dialogue：How Radio Frequency Identification（RFID）Readers Work 🎧 ········· 038
  - Listening Comprehension：Moore's Law 🎧 ········· 042
  - Dictation：Sensors Get Data We Never Had Before 🎧 ········· 042

Unit 3　Software for Systems ········· 045

- Part 1　Reading and Translating ········· 046
  - Section A：Web Apps and Mobile Apps ········· 046
  - Section B：Cloud Software ········· 050
- Part 2　Simulated Writing：Communicating with E-mail and Memos（Ⅰ） ········· 056
- Part 3　Listening and Speaking ········· 059
  - Dialogue：Making an Electronic Album Using Multimedia Editing Software 🎧 ········· 059
  - Listening Comprehension：IDE 🎧 ········· 061

Dictation: Open Source Software 062

Unit 4　Operating Systems 064

Part 1　Reading and Translating 065
　　　　Section A: Roles of an Operating System 065
　　　　Section B: Mobile versus Desktop Operating Systems 069
Part 2　Simulated Writing: Communicating with E-mail and Memos（Ⅱ） 074
Part 3　Listening and Speaking 077
　　　　Dialogue: Talking about Operating Systems 077
　　　　Listening Comprehension: Android 079
　　　　Dictation: Linus Torvalds and the Software Nobody Knows 080

Unit 5　Computer Programing 083

Part 1　Reading and Translating 084
　　　　Section A: Web Application Development 084
　　　　Section B: Mobile App Development 089
Part 2　Simulated Writing: Communicating with Social Media 094
Part 3　Listening and Speaking 098
　　　　Dialogue: Getting to Know Java Runtime Environment (JRE) and
　　　　　　　　　Java Virtual Machine (JVM) 098
　　　　Listening Comprehension: Writing the Code 101
　　　　Dictation: Agile Software Development 102

Unit 6　Database 104

Part 1　Reading and Translating 105
　　　　Section A: Normalization: Ensuring Data Consistency 105
　　　　Section B: NoSQL Databases 109
Part 2　Simulated Writing: Using Presentation Software to Write 116
Part 3　Listening and Speaking 121
　　　　Dialogue: Why is Big Data a Challenge 121
　　　　Listening Comprehension: Data Mining 124
　　　　Dictation: Data Warehouse 125

Unit 7　Computer Network 127

Part 1　Reading and Translating 128
　　　　Section A: OSI Reference Model: The Driving Force behind
　　　　　　　　　Network Communications 128
　　　　Section B: Ethernet (802.3) 134
Part 2　Simulated Writing: Writing Professional Letters（Ⅰ） 138

Contents

Part 3 Listening and Speaking ········· 144
    Dialogue: Setting up Wireless Network 🎧 ········· 144
    Listening Comprehension: IPv6 🎧 ········· 146
    Dictation: Router 🎧 ········· 147

Unit 8 The Internet and World Wide Web ········· 149

Part 1 Reading and Translating ········· 150
    Section A: Social Networking ········· 150
    Section B: 5G Internet: Transforming the Global Business Landscape ······ 156
Part 2 Simulated Writing: Writing Professional Letters (Ⅱ) ········· 163
Part 3 Listening and Speaking ········· 166
    Dialogue: Knowing the Myths about the Internet 🎧 ········· 166
    Listening Comprehension: How a World-Shaking Technology Came About:
    Tim Berners-Lee Invents the World Wide Web 🎧 ········· 169
    Dictation: How Web Search Engines Work 🎧 ········· 170

Unit 9 Ecommerce ········· 172

Part 1 Reading and Translating ········· 173
    Section A: How to Use Online AI—Artificial Intelligence for
           Ecommerce ········· 173
    Section B: Ecommerce Lessons for Why Amazon is so Successful ········· 179
Part 2 Simulated Writing: Writing for Employment (Ⅰ) ········· 186
Part 3 Listening and Speaking ········· 189
    Dialogue: Protecting Buyer's Privacy with Online Payment Services 🎧 ··· 189
    Listening Comprehension: Social Commerce 🎧 ········· 192
    Dictation: Mobile Payments 🎧 ········· 193

Unit 10 Computer Security and Privacy ········· 195

Part 1 Reading and Translating ········· 196
    Section A: Ways to Protect Your Personal Information Online ········· 196
    Section B: Using Computer Forensics against Cybercrime ········· 200
Part 2 Simulated Writing: Writing for Employment (Ⅱ) ········· 205
Part 3 Listening and Speaking ········· 210
    Dialogue: Using Antivirus Software 🎧 ········· 210
    Listening Comprehension: Hacker and Cracker 🎧 ········· 213
    Dictation: Trojan Horses 🎧 ········· 214

Unit 11 Software Engineering ········ 216

Part 1 Reading and Translating ········ 217
  Section A：How Software Engineering Works ········ 217
  Section B：Testers and Programmers Working Together ········ 221
Part 2 Simulated Writing：Progress Report ········ 227
Part 3 Listening & Speaking ········ 230
  Dialogue：Using Object-Oriented Analysis and Design Method 🎧 ········ 230
  Listening Comprehension：Extreme Programming 🎧 ········ 233
  Dictation：Unified Modeling Language（UML）🎧 ········ 234

Unit 12 Introduction to Artificial Intelligence ········ 236

Part 1 Reading and Translating ········ 237
  Section A：Benefits and Risks of Artificial Intelligence ········ 237
  Section B：Deep Learning, Machine Learning，and AI ········ 242
Part 2 Simulated Writing：Meeting Minutes ········ 248
Part 3 Listening and Speaking ········ 251
  Dialogue：Artificial Intelligence 🎧 ········ 251
  Listening Comprehension：Supervised Learning 🎧 ········ 255
  Dictation：Unsupervised Learning 🎧 ········ 256

Glossary ········ 258

Abbreviations ········ 280

Answers ········ 283

Bibliography ········ 301

Part 1

Reading and Translating

Section A: Cloud Computing

Cloud computing is **on-demand** access, via the Internet, to computing resources—applications, servers (physical servers and virtual servers), data storage, development tools, networking capabilities, and more—**hosted** at a remote data center managed by a cloud services provider (or CSP). The CSP makes these resources available for a monthly subscription fee or **bills** them according to usage.

If you use a computer or mobile device at home or at work, you almost certainly use some form of cloud computing every day, whether it's a cloud application like Google Gmail or Salesforce, streaming media like Netflix, or cloud file storage like Dropbox.

Compared to traditional **on-premises** IT, and depending on the cloud services you select, cloud computing helps do the following:

- Lower IT costs: Cloud lets you **offload** some or most of the costs and effort of purchasing, installing, configuring, and managing your own on-premises infrastructure.

- Improve **agility** and **time-to-value**: With cloud, your organization can start using enterprise applications in minutes, instead of waiting weeks or months for IT to respond to a request, purchase and configure supporting hardware, and install software. Cloud also lets you empower certain users—specifically developers and data scientists—to help themselves to software and support infrastructure.

- Scale more easily and **cost-effectively**: Cloud provides elasticity—instead of purchasing excess capacity that sits unused during slow periods, you can **scale** capacity **up and down** in response to **spikes** and **dips** in traffic. You can also take advantage of your cloud provider's global network to spread your applications closer to users around the world.

CLOUD COMPUTING SERVICES

SaaS (Software-as-a-Service)

SaaS—also known as cloud-based software or cloud applications—is application software that's hosted in the cloud and that you access and use via a Web browser, a **dedicated** desktop client, or an **API** that integrates with your desktop or mobile operating system. In most cases, SaaS users pay a monthly or annual subscription fee; some may offer "**pay-as-you-go**" pricing based on your actual usage.

Unit 1 Introduction to Computers

PaaS (Platform-as-a-Service)

PaaS provides software developers with on-demand platform—hardware, complete software stack, infrastructure, and even development tools—for running, developing, and managing applications without the cost, complexity, and inflexibility of maintaining that platform on-premises.

With PaaS, the cloud provider hosts everything—servers, networks, storage, operating system software, middleware, databases—at their data center. Developers simply pick from a menu to "spin up" servers and environments they need to run, build, test, deploy, maintain, update, and scale applications.

IaaS (Infrastructure-as-a-Service)

IaaS provides on-demand access to fundamental computing resources—physical and virtual servers, networking, and storage—over the Internet on a pay-as-you-go basis. IaaS enables end users to scale and shrink resources on an as-needed basis, reducing the need for high, up-front capital expenditures or unnecessary on-premises or "owned" infrastructure and for overbuying resources to accommodate periodic spikes in usage.

In contrast to SaaS and PaaS (and even newer PaaS computing models such as containers and serverless), IaaS provides the users with the lowest-level control of computing resources in the cloud.

Serverless computing

Serverless computing (also called simply serverless) is a cloud computing model that offloads all the backend infrastructure management tasks—provisioning, scaling, scheduling, patching—to the cloud provider, freeing developers to focus all their time and effort on the code and business logic specific to their applications.

What's more, serverless runs application code on a per-request basis only and scales the supporting infrastructure up and down automatically in response to the number of requests. With serverless, customers pay only for the resources being used when the application is running—they never pay for idle capacity.

TYPES OF CLOUD COMPUTING

Public cloud

Public cloud is a type of cloud computing in which a cloud service provider makes computing resources—anything from SaaS applications, to individual virtual machines (VMs), to bare metal computing hardware, to complete enterprise-grade infrastructures and development platforms—available to users over the public Internet.

The public cloud provider owns, manages, and assumes all responsibility for the data centers, hardware, and infrastructure on which its customers' workloads run, and it typically provides high-bandwidth network connectivity to ensure high performance and rapid access to applications and data.

Private cloud

Private cloud is a cloud environment in which all cloud infrastructure and computing resources are dedicated to, and accessible by, one customer only. Private cloud combines many of the benefits of cloud computing—including elasticity, scalability, and ease of service delivery—with the access control, security, and resource customization of on-premises infrastructure.

Many companies choose private cloud over public cloud because private cloud is an easier way (or the only way) to meet their regulatory compliance requirements. Others choose private cloud because their workloads deal with confidential documents, intellectual property, personally identifiable information, medical records, financial data, or other sensitive data.

Hybrid cloud

Hybrid cloud is just what it sounds like—a combination of public and private cloud environments. Specifically, and ideally, a hybrid cloud connects an organization's private cloud services and public clouds into a single, flexible infrastructure for running the organization's applications and workloads.

The goal of hybrid cloud is to establish a mix of public and private cloud resources—and with a level of **orchestration** between them—that gives an organization the flexibility to choose the optimal cloud for each application or workload and to move workloads freely between the two clouds as circumstances change. This enables the organization to meet its technical and business objectives more effectively and cost-efficiently than it could with public or private cloud alone.

Multicloud and hybrid multicloud

Multicloud is the use of two or more clouds from two or more different cloud providers. Having a multicloud environment can be as simple using email SaaS from one vendor and image editing SaaS from another. But when enterprises talk about multicloud, they're typically talking about using multiple cloud services—including SaaS, PaaS, and IaaS services—from two or more of the leading public cloud providers.

Hybrid multicloud is the use of two or more public clouds together with a private cloud environment.

Organizations choose multicloud to avoid vendor lock-in [1], to have more services to choose from, and to access to more innovation. But the more clouds you use—each with its own set of management tools, data transmission rates, and security protocols—the more difficult it can be to manage your environment. Multicloud management platforms provide visibility across multiple provider clouds through a central **dashboard**, where development teams can see their projects and deployments, operations teams can keep an eye on clusters and nodes, and the cybersecurity staff can monitor for threats.

Figure 1-1 shows these four types of cloud computing.

Cloud security

Traditionally, security concerns have been the primary obstacle for organizations considering cloud services, particularly public cloud services. In response to demand,

Unit 1　Introduction to Computers

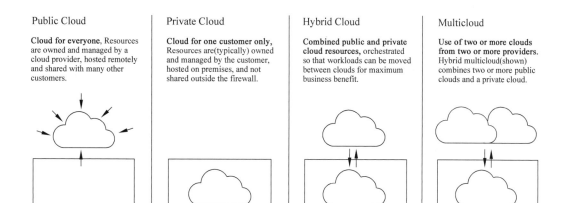

Figure 1-1 Four types of cloud computing

however，the security offered by cloud service providers is steadily **outstripping** on-premises security solutions.

 **Words**

on-demand 按需的,随需应变的
host[həust] v. 主办,主持（活动）
bill[bil] v. 发账单（要求付款）
on-premise 部署,预置
offload[ˌɔfˈləud] v. 减轻（负担）
agility[əˈdʒiliti] n. 灵敏性,敏捷
time-to-value 价值转换
cost-effective 有成本效益的
spike[spaik] n. 猛增
dip[dip] n. （使）下降
dedicated[ˈdedikeitid] v. 专用的,专门用途的
pay-as-you-go 先使用后付费

as-needed 按需的
up-front 预付的
accommodate[əˈkɔmədeit] v. 考虑到,顾及
provision[prəˈviʒn] v. 为……提供所需物品
per-request 每个请求
assume[əˈsjuːm] v. 承担（责任）
orchestration[ˌɔːkiˈstreiʃn] n. 和谐的结合
dashboard[ˈdæʃbɔːd] n. 仪表板
outstrip[ˌautˈstrip] v. 超过,胜过

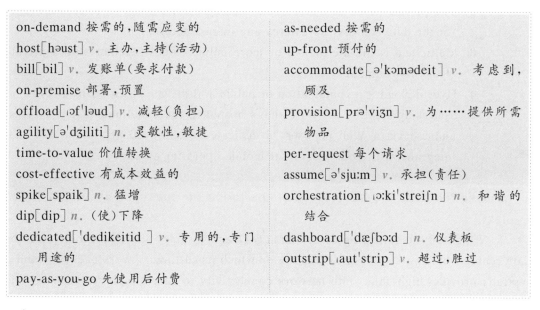 **Phrases**

scale up 增加
scale down 缩小
spin up 启动

Abbreviations

| API | Application Programming Interface | 应用程序接口 |

 Notes

［1］ 厂商陷阱（vendor lock-in，供应商套牢，供应商陷阱，厂商泥潭）：使一个系统过于依赖于外部所提供的组件/部件。

 Exercises

Ⅰ. Read the following statements carefully, and decide whether they are true (T) or false (F) according to the text.

____ 1. Public cloud is a cloud environment in which all cloud infrastructure and computing resources are dedicated to, and accessible by, one customer only.

____ 2. The private cloud provider owns, manages, and assumes all responsibility for the data centers, hardware, and infrastructure.

____ 3. Multicloud is the use of two or more public clouds together with a private cloud environment.

____ 4. Hybrid cloud is a combination of public and private cloud environments.

____ 5. SaaS is application software that's hosted in the cloud and that you access and use via a Web browser, a dedicated desktop client, or an API that integrates with your desktop or mobile operating system.

Ⅱ. Choose the best answer to each of the following questions according to the text.

1. Which of the following owns, manages, and assumes all responsibility for the data centers, hardware, and infrastructure on which its customers' workloads run, and it typically provides high-bandwidth network connectivity to ensure high performance and rapid access to applications and data?

  A. Private cloud provider   B. Public cloud provider
  C. Free cloud provider   D. None of the above

2. How many types of cloud computing are shown in Figure 1-1?
  A. One   B. Two   C. Three   D. Four

3. Which of the following is application software that's hosted in the cloud and that you access and use via a Web browser, a dedicated desktop client, or an API that

Unit 1 Introduction to Computers

integrates with your desktop or mobile operating system?

    A. PaaS   B. IaaS   C. HaaS   D. SaaS

Ⅲ. **Identify the letter of the choice that best matches the phrase or definition.**

    a. processing
    b. Uniform Resource Locator(URL)
    c. tablet computer
    d. computer
    e. Web site

    ____ 1. A collection of related Web pages usually belonging to an organization or individual.

    ____ 2. An Internet address, usually beginning with http：// that uniquely identifies a Web page.

    ____ 3. A programmable, electronic device that accepts data input, performs processing operations on that data, and outputs and stores the results.

    ____ 4. A portable computer about the size of a notebook that is designed to be used with a digital pen.

    ____ 5. Performing operations on data that has been input into a computer to convert that input to output.

Ⅳ. **Fill in the numbered spaces with the words or phrases chosen from the box. Change the forms where necessary.**

store	official	continue	seek	secret
view	notify	own	enforce	send

Is Data Stored in the Cloud Free from Prying Eyes?

    At an ever increasing rate, companies and individuals store Web sites and data in the cloud. For example, those who utilize Web-based email store their ____1____ and received email messages in the email provider's cloud environment. Those who use corporate or private email servers do not store their communications in the cloud. Important legal rulings highlight the differences between the two approaches for storing email messages. Law ____2____ agencies consider email ____3____ in the cloud to belong to the company that owns the cloud service, often an Internet access provider.

    Email stored on a private email server, however, is the property of the company or individual who ____4____ the server. When the law enforcement ____5____ need to read someone's email on a private email server, they must obtain a warrant that outlines exactly the information being ____6____. In the cloud, however, law enforcement officials simply may need to request the information from the company that owns the cloud service. The user might not be ___7___ of the search until up to 90 days later; further, the search may occur without limitations and may include ___8___ monitoring of an individual's email. While the government takes a liberal approach to ___9___ one's email in the cloud, individuals who ___10___ read others' email messages may be subject to felony computer crimes.

Ⅴ. Translate the following passage into Chinese.

Cloud Computing

As the demand for computing resources increases, companies may find that using outside computing resources is more economical than building new computing capacity internally. Cloud computing is a new technology that provides flexible and massive online computing power. Cloud computing is an Internet service that provides computing needs to computer users. For example, an employee working during the day in California could use computing power in a Paris network system located in an office that is closed for the evening. When the company uses the computing resources, they pay a fee based on the amount of computing time and other resources that they consume, much in the way that consumers pay utility companies, such as the electric company, based on how much electricity they use. Cloud computing allows a company to diversify its network and server infrastructure. Some cloud computing services automatically add more network and server capacity to a company's Web site as demand for services of the Web site increases. The network and server capacity may be duplicated around the world so that, for example, an outage of a single server does not affect the company's operations.

Section B: The Internet of Things

Many of us have **dreamed of** smart homes where our appliances do our **bidding** automatically. The alarm sounds and the coffee pot starts **brewing** the moment you want to start your day. Lights **come on** as you walk through the house. Some unseen computing device responds to your voice commands to read your schedule and messages to you while you get ready, then turns on the TV news. Your car drives you to work via the least congested route, **freeing** you **up** to **get caught up** on your reading or prep for your morning meeting while **in transit**.

We've read and seen such things in science fiction for decades, but they're now either already possible or on the brink of **coming into being**. And all this new tech is forming the basis of what people are calling the Internet of Things.

The Internet of Things (IoT), also sometimes referred to as the Internet of Everything (IoE), consists of all the Web-enabled devices that collect, send and act on data they acquire from their surrounding environments using embedded sensors, processors and communication hardware (Figure 1-2). These devices, often called "connected" or "smart" devices, can sometimes talk to other related devices, a process called machine-to-machine (M2M) communication, and act on the information they get from one another. Humans can interact with the **gadgets** to set them up, give them instructions or access the data, but the devices do most of the work on their own without human intervention. Their existence has been made possible by all the tiny mobile components that are available these days, as well as the always-online nature of our home and business networks.

Figure 1-2　The Internet of Things

Connected devices also generate massive amounts of Internet traffic, including loads of data that can be used to make the devices useful, but can also be mined for other purposes. All this new data, and the Internet-accessible nature of the devices, raises both privacy and security concerns.

But this technology allows for a level of real-time information that we've never had before. We can monitor our homes and families remotely to keep them safe. Businesses can improve processes to increase productivity and reduce material waste and unforeseen **downtime**. Sensors in city infrastructure can help reduce road congestion and warn us when infrastructure is in danger of **crumbling**. Gadgets out in the open can monitor for changing environmental conditions and warn us of **impending** disasters.

These devices are **popping up** everywhere, and these abilities can be used to enhance nearly any physical object.

The phrase "Internet of Things" was coined by Kevin Ashton, likely in 1999 as the title of a corporate presentation he made at his place of employment, Proctor & Gamble[1]. During his time there, Ashton **came up with** the idea of putting a **RFID** [2] tag on each **lipstick** and having them communicate with a radio receiver on the shelf to track sales and inventory and signal when **restocking** was needed. He **posits** that such data collection can be used to solve lots of problems in the real world.

Billions of connected devices are part of the Internet of Things. They use built-in hardware and software to send and receive data via various communication protocols. They might use our smartphones as their gateway to the Internet, connect to some other piece of hardware in our homes that's acting as a hub or connect directly through our home Internet service. They often send data to cloud-computing servers where it's then aggregated and analyzed. We can usually access the results via apps or browsers on our mobile devices or home computers. Some can even be set up to update your status on various social networks.

Despite the fact that most of us do not have smart homes full of interacting gadgets yet, the IoT is already quite huge. The estimates are all over the place, with researchers likely using different criteria for inclusion, but by some accounts, there are already between 50 and 25 billion connected devices, with the count expected to grow to anywhere from 50 to 212 billion by 2020. Some analysts even estimate that there will be around a trillion connected devices by 2025.

As huge as that number is, it seems less implausible when you realize that you can embed or attach sensors and tiny computing equipment to just about anything. Many of us have a smartphone, a device used as an access point for many connected gadgets, that's also an IoT device in its own right. Wearable fitness trackers are fairly common, too. And embedded processing, sensing and communication equipment is being added to nearly any device you can think of, from bathroom scales to refrigerators — even shoes. Smart thermostats, smoke alarms and security cameras can track your habits to help you save on energy bills, let you remotely see camera views of your home, send you a warning when something isn't right and make it easy to contact emergency services. You can even buy small tags to put on and track anything from your car keys to your pets and kids.

Lots more connected devices are either out already or hitting the market soon. Right now, we are likely to have a smattering of smart devices that we can interact with individually (often via separate phone apps), but that for the most part don't work in conjunction with one another. However, companies and industry groups are working to create standards and platforms to make it easier for all these devices to be programmed to work together more seamlessly, as well as to improve security. Outside the home, lots of industries and cities are adopting, or have already adopted, technologies that add to the Internet of Things, too.

Once there are more devices that can work with other devices, even those from different manufactures, we'll be able to automate lots of mundane tasks. We've essentially given common physical objects both computing power and senses. They can take readings from our surrounding environment (even our own bodies) and use the data to change their own settings, signal other devices to do so and aggregate it for us to peruse. A lot of them perform actions based on complex algorithms, not just the simple if-then directions of past embedded computing, that either occur within their own processors or on cloud servers.

There is still lots of innovation going on, so all these smart gadgets are bound to enable things we're not even considering right now.

 Words

bidding['bidiŋ] n. 吩咐,投标
brew[bru:] v. 煮(咖啡),酿制(啤酒),沏(茶)
gadget['gædʒit] n. 小装置,小器具
downtime['dauntaim] n. 停止运行时间
crumble['krʌmbl] v. 坍塌,损坏
impending[im'pendiŋ] adj. 即将发生的,迫在眉睫的
lipstick['lipstik] n. 口红,唇膏
restock[,ri:'stɔk] v. 补充(货源)
posit['pɔzit] v. 认为……为实
protocol['prəutəkɔl] n. (数据传递的)协议

gateway['geitwei] n. 网关
aggregate['ægrigət, 'ægrigeit] v. 总计,合计
around[ə'raund] adv. 大约
implausible[im'plɔ:zəbl] adj. 似乎不合情理的,不像真实的
scale[skeil] n. 磅秤
out[aut] adj. 面市的
mundane[mʌn'dein] adj. 单调的,平凡的
peruse[pə'ru:z] v. 细读,研读

 Phrases

dream of 渴望,梦想
come on (机器或系统)开始工作
free up 使解脱出来,使空出来
get caught up 被卷入,卷入到
in transit 在运送途中
come into being 开始存在
pop up 突然出现,冷不防冒出
come up with 提出(计划、想法等)
just about 几乎
hit the market 打入市场
a smattering of 少数,少量
in conjunction with 连同……,与……一起
be bound to 注定

011

Notes

[1] 宝洁公司(Proctor & Gamble)是 1837 年由威廉·普罗克特和詹姆斯·甘布尔两人在美国中西部的辛辛那提创办的主要生产肥皂和蜡烛的公司,两人的姓氏作为公司的名称一直沿用至今。宝洁公司目前是世界上最大的洗涤和护肤保健品制造商。

[2] 无线射频识别(Radio Frequency IDentification,RFID)即射频识别技术是自动识别技术的一种,通过无线射频方式进行非接触双向数据通信,利用无线射频方式对记录媒体(电子标签或射频卡)进行读写,从而达到识别目标和数据交换的目的,其被认为是 21 世纪最具发展潜力的信息技术之一。

 Exercises

Ⅰ. Read the following statements carefully, and decide whether they are true (T) or false (F) according to the text.

____ 1. The phrase "Internet of Things" was coined by Bill Gates from Microsoft.

____ 2. The Internet of Things (IoT) is also sometimes referred to as the Internet of Environment (IoE).

____ 3. Some analysts even estimate that there will be around a billion connected devices by 2025.

____ 4. M2M means Man-to-Man.

____ 5. The Internet of Things (IoT) consists of all the Web-enabled devices that collect, send and act on data they acquire from their surrounding environments using embedded sensors, processors and communication hardware.

Ⅱ. Choose the best answer to each of the following questions according to the text.

1. Who coined the phrase "Internet of Things"?
   A. Bill Gates   B. Steven Jobs
   C. Kevin Ashton   D. Mark Zuckerberg

2. When was the phrase "Internet of Things" coined?
   A. 1975   B. 1982   C. 1992   D. 1999

3. Which of the following description is right?
   A. The Internet of Things (IoT) is also sometimes referred to as the Internet of Environment (IoE).
   B. M2M means Man-to-Man.
   C. The Internet of Things (IoT) consists of all the Web-enabled devices that collect, send and act on data they acquire from their surrounding environments using embedded sensors, processors and communication hardware.

Unit 1 Introduction to Computers

D. Some analysts even estimate that there will be around a billion connected devices by 2025.

Ⅲ. **Identify the letter of the choice that best matches the phrase or definition.**
   a. wearable device
   b. Internet of Things
   c. mobile app
   d. RFID
   e. NFC

   ____ 1. Type of wireless connection that uses close-range radio signals to transmit data between NFC-enabled devices.
   ____ 2. Technology that uses radio signals to communicate with a tag placed in or attached to an object, an animal, or a person.
   ____ 3. An application you download from a mobile device's application store or other location on the Internet to a smartphone or other mobile device.
   ____ 4. Small mobile computing consumer device designed to be worn and that often communicate with a mobile device or printer.
   ____ 5. Term that describes an environment where processors are embedded in every product imaginable (things), and those 'things' communicate with each other via the Internet.

Ⅳ. **Fill in the numbered spaces with the words or phrases chosen from the box. Change the forms where necessary.**

   | efficient | high | access | agriculture | aware |
   | export | advantage | implant | develop | bring |

Does the Internet of Things Discriminate?

   Technology experts expect that the advantages __1__ by the expansion of the Internet of Things (IoT) will enhance the comfort, safety, and __2__ of a large population across the globe. Where does that leave people who are struggling to make ends meet? What about those who live in __3__ countries?

   Among the IoT technologies that exist or are in development include the following examples. Students can find accurate information quickly and use cloud-based apps to store data so that it is __4__. The coordination of traffic lights based on GPS data will lead to a lessening of commute times. Wearable and __5__ devices can collect and communicate health-related data. Sensors that monitor temperature, air and water quality and usage, and more, will reduce home ownership costs and security risks.

____6____ devices can monitor, track, and provide assessment of livestock and crops to lower costs and improve access to food.

Individuals or countries that cannot afford these and other IoT-related technologies may feel a negative impact as others take advantage of the effects brought by these technologies. Students without access to these technologies could be at a ____7____. Workers with shorter travel times may enjoy a better quality of life.

Those who cannot afford health-related devices may be at ____8____ risk for illnesses or medical complications. Homeowners without IoT-enabled homes may be more prone to dangers, such as fires. Countries involved in agricultural ____9____ may lose business as others are able to reduce costs.

As costs of these technologies decrease, it is likely that the divide between the more and less fortunate will decrease. ____10____ of the impact of the inequalities also may give rise to nonprofits or organizations that focus on providing IoT technologies to a larger population.

Ⅴ. Translate the following passage into Chinese.

How will the Internet of Things (IoT) Affect Our Daily Lives?

The Internet of Things (IoT) is one of the more intriguing topics on where technology is going and how it will impact almost every aspect of our daily lives. We are already seeing technology with embedded Internet connectivity emerge in things like cars, buildings, and more in order to develop a conversation between devices, the user, and the devices around them. While most IoT applications today are focused on information and entertainment, we foresee a big advancement in safety when cars are able to not only avoid traffic but also avoid accidents by getting "smarter" and having constant dialogue with other cars and the environment around them.

Part 2

Simulated Writing: Uncovering the Secrets of Clear Writing (I)

好的作者不是天生的。他们通过不断地练习和对细节的关注来培养自己的技能。我们也可以通过同样的方式来成为一个好的作者——不断练习并关注细节。我们培养出来的能够清晰明了地写作的技能会使我们在整个职业生涯中受益。一些人误以为清晰地写作就是文档里没有一点儿错误(比如拼写或语法错误)。清晰地写作实际上是指能够在最好地满足读者的需求和兴趣的情况下进行沟通。一个书写良好的文档具有特定的目的、明晰的观点，将支持性和相关性信息组织得富有逻辑，并且语法正确。

1. 使书面交流变得清晰明了

各个领域的专业人士必须能够在写作时清晰、简要并完整地表达想法。如果书面表达不清晰或者缺少重要的细节，读者会迷惑不解并且不能恰当地给出回复。要想清晰地写作，确保完成以下任务：准备、撰写以及修订，如图1-3所示。

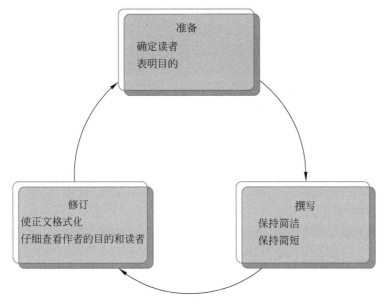

图1-3　清晰写作的过程

在开始写作之前，复习一下以下指导准则。

1）了解读者

以识别典型的读者来开始写作工作。通常情况下，作者需要帮助读者明白文档的主题和想法，说服他们支持文档的观点，或者动员他们采取行动。如果刚开始就从读者的角度而不是作者自己的角度来思考某个主题，那么作者就可以成功。如果文档很长、很复杂，或者非常重要，可以起草一个读者概况，写作的时候作为参考。

在与读者的经历和理解相关的理想情况下，作者的作品不会令读者感到惊讶。相反，作者应该增加读者的知识储备，并且和他们一起探索另一种想法。一个技能高超的作者可以确定他的读者所了解的主题并基于此来引入新的概念。考虑读者的经历可以帮助作者使写作更清晰明了，更易于理解，并且更具有相关性。

2）明确目标

在开始写作之前，要确定文档的确切目的。为什么要写作并且期望获得什么？大多数专业写作的目的都是为了告知某事，例如，宣布开会、概述决策或者列出流程。许多企业文档的目的都是为了说服，例如，为了说服经理或者同事，激励员工，或者刺激消费者采取行动。写作的时候，重复检查以确保每一个句子以及每一段话都有助于实现目标。

3）保持简洁

专业的写作应该是高效的，也就是说，易于阅读和理解。使文字、句子和段落简短并切中要点。去掉模糊用语和不必要的文字可以使文档"瘦身"。密切注意长句子并认真复查任何长于两行的内容。表1-1列出了使作品清晰明了的注意事项。

表 1-1　使作品清晰明了的注意事项

指导准则	适合提到	尽量避免
了解读者	• 确定是写给同事、决策者还是消费者 • 考虑有多少读者已经知道文档的主题 • 指出读者可以从这个文档中获得的好处	• 忽略次要读者 • 因为文档短而跳过此步骤
与读者关联	• 描述典型的读者 • 期待读者的反应 • 使文档符合读者 • 使用合适的词汇和语气 • 直接使用"你"来指代读者	• 使用不适合读者的语言,比如术语或缩写 • 选择可能被理解为偏见的词汇 • 忘了语气 • 仅仅关注需求和目标
明确目标	• 确定文档的目的 • 指出想要利用这个文档获得什么	• 包含不能满足目标的句子
保持简洁	• 使用简短、常见的词汇 • 使用短句子和段落	• 使用模糊或者不必要的词语 • 包含长于两行的句子
使文档具有吸引力	• 良好地组织并格式化文档,使其吸引读者	• 将文档格式化为一个大段的文本

4）使文档具有吸引力

读者会积极地确定是否去阅读作者已经准备的文档。影响该决定的一个重要因素就是作品看起来怎么样。那些使用清晰的书面语并使用了具有吸引力的布局的文档更吸引人,并且更有可能被人阅读。相反,大段的文档会吓跑读者,并且减少他们认真思考作者作品的机会。

总而言之,作品可以遵循以下指导准则：从读者角度出发,专注于能够满足目标的信息,并且仔细地选择语言。

2. 掌握标点符号

当和某人谈话时,说话的方式会传达很多意思。停顿、语调抑扬变化以及语速等会帮助表达想法并使意思清晰。书面交流使用一组称作标点的符号来实现这些任务,并且帮助读者解释文字。最常用的标点符号是句号、逗号和问号。表 1-2 总结了使用逗号和冒号时的注意事项。图 1-4 展示了某些类型的标点实例。

表 1-2　使用逗号和冒号时的注意事项

标点符号元素	适合提到	尽量避免
逗号	• 引出介绍性文字 例如,Generally, employees arrive on time • 列出一系列条目 例如,She writes, copies, and prints the articles • 使独立分句分开 例如,The Web page is colorful, but it doesn't provide much information	• 省略最后一个逗号,如果省略了,则会导致歧义 • 使用逗号将没有 FANBOYS 的独立分句分开
冒号	• 引出一个列表、例子或者引用 例如,You'll receive the following items at the conference: handouts, samples, and exhibition passes • 在商务信函中表示问候语的结束 例如,Dear Mr. Wolff: • 将标签(号)或短标题和文字信息分开 例如: Subject: Budget decisions	• 插入一个冒号,除非一边的文字形成了一个完整的句子

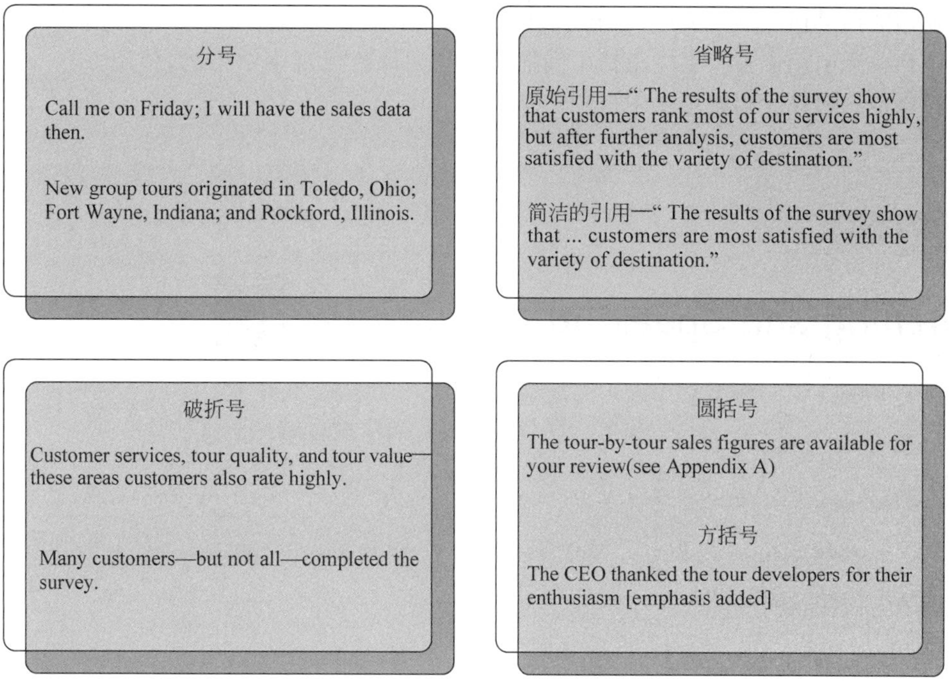

Unit 1　Introduction to Computers

分号

Call me on Friday; I will have the sales data then.

New group tours originated in Toledo, Ohio; Fort Wayne, Indiana; and Rockford, Illinois.

省略号

原始引用—" The results of the survey show that customers rank most of our services highly, but after further analysis, customers are most satisfied with the variety of destination."

简洁的引用—" The results of the survey show that ... customers are most satisfied with the variety of destination."

破折号

Customer services, tour quality, and tour value—these areas customers also rate highly.

Many customers—but not all—completed the survey.

圆括号

The tour-by-tour sales figures are available for your review(see Appendix A)

方括号

The CEO thanked the tour developers for their enthusiasm [emphasis added]

图 1-4　某些类型的标点实例

1）句号（。）和问号（？）

使用句号来结束一个完整的句子，甚至在项目符号列表或者编号列表中使用。使用问号来结束一个问句。

2）逗号（，）

插入逗号是向读者展示哪些词语在句子中是同属于一类。逗号的典型用法包括引出介绍性文字，列出 3 个或以上的一系列项目，使得用"for""and""not""but""or""yet""so"（这些都是连词，有时缩写为 FANBOYS）连接的独立分句分开。

3）分号（；）

当想要连接两个独立分句并且不使用像"and"或者"so"这样的连词，但要展示它们在意思上相关的时候使用分号。独立分句具有一个主语和一个动词，并且可以独立成句。

4）冒号（：）

使用冒号可以使读者意识到后面的信息是对当前想法的解释或提高。例如，一个冒号通常可以引出一个列表、例子或者引用。

5）省略号（…）

省略号表明已经省略了引用的一个或者多个单词。如果省略号出现在引用的句子的末尾，应在省略号之后加一个句号。

6）破折号（—）

插入破折号来引出或者强调句子的某一部分。一个单独的破折号强调紧随其后的内容；一对破折号强调包含在它们之间的内容。

7）圆括号（ ）和方括号[ ]

使用圆括号插入某一关注，对句子的意思来说不是必需的。也可以在圆括号中包含附加的解释或者引用。当想要在段落中间插入自己的评论或观察结果时，使用方括号。这些评论通常用来解释或阐明正文中提到的想法。

转 35 页

Part 3

Listening and Speaking

Dialogue: Buying a New Notebook Computer

(*After class, Sophie & Henry are standing by the door, waiting for Mark.*)

Henry: Excuse me, Sophie. May I ask you some questions about computers?

Sophie: Sure. What can I do for you?

Henry: I want to buy a new **notebook computer**, but I'm not sure which kind is better, the traditional notebook or **ultrabook**. What do you think?[1]

Sophie: Let me see. In my view, although these two categories of notebook computers have the same general appearance, they vary greatly in power, storage capacity, weight, and battery life. It depends on[2] your uses.

Henry: Well, I am a regular user. I need a desktop replacement and **portable** computer. I typically run office software, use the Internet, and listen to music.

Sophie: I see. My advice is that you should purchase an affordable traditional notebook computer that includes the following **specs**: middle-tier processors—not the fastest but not the slowest either; 8-GB of RAM; a 500-GB hard drive; and a 15-inch screen.

[1] Replace with:
1. What's your opinion on it?
2. What's your take on it?
3. What's your view on it?

[2] Replace with:
1. relies on
2. depends upon

Unit 1　Introduction to Computers

Henry: Is it expensive?

Sophie: Approximately $800 to $1000 currently. For maximum savings, as well as compatibility with most software, many buyers choose Windows-based PCs.

(When they are talking, Mark comes toward them.)

Sophie & Henry: Hi, Mark.

Mark: Hi, Henry and Sophie.

Sophie: You are just on time. Just before we were talking about Henry's buying a notebook computer. I heard that you want to purchase a new one also.

Mark: Yes. I am a power user. I need a portable computer that can handle the latest video games or process-intensive operations such as video editing, engineering, and design. Sophie, what do you recommend?

Sophie: I see. Well, I suggest that you should purchase a traditional notebook computer that includes the following minimum specs: the fastest categories of processors with large number of cores and high GHz count; a graphical processor (GPU) outside of the main CPU; 16-GB of RAM; a 1-TB hard drive; and a 17-inch screen.

Mark: How much does it cost?[3]

[3] Replace with:
1. How much does it take?
2. How much is it?
3. How much?

Sophie: Approximately $1000 to $1500, perhaps more. For games, many individuals choose Windows-based PCs. The video and design industries usually use Macs. What else do you want[4] to know?

Henry: Well, if I want a small, lightweight computer that I can carry, and hope it has a long battery life for extended use, can I purchase a computer like that?

[4] Replace with:
1. What else would you like
2. What other things do you want

Sophie:	Yes. You can purchase an ultrabook with 11- to 13-inch screen, **solid-state** hard drive, 8-GB RAM, and weight under 4 pounds.	3. What other things would you like
Mark:	I guess it is very expensive.	
Sophie:	Not really, $700 to $1000. Many ultrabooks will not include a DVD drive. Windows-based ultrabooks tend to [5] be more affordable. The MacBook is slightly more expensive, but it has always been considered a leader in the lightweight notebook field.	[5] Replace with: 1. are prone to 2. are inclined to 3. have a tendency to
Mark:	Ok, we've got it. Sophie, thanks for your valuable suggestions.	
Sophie:	My pleasure.	

 Exercises

Work in a group, and make up a similar conversation by replacing the statements with other expressions on the right side.

 Words

ultrabook 超薄笔记本电脑
portable[ˈpɔːtəbl] *adj.* 便携式的，易携带或移动的
specs[speks] *n.* 说明，规格（spec 的名词复数），规范

compatibility[kəmˌpætiˈbiliti] *n.* 兼容性，适合性
core[kɔː] *n.* 核，核心，芯
count[kaunt] *n.* 计数，计算
solid-state 固态的

Phrases

notebook computer 笔记本型电脑，笔记本式计算机，笔记型电脑
power user 高级用户，超级用户
outside of 在……的外面

Unit 1 Introduction to Computers

Listening Comprehension: Quantum Computer

Listen to the article and answer the following 3 questions based on it. After you hear a question, there will be a break of 15 seconds. During the break, you will decide which one is the best answer among the four choices marked (A), (B), (C) and (D).

Questions

1. What is the meaning of "a blend or superposition of these classical states"?
   (A) A qubit can exist as 0 or 1 alternatively
   (B) A qubit can exist as both 0 and 1 simultaneously
   (C) A qubit can exist as 0 or 1 in multiple bits
   (D) A qubit can exist as 0 or 1 in a classical bit

2. What kind of problems does quantum computer particularly fit for?
   (A) Problems about physical phenomenon in nature
   (B) Problems with three different states
   (C) Problems with a large amount of data or variables
   (D) Problems with not binary but rather more quaternary

3. What is the prospect of quantum computer according to this article?
   (A) Negative
   (B) Affirmative
   (C) Indifferent
   (D) Paradoxical

Words

quantum['kwɔntəm] *n.* 量子,量子论	coefficient[ˌkəui'fiʃnt] *n.* 系数
staple['steipl] *n.* 主要产品,日常必需品	uncrackable[ʌn'krækəbl] *adj.* 不可破解的
cage[keidʒ] *v.* 将……放入,将……限制于	cipher['saifə(r)] *n.* 密码
qubit 量子比特	infancy['infənsi] *n.* 初期
quaternary[kwə'tɜːnəri] *adj.* 四进制的	cryptography[krip'tɔgrəfi] *n.* 密码使用法,密码系统
superposition[ˌsjuːpəpə'ziʃn] *n.* 重叠	

Phrases

come of age 成熟,发达

Dictation: John von Neumann

This article will be played three times. Listen carefully, and fill in the numbered spaces with the appropriate words you have heard.

John von Neumann (1903—1957) was unquestionably one of the most **brilliant** scientists of the ___1___. He was born in Budapest, Hungary, in 1903. In 1930 he joined the Princeton Institute for Advanced Study. He became a U.S. ___2___ in 1937, and during the Second World War **distinguished** himself with his work in weapons development. In 1955 he was named a Commissioner of the Atomic Energy Commission, a position he held up to his death from cancer in 1957.

Von Neumann made major contributions to quantum **mechanics** and ___3___ physics and is perhaps best known for his work in the ___4___ of computers during his all-too-short ___5___ in computer science since 1943. In the now famous **EDVAC** report of 1945, von Neumann clearly stated the idea of a ___6___ program that **resides** in the computer's ___7___ along with the data it was to ___8___ on.

Instead of the ENIAC—the first ___9___ computer **unveiled** in 1946—having program instructions **rewired** in for each new ___10___ (typically requiring a half-day at least to prepare the machine for operation), stored-program computer kept its ___11___ instructions in its memory, storing the information in the same ___12___ as it would store any other information. **To this end**, the computer would necessarily contain five basic components: a ___13___, memory, a ___14___ (CPU), and input and output components for interacting with human users. The control unit would **delve** into memory, ___15___ an instruction or ___16___, and deal with what it found ___17___. Stored-program computer was an ___18___ over and was far more flexible than its **predecessor**. Moreover, its ___19___ has become the prototype of most of its **successors**, including the ___20___ of modern computers which exist to this day. Von Neumann's name has also become **synonymous** with modern computer architecture.

Words

brilliant['briljənt] *adj.* 超群的, 杰出的
distinguish [dis'tiŋwiʃ] *v.* 使杰出, 使
  著名
mechanics[mi'kæniks] *n.* 力学
reside[ri'zaid] *v.* 居住
unveil[ʌn'veil] *v.* 公布
rewire[ri:'waiə] *v.* 重接电线

delve[delv] *v.* 挖掘
predecessor['pri:disesə] *n.* 前任,(被取
  代的)原有事物
successor[sək'sesə] *n.* 后继者,后续
  事物
synonymous[si'nɔniməs] *adj.* 同义的

Unit 1　Introduction to Computers

 Phrases

to this end 为此

 Abbreviations

EDVAC　Electronic Discrete Variable Automatic Computer　离散变量自动电子计算机

Unit 2

Hardware for Systems

Unit 2　Hardware for Systems

Reading and Translating

Section A: Random Access Memory (RAM): The Genius of Memory

Inside your computer, RAM takes the form of separate microchip modules that plug in slots on the computer's motherboard. These slots connect through a line (bus) or set of electrical paths to the computer's processor. Before you turn on a computer, its RAM is a blank slate. As you start and use your computer, the operating system files, programs, and any data currently being used by the processor are written to and stored in RAM so that the processor can access them quickly.

How is this data written to and stored in RAM? In the most common form of RAM, Dynamic Random Access Memory (DRAM), transistors(in this case, acting as switches) and a capacitor(as a data storage element)create a memory cell, which represents a single bit of data.

Memory cells are etched onto a silicon wafer in a series of columns (bit lines) and rows (word lines), known as an array. The intersection of a column and row constitutes the address of the memory cell (Figure 2-1). Each memory cell has a unique address that can be found by counting across columns and then counting down by row. The address of a character consists of a series of memory cell addresses put together.

To write data to RAM, the processor sends the memory controller the address of a memory cell in which to store data. The memory controller organizes the request and sends the column and row address in an electrical charge along the appropriate address lines, which are very thin electrical lines etched into the RAM chip. [1] This causes the transistors along those address lines to close.

These transistors act as a switch to control the flow of electrical current in an either closed or open circuit. While the transistors are closed, the software sends bursts of electricity along selected data lines. When the electrical charge traveling down the data line reaches an address line where a transistor is closed, the charge flows through the closed transistor and charges the capacitor.

A capacitor works as electronic storage that holds an electrical charge. Each charged capacitor along the address line represents a 1 bit. An uncharged capacitor represents a 0 bit. The combination of 1s and 0s from eight data lines forms a single byte of data.

The capacitors used in dynamic RAM, however, lose their electrical charge. The

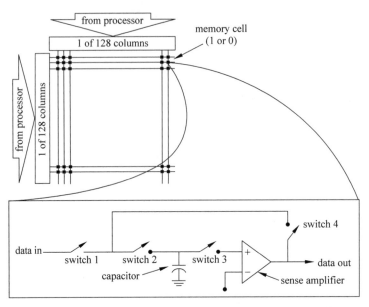

Figure 2-1　An illustration of one type of DRAM. When writing data, switches 1 and 2 in the circuit are closed and switches 3 and 4 are open. When reading data, switches 2,3,and 4 in the circuit are closed and switch 1 is open. Most DRAM chips actually have arrays of memory cells (upper-left corner of figure) that are 16 rows deep.

processor or memory controller continuously has to recharge all of the capacitors holding a charge (a 1 bit) before the capacitor **discharges**. During this refresh operation, which happens automatically thousands of times per second, the memory controller reads memory and then immediately rewrites it. This refresh operation is what gives dynamic RAM its name. Dynamic RAM has to be refreshed continually, or it loses the charges that represent bits of data. A specialized circuit called a counter tracks the refresh sequence to ensure that all of the rows are refreshed.

　　The process of reading data from RAM uses a similar, but reverse, series of steps. When the processor gets the next instruction it is to perform, the instruction may contain the address of a memory cell from which to read data. This address is sent to the memory controller. To locate the memory cell, the memory controller sends the column and row address in an electrical charge down the appropriate address lines.

　　This electrical charge causes the transistors along the address line to close. At every point along the address line where a capacitor is holding a charge, the capacitor discharges through the circuit created by the closed transistors, sending electrical charges along the data lines.[2]

　　A specialized circuit called a sense amplifier determines and amplifies the level of charge in the capacitor. A capacitor charge over a certain voltage level represents the binary value 1; a capacitor charge below that level represents a 0. The sensed and amplified value is sent back down the address line to the processor.

As long as a computer is running, data continuously is being written to and read from RAM. As soon as you shut down a computer, RAM loses its data. The next time you turn on a computer, operating system files and other data are again loaded into RAM and the read/write process starts *all over*.

Words

bus[bʌs] n. （计算机的）总线
slate[sleit] n. 石板，板岩
capacitor[kəˈpæsitə(r)] n. 电容器，电容
etch[etʃ] v. 蚀刻，侵蚀

wafer[ˈweifə(r)] n. 薄片，圆片，晶片
burst[bɜːst] n. 短暂的突然发作，一阵
charge[tʃaːdʒ] v. 使充电，收费
discharge[disˈtʃaːdʒ] v. 放电

Phrases

take the form of 表现为……的形式，采取……的形状
bit line 位线，数元线
word line 字线
work as 充当，担任
all over 到处，浑身

Notes

[1] **Original**: The memory controller organizes the request and sends the column and row address in an electrical charge along the appropriate address lines, which are very thin electrical lines etched into the RAM chip.
Translation：存储器控制器可将这些存储数据的请求组织起来，并通过沿着合适的地址线——蚀刻在 RAM 芯片上的很细的电线——发送电荷中的列和行的地址。

[2] **Original**: At every point along the address line where a capacitor is holding a charge, the capacitor discharges through the circuit created by the closed transistors, sending electrical charges along the data lines.
Translation：沿着电容器存放电荷的地址线上的每个点，电容器通过由闭合的晶体管所构成的电路来放电，并沿着数据线发送电荷。

Exercises

Ⅰ. Read the following statements carefully, and decide whether they are true (T) or false (F) according to the text.

____ 1. After you switch off a computer, RAM still keeps its data.

____ 2. A capacitor charge over a certain voltage level represents the binary value 0.

____ 3. A single byte of data consists of the combination of 1s and 0s from eight data lines.

____ 4. A series of memory cell addresses put together form the address of a character.

____ 5. An uncharged capacitor represents a 1 bit.

Ⅱ. **Choose the best answer to each of the following questions according to the text.**

1. Which of the following works as electronic storage that holds an electrical charge?

   A. External storage

   B. Controllers for video display

   C. Capacitor

   D. Peripheral devices

2. Which of the following components can make it access the operating system files, programs, and any data currently being used by it written to and stored in RAM?

   A. Power connectors

   B. Processor

   C. Expansion card slots

   D. Non-volatile memory chips

3. Which of the following is right about a capacitor?

   A. Each charged capacitor along the address line represents a 1 bit

   B. A capacitor works as electronic storage that holds an electrical charge

   C. An uncharged capacitor represents a 0 bit

   D. All of the above

Ⅲ. **Identify the letter of the choice that best matches the phrase or definition.**

a. ASCII

b. byte

c. parallel processing

d. RAM (random access memory)

e. Universal Serial Bus (USB)

____ 1. A processing technique that uses multiple processors or processing cores simultaneously, usually to process a single job as fast as possible.

____ 2. A fixed-length, binary coding system used to represent text-based data for computer processing on many types of computers.

____ 3. A group of 8 bits.

____ 4. A universal bus used to connect up to 127 peripheral devices to a computer without requiring the use of additional expansion cards.

____ 5. Chips connected to the motherboard that provide a temporary location for the computer to hold data and program instructions while they are needed.

Ⅳ. **Fill in the numbered spaces with the words or phrases chosen from the box. Change the forms where necessary.**

> lifetime   recognize   develop patent   legacy miniature
> microchip   award   credit   influence

Jack Kilby—Integrated Circuit Inventor

Jack Kilby is ___1___ with being one of the more ___2___ people in the world. He was ___3___ more than 60 patents during his ___4___, but none changed society as much as the one for his integrated circuit, or ___5___, that made microprocessors possible. His Nobel Prize in physics, awarded in 2005, ___6___ his part in the invention of the integrated circuit.

Kilby started his work with ___7___ electrical components at Centralab, where he developed transistors for hearing aids. He then took a research position with Texas Instruments and ___8___ a working model of the first integrated circuit, which was ___9___ in 1959. Kilby applied this invention to various industrial, military, and commercial applications, including the first pocket calculator. Kilby died in 2005, but his ___10___ lives on.

Ⅴ. **Translate the following passage into Chinese.**

Why does a Smartphone Need a Dual-core Processor?

Dual core processors allow smartphones to deliver increased performance, while delivering better battery life. The reason for this is that the tasks that run on a smartphone have widely different performance needs; for instance, compare writing an SMS text message with playing a 3D game.

To provide this scalability of performance and power in today's advanced chip manufacturing processes such as 28 nm (1 nm 1 billionth of a meter), it is better to have multiple smaller cores versus one large monolithic core. With dual-core processors, you can switch one core off for tasks such as SMS (to save power), and then you can switch both cores on when maximum performance is needed.

Section B: Touch Screen Technology: How the Screen Is So Smart

Touch screen technology is becoming a larger part of everyday life for many individuals. As we know, a touch screen is a touch-sensitive display device that users can interact with by touching areas of the screen. People have been using touch screens for more than 50 years, and this technology now is being used in more places, such as in smart phones, point-of-sale terminals, automated teller machines, remote controls, GPS receivers, home security systems, and Tablet PCs.

Touch screen technology has evolved since its creation in the late 1960s. The first touch screens developed allowed users to press only one area at a time with the tip of their finger, and they were much less accurate than today's touch screens. [1] As the technology is advancing, users are able to perform additional tasks: such as dragging their finger across the screen and touching more than one area of the screen at a time. For example, the iPhone and iPod touch allow you to zoom in pictures or other objects on the screen by placing two fingers close together on the screen, and then slowly moving them apart. Three types of touch screens most in use today are capacitive, resistive, and surface wave touch screens.

A capacitive touch screen has a layer of material that stores electrical charges coating the surface. When a finger touches the screen, it conducts a small amount of the electrical charge, reducing the charge on the capacitive layer. Circuits located at each corner of the capacitive touch screen measure the change in electrical charge. The circuits then send this data to the touch screen controller, or software that is running on the computer. The controller then uses the data to calculate the location where the finger is touching the screen. Capacitive touch screens typically are high-quality and unaffected by items that do not conduct electrical charges. An example of the components of a capacitive touch screen is shown in Figure 2-2.

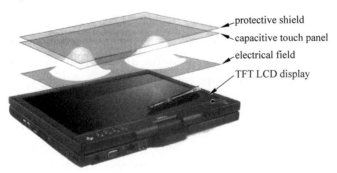

Figure 2-2 A capacitive touch screen identifies where someone touches the screen by measuring differences in electrical charges.

The second type of touch screen is a resistive touch screen. A metallic conductive and resistive layer held apart by spacers covers a resistive touch screen. When a user touches a resistive touch screen, the conductive and resistive layers connect in the location of the touch. An electronic current runs between the two layers, and the interruption in the current enables the touch screen controller to calculate the exact location of the touch. Although resistive touch screens usually are more affordable than capacitive touch screens, they are not as clear and can be damaged more easily.

The third type of touch screen uses surface wave technology. Surface wave technology passes ultrasonic waves over the touch screen. Touching the screen absorbs portions of the waves, which then allows the touch screen controller to calculate the position at which the object touched the screen. [2] Because ultrasonic waves pass over the touch screen, it is easy for outside elements to damage the device. Touch screens using surface wave technology are the most advanced and often the most expensive of the three types.

Additional types of touch screen technologies exist, but they are not used as widely as the capacitive, resistive, and surface wave touch screens. Optical touch screens use cameras mounted at two corners of the screen to detect objects close to the surface. Infrared touch screens use light emitting diodes and light detectors at the edges of the touch screen to detect objects that break the beams of light traveling across the screen.

As touch screen prices continue to decrease, they most likely will be incorporated in an increasing number of computers and devices. Touch screens have increased productivity by allowing people to interact with devices more quickly than they can with a mouse or keyboard.

Words

point-of-sale 销售点的,售货点的
capacitive[kə'pæsitiv] adj. 电容性的
resistive[ri'zistiv] adj. 抗(耐、防)……的,电阻的
coat[kəut] v. 给……涂上(或盖上、裹上)
metallic[mə'tælik] adj. 金属的,金属性的

spacer['speisə] n. 垫片,隔圈,隔离物,衬垫
affordable[ə'fɔːdəbl] adj. 买得起的,价格实惠的,经济适用的,价格适中的
infrared[ˌinfrə'red] adj. 红外线的
diode['daiəud] n. 二极管

Phrases

automated teller machine 自动出纳机,自动柜员机
remote control 遥控,远程控制,遥控装置
Tablet PC 平板电脑,平板型计算机
zoom in 拉近,放大
electrical charge 电荷

Abbreviations

GPS   Global Position System   全球定位系统,导航系统

 Notes

[1] **Original**:The first touch screens developed allowed users to press only one area at a time with the tip of their finger, and they were much less accurate than today's touch screens.
Translation:最初研制的触摸屏仅允许用户用手指一次触摸一个区域,并且它们的准确性和今日的同类产品相比相差甚远。

[2] **Original**:Touching the screen absorbs portions of the waves, which then allows the touch screen controller to calculate the position at which the object touched the screen.
Translation:当触摸屏幕时,部分声波会被吸收,从而使得触摸屏控制器可以计算出对象触摸屏幕的位置。

 Exercises

Ⅰ. **Read the following statements carefully, and decide whether they are true(T) or false(F) according to the text.**

_____ 1. The first touch screens developed were more accurate than today's touch screens.

_____ 2. Touch screens have decreased productivity by allowing people to interact with devices more quickly than they can with a mouse or keyboard.

_____ 3. Additional types of touch screen technologies are used as widely as the capacitive, resistive, and surface wave touch screens.

_____ 4. Capacitive, resistive, and surface wave touch screens are three types of touch screens most in use today.

_____ 5. A resistive touch screen has a layer of material that stores electrical charges coating the surface.

Ⅱ. **Choose the best answer to each of the following questions according to the text.**

1. When has touch screen technology evolved since its creation?
   A. in the late 1990s
   B. in the late 1970s

C. in the late 1960s

D. in the late 1980s

2. Which of the following is wrong about surface wave technology?
    A. It is easy for outside elements to damage the device because ultrasonic waves pass over the touch screen.
    B. The most advanced of the three types is touch screens using surface wave technology.
    C. Surface wave technology passes ultrasonic waves over the touch screen.
    D. Touch screens using surface wave technology are the cheapest of the three types.

3. Which of the following is right about a capacitive touch screen?
    A. Capacitive touch screens typically are low-quality.
    B. Although capacitive touch screens usually are more affordable than resistive touch screens, they are not as clear and can be damaged more easily.
    C. Capacitive touch screens typically are affected by items that do not conduct electrical charges.
    D. Optical touch screens is not used as widely as capacitive touch screens.

Ⅲ. Identify the letter of the choice that best matches the phrase or definition.
   a. cache
   b. flash memory
   c. multicore
   d. Plug and Play
   e. port
   _____ 1. A generic term that is associated with the ability to attach any device onto a computer and have it play or work immediately.
   _____ 2. A type of multiprocessor chip that provides two or more separate and independent CPUs.
   _____ 3. A socket for external devices to connect to the system unit.
   _____ 4. A type of memory that provides a combination of features of RAM and ROM.
   _____ 5. A type of memory that improves processing by acting as a temporary high-speed holding area between the memory and the CPU.

Ⅳ. **Fill in the numbered spaces with the words or phrases chosen from the box. Change the forms where necessary.**

> short   build   say   compute   locate
> bank   instead   announce   center   pay

Where Are Data Centers Located?

Some data centers are ___1___ close to their power source, such as secluded sites in Oregon near the power generators on the Columbia River, where Google, Yahoo!, Facebook, and Amazon have ___2___ enormous server farms. Others may be right near your neighborhood.

___3___ and high-frequency stock traders in New York City insist that the servers they use be as close to them as possible. "___4___ distances make for quicker trades," explains a New York Times accountant, and microseconds can mean millions of dollars made or lost. As a result, companies are ___5___ top dollar to lease server space in buildings across the Hudson River in New Jersey, in places such as Weehawken, Secaucus, and Mahwah.

___6___ the Times: When the [data] centers opened in the 1990s as quaintly termed Internet hotels; the tenants paid for space to plug in their servers with a proviso that electricity would be available. As ___7___ power has soared, so has the need for power, turning that relationship on its head: electrical capacity is often the ___8___ element of lease agreements, and space is secondary.

In June 2012 the online auction company eBay ___9___ it would build a new data center in South Jordan, Utah, that would rely less on coal-fired electricity to run. ___10___, it would use energy fuel cells.

Ⅴ. **Translate the following passage into Chinese.**

Cache Memory

It is instructive to compare the memory facilities within a computer in relation to their functionality. Registers are used to hold the data immediately applicable to the operation at hand; main memory is used to hold data that will be needed in the near future; and mass storage is used to hold data that will likely not be needed in the immediate future. Many machines are designed with an additional memory level, called cache memory. Cache memory is a portion (perhaps several hundred KB) of high-speed memory located within the CPU itself. In this special memory area, the machine attempts to keep a copy of that portion of main memory that is of current interest. In this setting, data transfers that normally would be made between registers and main memory are made between registers and cache memory. Any changes made to cache memory are then transferred collectively to main memory at a more opportune time. The result is a CPU that can execute its machine cycle more rapidly because it is not delayed by main memory communication.

Part 2

Simulated Writing: Uncovering the Secrets of Clear Writing (II)

接 18 页

3. 说明数据

当需要对比数据时,可以使用图表来说明。使用图形来表示数据可以使信息更易于理解和记忆。图形可以使数字信息有意义,可揭示其背后的趋势和模式,简化复杂的关系,并为文档增加视觉吸引力。要熟悉最流行的图表类型、它们的优缺点,以及什么时候使用它们才合适。表 2-1 列出了在企业文档中使用图表的注意事项。

表 2-1 使用图表的注意事项

图表类型	适合提到	尽量避免
条形图和柱状图	• 展示随时间变化的数据 • 比较项目 • 在比较持续时间时选择柱状图	• 比较过多的项目,5 个或 6 个是比较典型的上限 • 当类别有很长的名字时不要使用条形图,而是使用柱状图
线形图	• 展示数据的趋势或模式	• 如果数值被均匀分割,使用线形图,例如按月或年划分
饼图	• 展示一类数据的大小相对于其他类和整体的比例	• 在饼图中展示多于一个类别的数据
过程图	• 展示过程中的步骤 • 使用常见的形状来表示过程中的部分	• 改变常见形状的意义
组织结构图	• 展示一个组织中的汇报关系	• 在图内的每个方框中包含过多的细节

1) 条形图和柱状图

条形图和柱状图表示以间距归类的分类数据和数字数据,例如,每月的销售额或每个产品的费用。条形图的每一个类别都包含一个横条,并且,每一个条形的高度或长度代表着那一类别的值。柱状图与其相似,只是使用纵向的条形。图 2-3 展示了柱状图的实例。

2) 线形图

线形图揭示了数据的趋势和模式。线形图展示了两个数值是如何彼此关联的。纵轴(y)通常表示数量,例如,金额或者百分比。横轴(x)通常表示时间单元。因此,用线形图展示随时间变化的数量最为理想。图 2-3 同样展示了线形图。

3）饼图

饼图可以被分割成若干个楔形块，每块都代表一个类别。有时，为了特别强调，将一个楔形块从饼图中分离出来。饼图可以将整体和其各部分进行对比。图2-3同样展示了带有重点强调的楔形块的饼图。

4）过程图

过程图展示了一个过程中的若干步骤，有时称作流程图。不同的形状代表各种不同类型的活动。例如，圆形或椭圆代表过程的开始和结束，菱形代表必须进行的决策和选择，而矩形代表过程的主要活动或者步骤。

5）组织结构图（或层次图）

当人们和物体按照一定层次组织在一起时，可以使用一个组织结构图来代表它们。组织结构图通常画为一棵水平或竖直放置的树，使用几何图形来代表其不同的元素。线将各种形状连接起来表明元素之间的关系。

组织结构图展示了企业的正式结构和对象间的关系。图2-3同样展示了一个组织结构图的例子。

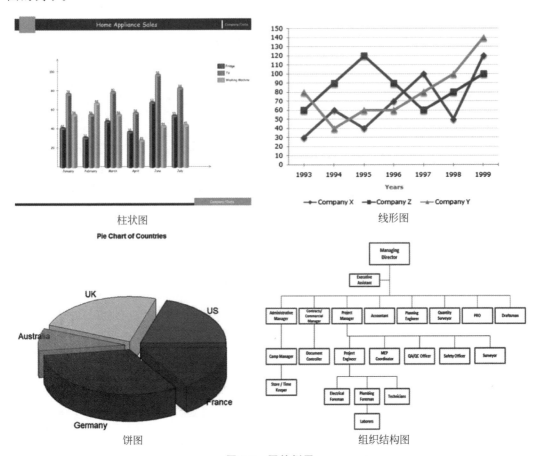

图2-3　图的例子

4. 在文档中添加表格和图片

让文档变得更有吸引力和易于阅读的一个方法就是插入图形、照片等。这些视觉元素可以吸引眼球，并且有助于将读者的注意力吸引到文字上来。表格也提供视觉上的吸引力，而且被设计用来比较信息的列表。

1）在合适的时候使用插图

仅当它们能够提升文档的价值并且支持内容的时候才插入图形。例如，在公司文档中使用公司徽标。插入图形不要仅仅为了装饰页面、分割文本或增加文档长度的视觉资料。图 2-4 展示了带有附加图片的 InfoSource 手册。

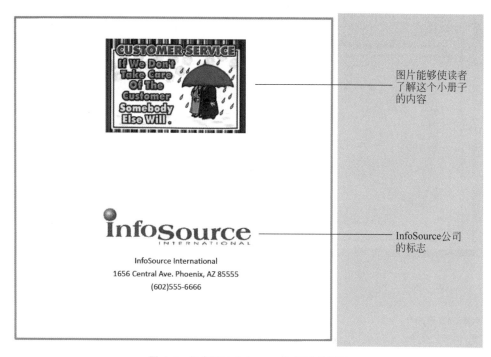

图 2-4 添加到 InfoSource 小册子的图片

2）给图片加上标签

每一张图片和表格通常都包含一个标签和题注来标记它们。使用"图♯"来标记图片，比如图表、示意图、照片、地图和绘图。使用"表♯"来标记表格。给图片和表格单独按顺序编号。表格的标签通常出现在表格的上方，图片的标签出现在插图的下方。在标签后面加一个简短的说明来描述展示的内容。

3）引用每一张图片或表格

在文字的附近，插入所包含的每一张引用图片和表格。参考图号理论上应该出现在图片的前面，例如，图 2-5 展示了云端的客户服务的照片。

4）调整插图的大小

当在文档中插入照片、图表和图形时，它们会以原始大小和分辨率显示。如果必要，调整图像的大小来适应页面和平衡内容。确保在调整大小的时候保持纵横比不变。

5）将插图放在适当的位置

将图片放在适当的位置以使页面布局平衡。例如，两张图片都在页面的左边而所有的文字都在右边，这可能看起来不平衡。

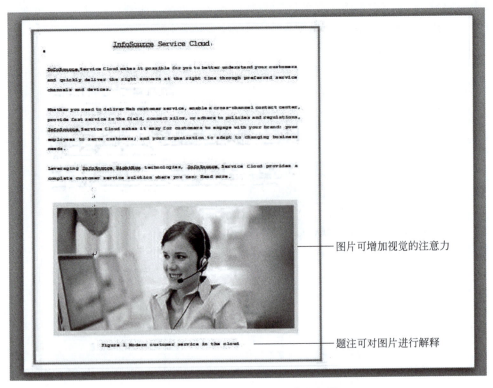

图 2-5 添加小册子中的图片和标题

Part 3

Listening and Speaking

Dialogue: How Radio Frequency Identification(RFID) Readers Work

(*Today is Monday. Henry and Mark are on the way to the classroom when they* ***come across*** *Sophie who is going to the classroom too.*)

Henry & Mark: Good morning, Sophie.

Sophie: Good morning, Henry and Mark.

Henry: How's your weekend going, Sophie?

Sophie: Not bad. I'm learning hardware. I heard **RFID** is very popular now. Do you know anything about it?

Unit 2　Hardware for Systems

Henry: As I know,[1] Radio Frequency Identification (RFID) is a technology that can store, read, and transmit data located in RFID tags. RFID tags contain tiny chips and radio antennas; they can be attached to objects, such as products, price tags, shipping labels, ID cards, assets (such as livestock, vehicles, computers, and other expensive items), and more.

[1] Replace with:
1. As far as I know,
2. So far as I know,
3. As for as I know,

Mark: Yes. The data in RFID tags is read by RFID readers. Whenever an RFID-tagged item is within range of an RFID reader (from two inches up to 300 feet or more, depending on the type of tag and the radio frequency being used), the tag's built-in antenna allows the information located within the RFID tag to be sent to the reader.

Sophie: So interesting.

Henry: Unlike barcodes, RFID tags only need to be within range (not within line of sight) of a reader. This enables RFID readers to read the data stored in many RFID tags at the same time and read them through cardboard and other materials—a definite advantage for shipping and inventory applications.

Mark: You are right. Another advantage over barcodes is that the RFID tag attached to each item is unique (unlike UPC codes, for instance, that have the same code on all instances of a single product), so each tag can be identified individually and the data can be updated as needed.

Sophie: Any other advantages?

Henry: Yes. RFID technology is cost-prohibitive [2] for low-cost items at the present time; however, the many advantages of RFID over barcodes make it possible that RFID may eventually replace barcodes on product labels and price tags—especially as the costs

[2] Replace with:
1. prohibitive
2. costly
3. expensive

039

associated with RFID technology go down and its usage becomes even more commonplace. Because RFID technology can read numerous items at one time, it is also possible that, someday, RFID will allow a consumer to perform self-checkout at a retail store by just pushing a shopping cart past an RFID reader, which will ring up all items in the cart at one time.

Sophie: Really? I guess there are many different kinds of RFID readers.

Mark: Yes. A variety of RFID readers, including handheld, portal, and stationary RFID readers, are available to fit the various RFID applications in use today.

Henry: Handheld RFID readers are used by workers to read RFID tags on the go or to read RFID-enabled tickets at a venue entrance. Portal RFID readers are used to read all the RFID tags on all the products located inside sealed shipping boxes on a palette at one time when the palette passes through the portal. Stationary RFID readers are used at checkstands, border crossings, and other locations where RFID tags need to be read on a continual basis.

Sophie: So, does it mean that we can use RFID in the retail industry very easily?

Mark: Not really. RFID growth in the retail industry has been slower than initially expected. This is primarily because of [3]cost constraints and a number of privacy and security issues, such as concerns that others might be able to read the data contained in an RFID tag attached to your clothing, passport, or other personal item, or they might be able to make fraudulent charges via your smartphone.

[3] Replace with:
1. due to
2. owing to
3. on account of
4. as a result of
5. as a consequence of

Henry: Precautions against fraudulent use—such as using high-frequency tags that need to be within a few inches of the reader, and requiring a PIN code, signature, or other type of authorization when an RFID payment system is used—are being developed.

Sophie: Well, from your descriptions, I'm sure RFID will have a good future.

Mark: I think so.

Henry: I'm pretty confident.

Exercises

Work in a group, and make up a similar conversation by replacing the statements with other expressions on the right side.

Words

livestock ['laivstɔk] n. 牲畜, 家畜
barcode 条形码, 条码技术
cardboard ['kɑːdbɔːd] n. 硬纸板
cost-prohibitive 成本高昂的
commonplace ['kɔmənpleis] adj. 普通的, 普遍的
checkout ['tʃekaut] n. (在超级市场) 对购物的核算付款, 结账
portal ['pɔtl] n. 壮观的大门, 门户网站

palette ['pælit] n. 调色板, 颜料
checkstand ['tʃekˌstænd] n. (超级市场的) 点货收款台
fraudulent ['frɔːdjulənt] adj. 欺骗性的, 不诚实的
charge [tʃɑːdʒ] n. 费用
authorization [ˌɔːθəraiˈzeiʃən, -riˈz-] n. 授权, 认可

Phrases

come across 偶然遇见
line of sight 视线, 瞄准线
ring up 把(售货金额)记入现金收入记录机, 给……打电话

Abbreviations

RFID Radio Frequency Identification 无线射频识别
UPC   Universal Product Code 商品通用条码(扫描后可结账、盘存货物等)

| PIN | Personal Identification Number | 个人识别密码 |

Listening Comprehension: Moore's Law

Listen to the article and answer the following 3 questions based on it. After you hear a question, there will be a break of 15 seconds. During the break, you will decide which one is the best answer among the four choices marked (A), (B), (C) and (D).

Questions

1. How many years does it take for the number of transistors per square inch on chips Gordon Moore observed to double since the integrated circuit was invented?

  (A) One   (B) Two   (C) Three   (D) Four

2. Which of the following is right in terms of Moore's Law?

  (A) Chip speed doubles about every 24 months
  (B) Storage capacity doubles approximately every 20 months
  (C) The number of transistors per square inch on chips doubles every two years
  (D) All of the above

3. In which year did Gordon Moore make Moore's Law?

  (A) 1945   (B) 1955   (C) 1965   (D) 1975

 Words

| co-founder 共同创立者
double['dʌb(ə)l] v. 加倍
breakthrough['breikθruː] n. 突破,突破性进展 | cram[kræm] v. 填满,塞满 |

 Phrases

integrated circuit 集成电路
all the time 一直
in sight 在望,迫近

Dictation: Sensors Get Data We Never Had Before

This article will be played three times. Listen carefully, and fill in the numbered spaces with the appropriate words you have heard.

The rapid spread of low-cost sensors, **notes** Harvard technology expert DavidB. Yoffie, makes it possible to ___1___ all kinds of physical objects—"from fruit shipments (**sniffing** for signs of **spoilage**) to ___2___ engines (tracking **wear** to predict when ___3___ is needed)." The **prevalence** of sensors is new, says Yoffie. "The sensors make it possible to get data we never ___4___ before."

Your plant needs water? Your child opens the **cookie jar** one too many times? You want to ___5___ your home **thermostat** as electricity prices rise and fall during the day? All such information can be ___6___ with sensors.

Sensors also help keep society's ___7___ going. In Los Angeles, ___8___ sensors in the road ___9___ the flow of ___10___ and help in **synchronizing** every red light **throughout** the city. In San Diego, researchers have developed ___11___ sensors that send air-pollution data to smartphones. In wintertime Iowa, sensors are used on ___12___ to tell workers when to roll out **snowplows**. In ___13___, sensors are used to detect **ice buildup** on airplane wings or to ___14___ pilots to sudden changes in wind direction.

Sensors are also a great aid to research. At Stanford University, scientists have put sensors in football **helmets** to help **gauge** what ___15___ cause **concussions** on the field. Sensors on the small unmanned aerial systems known as ___16___ are used to make more accurate counts of bird populations. In California, sensors have been **planted** along **major** earthquake ___17___ lines in an experiment to see whether scientists can predict ___18___ earth movements. Indeed, ocean- and land-based sensors in and near Japan were shown to have provided a ___19___ alert to officials **prior to** the 2011 earthquake and **tsunami**, allowing them 10 minutes to ___20___ a public warning system, probably saving hundreds of lives.

Words

note[nəut] v. 着重提到,强调,指出,表明
sniff[snif] v. 嗅
spoilage['spɔilidʒ] n.（食物的）变质,腐败
wear['wɛə] n. 磨损,损耗,损耗量
prevalence['prevələns] n. 流行,卓越
thermostat['θɜːməstæt] n. 温度自动调节器,恒温器

synchronize['siŋkrənaiz] v. 同步,同时发生
throughout[θruːˈaut] prep. 遍及
snowplow['snəuplau] n. 雪犁,扫雪机,犁雪机（等于 snowplough）
helmet['helmit] n. 钢盔,头盔
gauge[geidʒ] v. 判定,估计,估算

concussion[kən'kʌʃən] n. 冲击,震荡,脑震荡

plant[plɑːnt, plænt] v. 安置,置放,插

major['meidʒə] adj. 较大的,重要的

tsunami[tsu'nɑːmi] n. 海啸

 Phrases

cookie jar 饼干罐
ice buildup 冰堆积
prior to 在……之前,居先

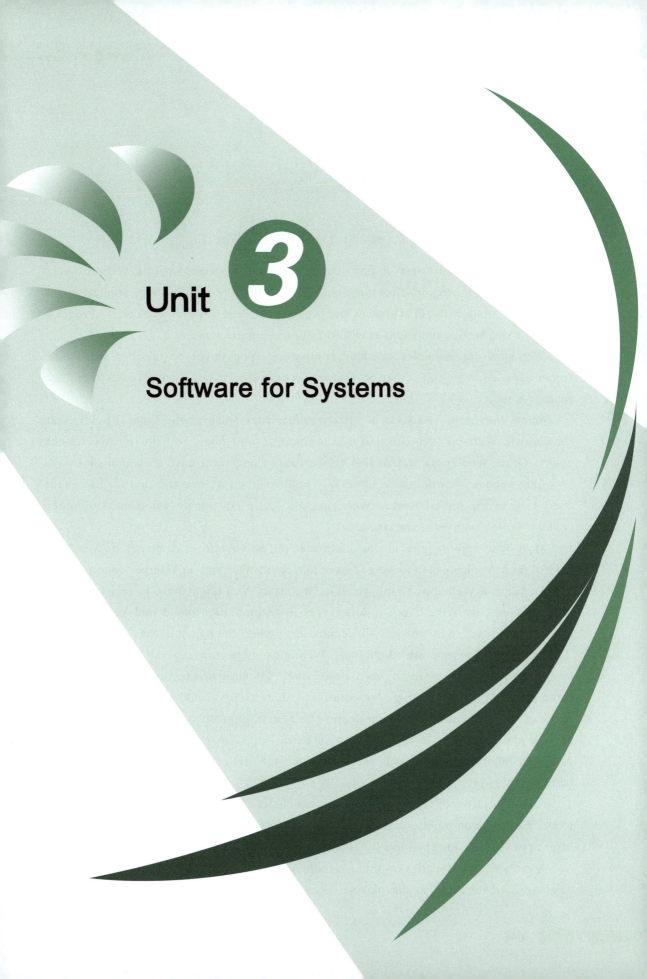
Unit 3
Software for Systems

Part 1

Reading and Translating

Section A: Web Apps and Mobile Apps

A Web application (or Web app) is software that is accessed with a Web browser. Instead of running program files that are stored locally, the code for Web applications is downloaded along with HTML pages and is executed **client-side** by the browser. Program code for some Web applications may also run on a remote server.

Web apps are examples of cloud computing. You might be familiar with some frequently used Web apps, such as Gmail, Google Docs, and Turnitin, but there are thousands more.

Many Web apps **are associated with** consumer sites, such as the Color Visualizer at the Sherwin-Williams Web site that uses a photo of your house to help you select paint colors. Other Web apps, such as the XE Currency Converter, have dedicated sites.

Chromebook[1] owners depend on Web apps for the software they use for just about every task in the digital world. Web apps also have advantages for owners of other devices, from desktops to smartwatches.

Most Web apps require no installation at all on your local computer or handheld device. Your device must, however, have a Web browser and an Internet connection.

To access a Web app, simply go to its Web site. You might have to register before your first use, and then log in using your registered user name and password for subsequent visits. Your browser will remain open while the app is in use.

Just about everyone uses Web apps. Web apps **are** particularly **suited for** consumer-level activities, such as basic word processing, spreadsheet creation, photo editing, audio recording, video editing, presentation design, and personal finance management. Although they may not yet provide features required by professionals, the **sophistication** of Web apps continues to increase. As an extra **bonus**, many Web apps allow several people to collaborate on projects because the project files are stored on the Web and can be easily shared.

Although just about every mobile device includes a browser, the current trend is not to use Web apps on mobile devices. Following Applet[2] lead, most mobile developers offer apps that are installed locally on a smartphone or tablet.

A mobile app is designed for a handheld device, such as a smartphone, tablet computer, or enhanced media player. They are generally small, focused applications sold through an online app store.

Most handheld devices can use both Web apps and mobile apps. The difference between the two is that the program code for Web apps arrives only when you use the app, whereas mobile apps are stored on the handheld device, so they have to be downloaded and installed.

Some mobile apps, such as Yelp and Pandora, are hybrids. A thin client is downloaded from an app store, but during use, data is accessed from the Web. These hybrid apps can only function correctly when the device is connected to the Internet, and their use can rack up megabytes on your mobile plan. Figure 3-1 summarizes software options for mobile devices.

Figure 3-1　Software for mobile devices

iPads, iPhones, and iPods are only allowed to download apps from the official iTunes App Store [3]. Apps are available from other sources, but using them requires an unauthorized change to the device's software called a jailbreak. After downloading and installing the jailbreak software, your device will be able to install apps from a variety of sources other than the iTunes App Store. The jailbreak lasts until you accept a software update from Apple. Updates wipe out the jailbreak software, forcing you to reinstall it.

Android phones are not limited to a single app store, so there is no need to jailbreak them to access more apps. There are various ways to make unauthorized modifications to any mobile device to overcome limitations imposed by mobile service providers. The process is called rooting [4], but most consumers have no need to root their mobile devices.

Words

client-side 客户端
sophistication[səˌfistiˈkeiʃn] n. （技术、
　产品等的）复杂性，精密性，尖端性
bonus[ˈbəunəs] n. 额外给予的东西，意
　外获得的东西，赠品

arrive[əˈraiv] v. （东西）被送来，到达
client[ˈklaiənt] n. 客户端
jailbreak[ˈdʒeilbreik] n. 越狱，破解

Phrases

be associated with 与……有关,与……有关系
be suited for 适合于,适合做
rack up 积累,击倒,获胜
wipe out 摧毁,毁灭

 Notes

[1] Chromebook 是 Google 推出的网络笔记本。这是一种全新的笔记本电脑,号称"完全在线",能提供完善的网络应用服务。

[2] Applet 是采用 Java 编程语言编写的小应用程序,该程序可以包含在 HTML(标准通用标记语言的一个应用)页中,与在页中包含图像的方式大致相同。

[3] App Store 是 iTunes Store 中的一部分,是 iPhone、iPod Touch、iPad 以及 Mac 的服务软件,允许用户从 iTunes Store 或 Mac App Store 浏览和下载一些为 iPhone SDK 或 Mac 开发的应用程序。

[4] 安卓(Android)手机的 ROOT,是为了获取最高的权限而设定的,就与计算机获取超级管理员权限一样的;厂家怕用户不懂手机系统就设置了这样一个权限。用户的手机没有 ROOT 之前,就是以一个使用者的身份在用这个手机。用户只能被动地使用里面的一些功能,或者在不影响系统全局的情况下安装一些新的程序。而 ROOT 之后,用户就变成了一个开发者的身份,就是说可以深入地编辑这部手机了。

 Exercises

Ⅰ. Read the following statements carefully, and decide whether they are true(T) or false(F) according to the text.

　　____ 1. Web apps are examples of local area network.
　　____ 2. A mobile app is designed for a desktop.
　　____ 3. Both Web apps and mobile apps can be used by most handheld devices.
　　____ 4. If your device wants to use Web apps, it must have a Web browser and an Internet connection.
　　____ 5. A Web application (or Web app) is software that is accessed with a word processor.

Ⅱ. Choose the best answer to each of the following questions according to the text.
　1. Where are iPads, iPhones, and iPods only allowed to download apps from?
　　A. Google play
　　B. Amazon

C. The official iTunes App Store

D. All of the above

2. Web apps are examples of which of the following?
   A. Local Area Network
   B. Wide Area Network
   C. Cloud computing
   D. Bluetooth

3. If you want to use Web apps, which of the following do you need?
   A. A Web browser
   B. An Internet connection
   C. A local computer or handheld device
   D. All of the above

III. Identify the letter of the choice that best matches the phrase or definition.

   a. cell
   b. field
   c. shareware
   d. label
   e. domain software

   ____ 1. A single category of data to be stored in a database, such as a person's name or phone number; also called a column.
   ____ 2. A text-based entry in a worksheet cell that identifies data on the worksheet.
   ____ 3. Copyrighted software that is distributed on the honor system; consumers should either pay for it or uninstall it after the trial period.
   ____ 4. Software that is not copyrighted and may be used without restriction.
   ____ 5. The location at the intersection of a row and column on a worksheet into which data can be typed.

IV. Fill in the numbered spaces with the words or phrases chosen from the box. Change the forms where necessary.

   | market   offshoot   program   source   reason |
   | license   feature   perform   free   introduce |

Dan Bricklin—VisiCalc Developer

Dan Bricklin ____1____ wikiCalc in 2007 as a ____2____ software tool for Web pages that have data in lists and tables. This program is an ___3___ of a prototype program he had developed 30 years earlier, named VisiCalc, that ___4___ a series of calculations automatically when numbers were entered.

Bricklin and a friend founded a company, Software Acts, to develop VisiCalc, short for Visible Calculator. They ___5___ the software using Apple Basic on an Apple II computer. This small program was the first type of application software that provided a ___6___ for businesses to buy Apple computers. It included many ___7___ found in today's spreadsheet software.

Bricklin founded a small consulting company, Software Garden, to develop and ___8___ software such as wikiCalc. The company also distributes resources to help programmers learn about ___9___ their products and about open ___10___ software.

Ⅴ. Translate the following passage into Chinese.
How Should Schools Deal with Internet Plagiarism?

A high school teacher failed 28 students for plagiarizing, or copying, material from the Internet. When parents complained, the school board passed the students, and the teacher resigned. Word processing software and the Internet make plagiarism easier than ever. Students can use term paper Web sites, such as CheatHouse.com or Research Papers Online, to copy complete papers on a variety of topics. According to one survey, half of those who responded said that cheating does not or may not matter in the long run, and 60 percent had plagiarized in the past. Students who plagiarize blame peer pressure, classroom competition, the "busy work" nature of some assignments, and the permissive attitude that pervades the Internet. Teachers have several tools to catch plagiarists, including a variety of Internet-based services, such as Turnitin, that compare suspected papers to papers found on the Internet and produce an originality report highlighting text that may have been copied. Some instructors, however, are reluctant to investigate the integrity of a students work and possibly ruin an academic career.

Section B: Cloud Software

Instead of being available in an installed format, some software is run directly from the Internet as cloud software, also referred to as Software as a Service (SaaS) and cloudware. Cloud software is delivered **on demand** via the Web to wherever the user is at the moment, **provided** he or she has an Internet connection (and has paid to use the software if a payment is required).[1] The use of cloud software is growing rapidly and research firm IDC estimates that the enterprise SaaS market alone will exceed $307.3 billion by 2026. Typically, documents created using cloud software are stored online so that they are accessible via any Internet-enabled device.

There is a wide range of both free and fee-based cloud software available (Figure 3-2). For instance, many free interactive games are available through Web sites and there are

Unit 3 Software for Systems

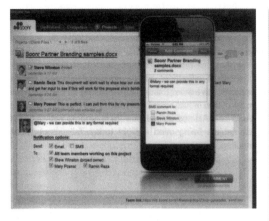

BUSINESS SAAS APPLICATIONS
This program allows you to share documents and collaborate on projects online.

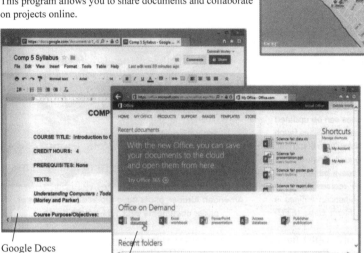

WEB DATABASE APPLICATIONS
This application allows you to retrieve property information, such as home values and homes for sale.

Google Docs

Office on Demand

CLOUD PRODUCTIVITY APPLICATIONS
These programs allow you to create documents online.

Figure 3-2 Cloud software is commonly used with both computers and mobile devices

several free online office suites (such as Google Docs, ThinkFree Online, CloudOn, and Zoho Docs) that can be used on computers and mobile devices as an alternative to the Microsoft Office suite. Some software is offered in both installed and cloud versions. For instance, the latest version of Microsoft Office is available as a traditional installed version (Office 2019) or a **subscription**-based cloud version (Office 365); Office 365 users can install and use the program on their computers, as well as **stream** the program over the Internet via the Office on Demand feature. In addition, many business software services are offered as SaaS, including applications **geared** for collaboration, scheduling, customer service, accounting, project management, and more. Typically, business SaaS applications use a subscription (often per user, per month) pricing scheme; companies that deliver SaaS are sometimes referred to as Application Service Providers (ASPs). As it evolves, cloud software is beginning to move from single stand-alone applications to groups of products that can work together to **fulfill** a wide variety of needs. For instance, the Google Docs Home page provides access to the Google Docs applications, but it also allows easy access to other Google online services, such as Gmail, Calendar, Photos, and Web search.

One advantage of cloud software **over** installed software is that the programs and your files can be accessed from any computer with an Internet connection regardless of the type of computer or operating system used; some can also be accessed via a smartphone, media tablet, or other type of Internet-enabled mobile device. This makes cloud software especially appropriate for applications like shared scheduling and collaboration applications that are **time-critical** because documents and other data can be shared regardless of an individual's location or device. Other advantages of cloud software include ease of implementation, potential lower cost of ownership, improved collaboration capabilities, and always working with the most current version of the software without having to perform software updates on company computers. In addition, cloud applications can easily **interface** with existing online databases, such as online maps and property records (for instance, the real estate applications accessible via the Zillow Web site utilize maps, property record information, and real estate listing information pulled from various online databases).

Some potential disadvantages of cloud software are that online applications tend to run more slowly than applications stored on a local hard drive, that many online applications have a limit regarding the file size of the documents you create, and that the cost may eventually exceed the cost of buying a similar installed software program.[2] In addition, you cannot access cloud software and your data if the server on which they reside **goes down** or if you are in a location with no Internet access, such as while traveling or in a rural area. To eliminate this last concern, a growing trend is for online applications to also **function**, at least in part, offline. For instance, Google Docs includes offline capabilities so that users can access the Google Docs applications and their documents locally on their computers, when needed. Edits are stored locally on the computer when a user is offline and, when the user reconnects to the Internet, the changes are synchronized with the documents stored on the Google Docs servers.

 Words

provided[prə'vaidid] *conj.* 如果,假如
subscription[səb'skripʃən] *n.* (报刊等的)订阅费
stream[stri:m] *v.* 流,流动
gear[giə] *v.* 准备好,使适应
fulfill[ful'fil] *v.* 达到(目的),履行(诺言等)

over[ˈəuvə(r)] prep. 超过
time-critical 时间敏感的,时序要求严格的

interface[ˈintəfeis] v. (使通过界面或接口)接合,连接
function[ˈfʌŋkʃən] v. 有或起作用

 Phrases

on demand 一经要求,点播
go down 停止,被打败

 Notes

〔1〕 **Original**:Cloud software is delivered on demand via the Web to wherever the user is at the moment, provided he or she has an Internet connection (and has paid to use the software if a payment is required).

Translation:如果需要,云软件可以通过 Web 向用户递送,不论用户此时身处何地,前提是用户具有因特网连接(如果为付费软件,则需要交费)。

〔2〕 **Original**:Some potential disadvantages of cloud software are that online applications tend to run more slowly than applications stored on a local hard drive, that many online applications have a limit regarding the file size of the documents you create, and that the cost may eventually exceed the cost of buying a similar installed software program.

Translation:云软件的潜在劣势在于在线应用往往要比存储在本地硬盘中的应用程序慢得多,很多在线应用程序因为所创建文档的文件大小具有限制,价格也许最终会超过购买一个类似的已安装的软件程序。

 Exercises

Ⅰ. Read the following statements carefully, and decide whether they are true (T) or false (F) according to the text.

____ 1. Office 2019 is one kind of cloud software.
____ 2. SaaS means Solider as a Stronghold.
____ 3. Office 365 is a traditional installed software.
____ 4. Google Docs is a cloud software which is not free.
____ 5. You cannot access cloud software if you are in a location with no Internet access.

Ⅱ. Choose the best answer to each of the following questions according to the text.
 1. Which of the following items is the traditional installed software?
    A. Zoho Docs

B. Google Docs
  C. Office 2019
  D. All of the above

2. Which of the following is not the advantage of cloud software over installed software?
  A. Online applications tend to run more slowly than applications stored on a local hard drive
  B. Improved collaboration capabilities
  C. Potential lower cost of ownership
  D. Ease of implementation

3. Which of the following can be an alternative to the Microsoft Office suite?
  A. Google Docs
  B. CloudOn
  C. ThinkFree Online
  D. All of the above

Ⅲ. Identify the letter of the choice that best matches the phrase or definition.
  a. buttons
  b. cloud
  c. database
  d. galleries
  e. image editor

  ____ 1. Also known as a photo editor, this specialized graphics program edits or modifies digital photographs.
  ____ 2. Toolbars typically appear below the menu bar and include small graphic elements called.
  ____ 3. Simplifies the process of making a selection from a list of alternatives by graphically displaying the effect of alternatives before being selected.
  ____ 4. A type of suite that is stored at a server on the Internet and is available anywhere you can access the Internet.
  ____ 5. A collection of related data.

Ⅳ. Fill in the blanks with the words or phrases chosen from the box. Change the forms where necessary.

| sensor | technology | find | feel | be |
| imagine | recent | dimension | market | project |

Unit 3 Software for Systems

Virtual Reality

Virtual reality is an artificial hardware-and-software-created environment that seems "real" and can be manipulated in real time.

Virtual reality (VR), a computer-generated artificial reality, ___1___ a person into a sensation of three-dimensional space.

To put yourself into virtual reality, you need software and special headgear; then you can add gloves, and later perhaps a special suit. The headgear—which is called a head-mounted display (___2___ as a VR headset)—has two small video display screens, for each eye, to create the sense of three-___3___. Headphones pipe in stereophonic sound or even 3-D sound so that you think you are hearing sounds not only near each ear but also in various places all around you. The glove has sensors for collecting data about your hand movements. Once you are wearing this equipment, software gives you interactive ___4___ feelings similar to real-world experiences.

Virtual reality is used in arcade-type games, most ___5___ the VR Oculus version of SoundSelf, but there are far more important uses—for example, in simulators for training. Simulators are devices that represent the behavior of physical or abstract systems. Virtual reality simulation ___6___ are applied a great deal in training.

Virtual reality is also ___7___ used in research. In one Stanford University study of people's ___8___ about conservation, subjects were immersed in a three-dimensional virtual forest and told to saw through a towering sequoia redwood tree until it crashed in front of them. Later these subjects were ___9___ to use less paper in the real world than did people who only ___10___ what it was like to cut down a tree. "We found that virtual reality can change how people behave," said researcher Sun Joo Ahn.

Ⅴ. **Translate the following passage into Chinese.**

Cross-Platform Software

A typical application program must rely on the operating system to perform many of its tasks. It may require the services of the window manager to communicate with the computer user, or it may use the file manager to retrieve data from mass storage. Unfortunately, different operating systems dictate that requests for these services be made in different ways. Thus for programs to be transferred and executed across networks and Internets involving different machine designs and different operating systems, the programs must be operating-system independent as well as machine independent. The term cross-platform is used to reflect this additional level of independence. That is, cross-platform software is software that is independent of an operating systems design as well as the machines hardware design and is therefore executable throughout a network.

Part 2

Simulated Writing：Communicating with E-mail and Memos（I）

当我们需要和同事或者所在组织的其他人交流的时候，通常会发送电子邮件或者发布备忘录。电子邮件是组织内部交换信息最流行的手段，是必不可少的生产力工具，例如，我们可以使用电子邮件来收集信息，对请求做出回复，或者对决策做出确认。然而，当我们想创建一个永久的或者更加正式的记录时，备忘录是更合适的选择。

1. 什么是电子邮件和备忘录

电子邮件和备忘录是企业交流的标准形式，可用于员工通知、政策传达、信息请求，提供回复和决策确认。图 3-3 展示了专业的电子邮件和备忘录。然而，正如表 3-1 所描述的那样，电子邮件和备忘录都有其不同的目的。

图 3-3　电子邮件和备忘录的样例

表 3-1 恰当使用电子邮件和备忘录

场　　景	使用电子邮件	使用备忘录	使用其他
许多人都收到相同的短消息	√		
快速回答一个或多个问题	√		
回复同事的电子邮件	√		
上司要求你确认一个决策	√		
邀请其他人来开会	√		
更新一个简单的流程	√	√	
与会者回顾计划的细节		√	
传递新的正式的公司政策		√	
对同事表现出热情			打电话或者拜访
解决争端			面对面协商
消息是机密的			用信封封装的信

2. 在撰写电子邮件或者备忘录之前，先回答下面的问题

- 这封邮件或备忘录的目的是什么，对象是谁？

首先要分析通过发送电子邮件或者发布备忘录来达到什么目的，这应该是主题，并且要明确地分辨发送的对象。写给同事的邮件可以写得不太正式，但是写给上司的邮件就应该更加专业。

- 电子邮件还是备忘录？

电子邮件一般来说比备忘录更短、更具有时效性，并且没有备忘录那样正式。邮件也可以包含存储在计算机、网络或者因特网上的电子信息。

3. 使用电子邮件可完成下列任务

- 与同一组织的其他人交流想法和信息。

电子邮件之所以流行是因为它允许快速地交换简短的消息，尤其是那些需要快速回复、确认决策或者提供简要信息的消息。

- 告知人们未来计划的变更。

当时间是一个要素的时候，电子邮件是用于交流计划变更的理想工具，例如，会议改期、项目更新，以及截止日期延后。

- 请求信息或者行动和回复请求。

发送电子邮件而不是打电话来请求的信息，可以让同事查阅询问或者请求行动的文字记录。电子邮件软件也允许用户很方便地回复别人发来的邮件，并且在回复中包含他们发来的原始邮件的内容。

- 向许多人发布信息。

因为可以方便地同时向许多人发送电子邮件，所以可以使用邮件来发布信息，例如，职位空缺、新产品或者推广信息。

4. 使用备忘录可以完成下列任务

- 创建一个永久的记录。

当需要一份交流内容的实体记录的时候，可以传递备忘录，例如，列举流程、提供指导或

者在中心地带发布信息。

- 传递正式的消息。

书面的备忘录比电子邮件更加正式,这使得备忘录很适合进行官方的交流,例如,公司政策、雇佣决策以及其他重要事项。

5．撰写电子邮件的主要元素

当撰写电子邮件时,电子邮件应该包含4个基本元素:

(1) 能够提供邮件内容预览的一个标题;

(2) 能够传达主要思想的一个起始句;

(3) 能够解释、支持或者证明主要思想的邮件的正文;

(4) 一个合适的结束语。

图 3-4 展示了具有这 4 个元素的一封电子邮件。

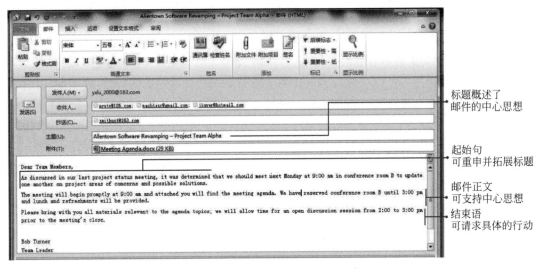

图 3-4　电子邮件中的 4 个基本元素

1) 标题

使用简明的语句概述邮件的主要思想。忙碌的人往往基于标题来决定是否打开一封电子邮件。例如,"周二上午 10 点有会议"和"在秋季贸易展上的报告"都是有效的标题,而"重要的""问题""会议"就不太好。表 3-2 列出了有关标题和其他电子邮件元素的注意事项。

2) 起始句

第一句就可以传达邮件的中心思想。可以通过重申标题或者拓展标题来做到这一点,例如,"请告诉我你是否能参加预定于 4 月 4 日周二上午 10 点的项目会议。"如果所传递的是一个坏消息,无论怎样,都应该以一个温和的语气来开始。

3) 邮件的正文

用更多的信息来支持邮件的中心思想,解释为什么要写这封邮件。将邮件限制在某个主题,并且尽可能地组织材料使其更加易于阅读。例如,使用短句子、章节标题、列表、表格和图形标出法,比如加粗和着重号。要避免冗长的文本段落。

表 3-2 电子邮件基本元素的注意事项

基本元素	适合提到	尽量避免
标题	• 概述邮件的中心思想 • 使用简短的句子	• 使用模糊的或冗长的语言 • 写完整的句子 • 使用可能被过滤为垃圾的词语
起始句	• 重申中心思想（除非是个坏消息） • 确保请求或者回复是直接针对某个问题的	• 以其他主题开始 • 在做出请求之前解释 • 在回复中重申请求
邮件正文	• 专注于某个主题 • 有逻辑地组织可支持性观点 • 使用短句子、章节标题和列表 • 将补充材料包含在附件中	• 让读者淹没在冗长的陈述中 • 包含与主题无关的信息
结束语	• 如果要做出一个请求的话，请包含一个行动号召 • 在合适的时候提供一个截止日期 • 概述长邮件或者以一个结束观点来结束	• 遗漏联系方式 • 突然结束

4）结束语

以对读者具体行动的请求、申明截止日期、概述复杂邮件的关键点来结束，或者以正面观点来结束。例如，"请在 9 月 3 日之前提交产品描述"是一个有效的行动号召。如果要写一个简单的不需要读者行动的邮件，以礼貌的陈述结束即可，比如，"感谢你对这个项目的帮助。"

转 74 页

Part 3

Listening and Speaking

Dialogue：Making an Electronic Album Using Multimedia Editing Software

（Today is the first day after the National Day holiday．Henry met Mark in the hall．）

Henry： Hi，Mark．How was your National Day holiday?

Mark： It was wonderful! During this holiday，I went to Hangzhou with my family．It's a very beautiful city．We took a lot of photos and made many pieces of video with my video camera．

Henry: Really? Sounds exciting! All of these will be precious memories. I think you can make a family album about your journey in Hangzhou with that material, so that you can enjoy it on your computer at any time. Furthermore,[1] if you like, you can release it on your blog so as to allow more people to share with you.

[1] Replace with:
1. In addition
2. Moreover
3. What is more
4. Additionally
5. Besides
6. Plus
7. Also

Mark: Oh, that's a good idea! But I don't know how to do that at all. Could you help me?

Henry: Sorry, I'm a layman too. But Sophie is good at multimedia editing software, maybe she can help you.

Sophie: According to my experience, graphics software is necessary, Mark. It can help you create, manipulate and print graphics.

Henry: There are many types, right?

Sophie: Yes, they include painting software, photo editing software, drawing software, 3D graphics software, CAD software, and presentation software, etc. However,[2] in your case, Mark, photo editing software is enough, such as Photoshop.

[2] Replace with:
1. Nevertheless
2. Even so
3. Yet

Mark: Oh, yes. I've heard that it's a very nice photo editing software. And what about those pieces of video?

Sophie: Don't worry. You can edit those pieces of video with video editing software. It provides a set of tools for transferring video footage from a camcorder to a computer, clipping out unwanted footage, assembling video segments in any sequence, adding special visual effects and adding a sound track.

Henry: I have heard that one brand of this software is Adobe Premiere.

Sophie: That's right! Besides, DVD authoring software offers tools for creating DVDs with Hollywood-style menus. For example, Sonic DVDit, ULead DVD MovieFactory, Apple iDVD and Adobe Encore DVD.

Mark: Thank you very much for your helpful guide, Sophie. Would you like to tell me some details about how to use them to make a complete electronic album?

Sophie: No problem! If you have time, I'll show you how to use these kinds of software.

Henry: Well, we look forward to your wonderful work, Mark!

Mark: Ok, I'll try my best!

Sophie: May you succeed! We'd say "Good luck!"

 Exercises

Work in a group, and make up a similar conversation by replacing the statements with other expressions on the right side.

 Words

layman ['leimən] n. 外行
manipulate [mə'nipjuleit] v. （熟练地）操作，使用
footage ['futidʒ] n. 连续镜头，电影胶片
camcorder ['kæmkɔːdə] n. 便携式摄像机
author ['ɔːθə(r)] v. 编写

 Phrases

clip out 剪辑，剪辑出

 Abbreviations

CAD   Computer Aided Design   计算机辅助设计
DVD   Digital Video Disc   数字化视频光盘

Listening Comprehension: IDE

Listen to the article and answer the following 3 questions based on it. After you hear a question, there will be a break of 15 seconds. During the break, you will decide which one is the best answer among the four choices marked (A), (B), (C) and (D).

Questions

1. What is the correct full name of the abbreviation "IDE" in this article?

(A) Interface Development Environment

(B) Integrated Development Environment

(C) Integrated Development Editor

(D) Interface Debugging Editor

2. What is the greatest benefit brought by IDE for software developers according to this article?

(A) Learning a language

(B) Increasing developing productivity

(C) Piecing together command lines

(D) Compiling code

3. Which of the following items is not integrated in the IDE first used in Dartmouth BASIC?

(A) File management

(B) Compilation

(C) Debugging

(D) Graphical user interface

 Words

abbreviate[əˈbriːvieit] v. 缩写，简写
facility[fəˈsiliti] n. 工具，便利
interpreter[inˈtəːpritə] n. 解释程序
build[bild] n. 构建
configuration[kənˌfigjuˈreiʃən] n. 配置

cohesive[kəuˈhiːsiv] adj. 使内聚的，黏着的
flowchart[ˈfləutʃaːt] n. 流程图
keypunch[ˈkiːpʌntʃ] n. 键盘穿孔机

 Phrases

be characteristic of 具有……特色的

Dictation: Open Source Software

This article will be played three times. Listen carefully, and fill in the numbered spaces with the appropriate words you have heard.

Unit 3　Software for Systems

　　The use of open source software has grown over the past few years, ___1___ for cost reasons. One of the first widely known open source programs was the Linux operating system. However, there are also low-cost or no-cost open source **alternatives** for a wide ___2___ of application programs today. For instance, the free LibreOffice office ___3___ can be used as an alternative to Microsoft Office, and the ___4___ **GIMP** program can be used to **retouch** photos ___5___ Adobe Photoshop or another **pricey** image ___6___ program. In addition to saving you money, these alternative programs often require less disk space and memory than their ___7___ software **counterparts** ___8___.

　　Other possible ___9___ of using open source software include increased ___10___ and security (because they are tested and improved by a wide variety of programmers and users), and the ability to modify the application's source code. **Perceived** ___11___ of using open source software include ___12___ of support and ___13___ issues. However, both Linux and open source application programs are continuing to gain ___14___ and their use is growing. Some **insiders** ___15___ that the open source movement is finally ___16___ the **momentum** it **deserves**.

　　A ___17___ **survey** of **executives** found that most executives ___18___ open source as beneficial to both ___19___ and collaboration. It also **revealed** that more than half of all software purchased five years from now is expected to be open source, with the top factors driving this increased ___20___ of open source software being improved quality and flexibility of software **libraries**.

 Words

alternative[ɔːlˈtɜːnətiv] n. 二中择一,供替代的选择	momentum [məuˈmentəm] n. 势头,动量,动力
retouch[ˌriːˈtʌtʃ, ˈriːtʌtʃ] v. 修描(底片等)	deserve[diˈzɜːv] v. 值得,应得,该得
pricey[ˈpraisi] adj. 高价的,过分昂贵的	survey[sɜːˈvei, ˈsɜːvei, sə-] n. 民意调查,民意测验,抽样调查
counterpart[ˈkauntəpɑːt] n. 配对物,极相似的人或物	executive[igˈzekjutiv] n. 管理人员,主管业务的人,经理
perceive[pəˈsiːv] v. 察觉,发觉,感知	reveal[riˈviːl] v. 显示,透露,揭露
insider[ˌinˈsaidə] n. 知情人,了解内幕的人,消息灵通人士	library[ˈlaibrəri] n. (程序)库,文件库

 Abbreviations

GIMP　GNU Image Manipulation Program　GNU 图像处理程序

063

Unit 4

Operating Systems

Unit 4　Operating Systems

Reading and Translating

Section A: Roles of an Operating System

The operating system of a computer is the core of its system software. An operating system manages computer resources, such as memory and input/output devices, and provides an interface through which a human can interact with the computer. Other system software supports specific application goals, such as a library of graphics software that **renders** images on a display. The operating system allows an application program to interact with these other system resources.

Figure 4-1 shows the operating system in its relative position among computer system elements. The operating system manages hardware resources. It allows application software to access system resources, either directly or through other system software. It provides a direct user interface to the computer system.

A computer generally has one operating system that becomes active and takes control when the system is turned on. Computer hardware is **wired** to initially load a small set of system instructions that is stored in permanent memory (ROM). These instructions load a larger portion of system software from secondary memory, usually a magnetic disk.

Eventually all key elements of the operating system software are loaded, **start-up** programs are executed, the user interface is activated, and the system is ready for use. This activity is often called **booting** the computer. The term "boot" comes from the idea of "pulling yourself up by your own **bootstraps**," which is essentially what a computer does when it is turned on.

A computer could have two or more operating systems from which the user chooses when the computer is turned on. This configuration is often called a dual-boot or multi-boot system. Only one operating system controls the computer at any given time, however.

You've likely used at least one operating system before. The various versions of Microsoft Windows (Windows NT, Windows XP, Windows Vista, Windows 7, Windows 10) are popular choices for personal computers. The different versions of these operating systems indicate how the software evolves over time as well as how changes occur in the way services are provided and managed. The macOS family is the operating system of choice for computers manufactured by Apple Computer. UNIX has been a favorite of serious programmers for years, and a version of UNIX called Linux is popular for personal computer systems.

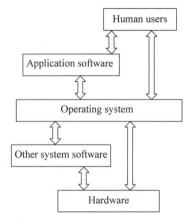

Figure 4-1　An operating system interacts with many aspects of a computer system

Mobile devices, such as smartphones and tablet computers, run operating systems that are tailored to their needs. The memory constraints and the smaller set of peripherals involved, for example, are different than those of a typical desktop or laptop computer. Apple Computer's iPod Touch, iPhone, and iPad all run the iOS mobile operating system, which is derived from macOS. The Android operating system, developed by Google as an open source project through the Open Handset Alliance, is the underlying system run on a variety of phones, and has become the most popular platform for mobile devices. Android and iOS dominate the current market for mobile operating systems, though there are still several others.

The various roles of an operating system generally revolve around the idea of "sharing nicely." An operating system manages resources, and these resources are often shared in one way or another among the various programs that want to use them. Multiple programs executing concurrently share the use of main memory. They take turns using the CPU. They compete for an opportunity to use input/output devices. The operating system acts as the playground monitor, making sure that everyone cooperates and gets a chance to play.

 Words

render['rendə] v. 着色,致使,提出 wire['waiə] v. 将……连入(计算机网络) start-up 启动,新成立的企业,创业者 boot[bu:t] v. & n. 引导,引导程序(= bootstrap)	bootstrap['bu:tstræp] n. 解靴带,引导程序,辅助程序 tailor['teilə] v. (为某一特定目的而)剪裁,制作

Unit 4 Operating Systems

peripheral[pəˈrifərəl] n. 外围设备,辅助设备(如打印机、扫描仪等)(亦作 peripheric)
underlying [ˌʌndəˈlaiiŋ] adj. 基础的,根本的,在下面的

concurrent [kənˈkʌrənt] adj. 并发的,一致的,同时发生的
playground[ˈpleigraund] n. 活动场所

Phrases

revolve around 以……为中心
take turn 轮流
act as 充当,用作,当作,起……的作用

Exercises

Ⅰ. Read the following statements carefully, and decide whether they are true (T) or false (F) according to the text.

____ 1. The operating system allows application software to access system resources, either directly or through other system software.

____ 2. The memory constraints for smartphones and tablet computers are different than those of a typical desktop or laptop computer.

____ 3. A computer could have only one operating system.

____ 4. The operating system supports specific application goals, such as a library of graphics software that renders images on a display.

____ 5. The operating system of a computer is application software.

Ⅱ. Choose the best answer to each of the following questions according to the text.

1. Which of the following computer resources does an operating system manage?
    A. Input devices
    B. Output devices
    C. Memory
    D. All of the above

2. Which of the following runs the iOS mobile operating system?
    A. iPhone
    B. iPad
    C. iPod Touch
    D. All of the above

3. Which of the following is wrong about the operating system?
   A. Android and iOS dominate the current market for mobile operating systems, though there are still several others.
   B. A computer could have two or more operating systems from which the user chooses when the computer is turned on.
   C. Mobile devices, such as smartphones and tablet computers, have the same operating systems as those of a typical desktop or laptop computer.
   D. The operating system allows application software to access system resources, either directly or through other system software.

Ⅲ. Identify the letter of the choice that best matches the phrase or definition.
   a. Android
   b. antivirus
   c. driver
   d. fragmented
   e. multitasking

   ____ 1. Type of program that guards computer systems from viruses and other damaging programs.
   ____ 2. Program that works with the operating system to allow communication between a device and the rest of a computer system is called a device ____.
   ____ 3. If a file cannot be saved on a single track, it has to be ____.
   ____ 4. Switching between different applications.
   ____ 5. Mobile operating system that is owned by Google and is widely used in many smartphones.

Ⅳ. Fill in the numbered spaces with the words or phrases chosen from the box. Change the forms where necessary.

> typical   specific   run   use   consider
> version   while   however   design   camera

Operating Systems for Mobile Devices

____1____ notebook, hybrid notebook-tablets, and other portable personal computers ____2____ use the same operating systems as desktop computers, mobile phones, media tablets, and other mobile devices usually use mobile operating systems—either mobile ____3____ of personal operating systems (such as Windows 10 or Linux) or special operating systems (such as Android or Apple iOS) that are designed ____4____ for mobile devices. ____5____, the current trend with both Microsoft and Apple operating systems is to make computers and mobile devices ___6___ their respective operating systems work more seamlessly together. There are also embedded operating systems ___7___ to be used with everyday objects, such as home appliances, gaming consoles, digital ___8___, e-readers, digital photo frames, ATMs, toys, watches, GPS systems, home medical devices, voting terminals, and cars. Most users select a mobile phone by ___9___ the mobile provider, hardware, and features associated with the phone, instead of considering the operating system used. However, users should understand that the operating system ___10___ with a phone or other device determines some of the capabilities of the device, the interface used, and the applications that can run on that device.

Ⅴ. **Translate the following passage into Chinese.**
Microsoft's Task Manager

You can gain insight to some of the internal activity of a Microsoft Windows operating system by executing the utility program called Task Manager (Press the Ctrl, Alt, and Delete keys simultaneously.) In particular, by selecting the Processes tab in the Task Manager window, you can view the process table. Here is an experiment you can perform: Look at the process table before you activate any application program. (You may be surprised that so many processes are already in the table. These are necessary for the system's basic operation.) Now activate an application and confirm that an additional process has entered the table. You will also be able to see how much memory space was allocated to the process.

Section B: Mobile versus Desktop Operating Systems

A desk operating system, sometimes called a **stand-alone** operating system, is a complete operating system that works on desktops, laptops, and some tablets. Desktop operating systems sometimes are called client operating system because they also work in conjunction with a server operating system. Client operating systems can operate with or without a network.

Examples of the more widely used desktop operating systems are Windows, macOS, UNIX, Linux, and Chrome OS.

The operating system on mobile devices and many consumer **electronics** is called a mobile operating system and resides on **firmware.** Mobile operating systems typically include or support the following: calendar and contact management, text messaging, email, touch screens, **accelerometer** (so that you can rotate the display), digital cameras, media players, speech recognition, GPS navigation, a variety of third-party apps, a browser, and wireless connectivity such as **cellular**, Wi-Fi, and Bluetooth.

An operating system has the same role, whether for a desktop or mobile device (Figure 4-2). It manages operations and provides a user interface. Because of this shared role, many similarities exist between the functions of desktop and mobile operating systems. From a user's **perspective**, operating systems enable you to work with apps and to monitor and maintain the functions of the computer or device. Typical functions included in mobile operating systems include the following:

- Main areas, such as a desktop or **home screen**, enable you to access and organize apps.
- Methods to return to the main area quickly.
- The ability to organize the app **icons** or **tiles** in the main areas easily by moving them to pages or folders or by adding them to menus.
- System tools, such as to manage battery power and Internet connections.
- Options for security settings.

Category	Name
Desktop	Windows
	macOS
	UNIX
	Linux
	Chrome OS
Server	**Windows Server**
	macOS Server
	UNIX
	Linux
Mobile	Google Android
	Apple iOS

Figure 4-2　Examples of operating system by category

Whether you are purchasing a computer or mobile device, the choice of an operating system plays an important role.

Historically, the two types of operating systems have had different uses and **capabilities**. The differences are due **in part** to the **disparity** in screen size, keyboards, and processing power. Because of **convergence**, as well as the increased reliance on mobile devices for communications and productivity, the use and function of mobile and desktop operating systems are becoming more similar. The prevalence of Web apps and cloud storage services enables users to access the same programs and files they work with on their desktop from a mobile device. Some developers now create operating systems that share code and have common features, regardless of whether they are installed on a computer or mobile device. Features, such as tiles and icons (typically used in mobile devices), make the transition between using a mobile device and computer easier. For example, mobile device operating systems include capabilities that allow users to **take advantage of** the touch screen displays. As more computer desktop monitors today are touch enabled, computer users can take advantage of this feature.

Many differences exist in the way a user interacts with a mobile operating system.

- A desktop operating system may use menus, windows, and bars to run apps and to access features within apps. On a desktop, you can run multiple programs simultaneously and seamlessly due to the large screen and the use of pointing devices. This feature makes desktops more relevant than mobile operating systems to productivity and multitasking.

- A mobile operating system typically has one program running at a time, although others may be running in the background. Quick movements and gestures are often all that you need to perform tasks on a mobile device. Mobile operating systems use technologies such as cellular, Bluetooth, Wi-Fi, GPS, and NFC [1] to communicate with other devices and to connect to the Internet. Mobile devices also typically include cameras, video cameras, voice recorders, and sometimes speech recognition.

Words

stand-alone（计算机）独立的
electronics[ilek'trɔniks] n. 电子器件，电子学
firmware['fɜːmweə(r)] n. （计算机的）固件[就是写入 EROM 或 EEPROM（可编程只读存储器）中的程序]
accelerometer[əkˌseləˈrɔmitə(r)] n. 加速度计
cellular[ˈseljələ(r)] n. 手机，移动电话，蜂窝电话（= cellular telephone）

perspective[pəˈspektiv] n. 观点，看法
icon[ˈaikɔn] n. 图标，图符
tile[tail] n. 平铺
capability[ˌkeipəˈbilitiː] n. 功能，才能
disparity[diˈspærəti] n. 不同，不等
convergence[kənˈvɜːdʒəns] n. 一体化，集中，收敛

Phrases

home screen 首页，主屏幕
in part 在某种程度上，部分地，一半
take advantage of 利用
at a time 每次，依次，逐一

Notes

[1] 近场通信（Near Field Communication，NFC）是一种短距高频的无线电技术，以 13.56MHz 频率运行于 20cm 距离内。其传输速度有 106kb/s、212kb/s 或者 424kb/s 三种。目前近场通信已通过成为 ISO/IEC IS 18092 国际标准、ECMA-340 标准与 ETSI TS 102 190 标准。NFC 采用主动和被动两种读取模式。NFC 近场通信技术是由非接触式射频识

别（RFID）及互联互通技术整合演变而来，在单一芯片上结合感应式读卡器、感应式卡片和点对点的功能，能在短距离内对兼容设备进行识别和与之进行数据交换。

 Exercises

Ⅰ. Read the following statements carefully，and decide whether they are true（T）or false（F）according to the text.

　　____ 1. It is not so important to choose an operating system when you buy a computer or mobile device.

　　____ 2. Client operating systems can operate with or without a network.

　　____ 3. In general，a mobile operating system has many programs running at a time.

　　____ 4. A mobile operating system resides on a hard disk.

　　____ 5. Sometimes we call desktop operating system server operating system.

Ⅱ. Choose the best answer to each of the following questions according to the text.

1. Which of the following is not the desktop operating system?

　　A. Windows

　　B. macOS

　　C. iOS

　　D. None of the above

2. Which of the following technology does the mobile operating system use?

　　A. NFC

　　B. Bluetooth

　　C. GPS

　　D. All of the above

3. Which of the following role does an operating system have?

　　A. It manages operations

　　B. It maintains the functions of the computer or device

　　C. It provides a user interface

　　D. All of the above

Ⅲ. Identify the letter of the choice that best matches the phrase or definition.

　　a. Android

　　b. backup

　　c. device driver

　　d. utility program

e. virtual memory

___ 1. A duplicate copy of data or other computer content for use in the event that the original version is destroyed.

___ 2. A Linux-based operating system designed for mobile devices and developed by the Open Handset Alliance, which is a group of companies led by Google.

___ 3. A memory-management technique that uses hard drive space as additional RAM.

___ 4. A program that enables an operating system to communicate with a specific hardware device.

___ 5. A type of software that performs a specific task, usually related to managing or maintaining a computer system.

Ⅳ. **Fill in the numbered spaces with the words or phrases chosen from the box. Change the forms where necessary.**

> support   program   create   close   virus
> develop   know   variant   hinder   separate

Are Open Source or Closed Source Operating Systems Better?

One feature that ___1___ Linux from other operating systems is that its source code, along with any changes, remains public. Closed source operating systems, where developers refuse to share some or all of the code, may ___2___ third party software developers who create programs and apps for the operating system.

___3___ of open source, such as the GNU Project, maintain that open source software enables ___4___ to examine, correct, and enhance code to create better programs. Communities of open source ___5___ can make changes immediately, which they claim results in higher-quality software. For example, proponents of open source software use Linux, which is ___6___ for its speed and stability. Of the 500 fastest supercomputers, 90 percent use ___7___ of Linux. Companies and non-profit organizations can distribute and sell their versions of Linux. This enables those without the expertise to modify open source software to benefit from the ___8___ efforts of the Linux community.

Fear of ___9___ and other security concerns can lead some to question about whether open source software is worthwhile. Dishonest and anonymous developers can use open source software to create programs that may be malware. Proponents of ___10___ source software also argue that companies and developers should be able to control, and profit from, the operation systems they create.

Ⅴ. **Translate the following passage into Chinese.**

Multi-Core Operating Systems

Traditional time-sharing/multitasking systems give the illusion of executing many processes at once by switching rapidly between time slices faster than a human can perceive. Modern systems continue to multitask in this way, but in addition, the latest multi-core CPUs are genuinely capable of running two, four, or many more processes simultaneously. Unlike a group of single-core computers working together, a multi-core machine contains multiple independent processors (in this case called cores) that share the computer's peripherals, memory, and other resources. For a multi-core operating system, this means that the dispatcher and scheduler must consider which processes to execute on each core. With different processes running on different cores, handling competition among processes becomes more challenging because disabling interrupts on all cores whenever one needs to enter a critical region would be highly inefficient. Computer science has many active research areas related to building operating system mechanisms better suited to the new multi-core world.

Part 2

Simulated Writing：Communicating with E-mail and Memos（Ⅱ）

接 59 页

6. 撰写专业的电子邮件

电子邮件是一种企业交流方式，有一些有关撰写专业电子邮件的惯例和一般准则。图 4-3 展示了一个按照这些准则撰写的电子邮件的开始部分，包括完整的邮件地址和一个简单的敬语。

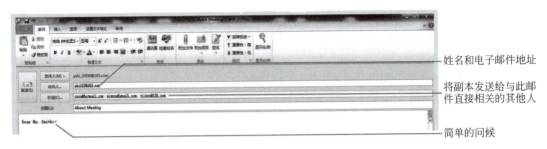

图 4-3　给电子邮件添加地址

（1）完整的名字和地址

类似 flower1972@gmail.com 这样的电子邮件地址不能明确地标识出发送者的身份，可以在电子邮件的 To 和 From 栏中填写完整的名字和电子邮件地址。像 Microsoft Office

Outlook 这样的电子邮件软件允许在姓名之后紧接着输入电子邮件地址（例如，Dan Lionel <flower1972@gmail.com>）。

（2）抄送

除了主要的收信人之外，可以将邮件的副本发送给其他人，只需要将他们的电子邮件地址填写在 Cc 栏中即可。确保在 Cc 栏中列出的人直接和邮件相关，并且可以从邮件的信息中获益——大部分人都只想收到他们想要阅读的邮件。

（3）敬语

用类似于 Greetings、Dear Mr. Dawson、Hi, Katie 或者 Ron. 等来开始电子邮件。敬语可以使交流有一个友好的开始，并且表明邮件已经开始了，这在别人转发或者回复给你的时候尤其有用。

（4）正文格式和内容

将开始行和其余部分进行相应的格式化，可以使其更容易阅读，见表 4-1。正文要关注于一个主题并且使用简练的文字，尽可能不要超过 25 行。理想情况下，读者在读取消息时不应该滚动一次以上。如果需要一次讨论多个主题，每个主题分别发送一封电子邮件。图 4-4 展示了发送的电子邮件的开始行和正文部分。

表 4-1 撰写电子邮件的注意事项

邮件	适合提到	尽量避免
To 和 From	• 每一行应包含姓名和电子邮件地址	• 仅仅依赖电子邮件地址来标识身份
抄送	• 发送一份副本到与此邮件直接相关的人	• 发送给与此消息无关的人
敬语	• 以一个简短的问候开始	• 省略敬语或者使用过于不正式的敬语，除非给朋友或者亲密的同事写信
正文格式	• 使用标准的大写和小写字符 • 插入空行和分割文档来提高可读性	• 使用全大写或全小写的文字 • 在一个长段落里包含所有的邮件内容
结束	• 如果适合提及的话，包括对行动的建议或者截止日期 • 以一个签名块结束	• 没有结论就结束 • 忘记提供联系方式

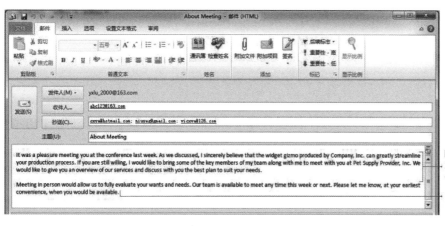

图 4-4 撰写电子邮件的正文

（5）结束语

以一个包含名字和联系方式的签名块结束，例如，所在组织的名称、地址、电话号码。大多数电子邮件软件都可以添加签名块。

7. 撰写专业的备忘录

专业人士偶尔使用传统的硬副本形式的备忘录在组织内部传递信息，尽管备忘录不像电子邮件那样常见。当需要正式的或者书面的、格式化的沟通记录的时候，就要写一个备忘录。不要像电子邮件那样，应该仅仅向组织内部的人发送备忘录。表4-2列出了撰写专业的备忘录所需注意的事项。

表 4-2 撰写备忘录的注意事项

备忘录元素	适合提到	尽量避免
首部	• 包含格式化为两列的标准首部行	• 遗漏首部的标签
发件人（From）行	• 在发件人（From）行的姓名后面签上名字的首字母	• 在备忘录的结尾处签名
起始行	• 以主要想法或请求开始	• 以敬语开始
正文格式	• 单倍行距 • 在段落之间插入空行 • 使用章节标题、列表和加粗来强调信息	• 双倍行距 • 用很长的段落

（1）使用印刷格式或者包含一个标题

如果所在组织提供了印刷格式或者备忘录的电子模板，要充分利用它们来保持和其他备忘录的一致。否则，可以在页面顶端添加 Memo 或 Memorandum 等抬头。图4-5展示了使用公司格式的备忘录。

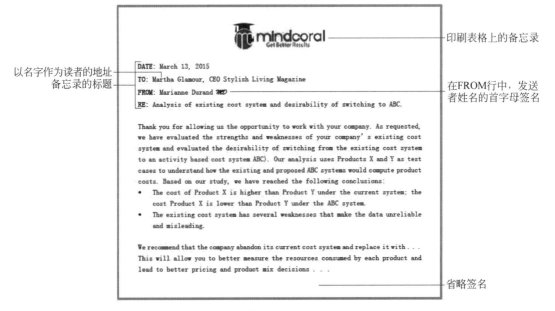

图 4-5 某个公司的备忘录

Unit 4　Operating Systems

（2）包含一个标准的首部

备忘录的首部列出了该文档的基本信息。大多数备忘录的首部至少有 4 行，类似于电子邮件：日期（Date）、收信人（To）、发件人（From）和标题（Subject）（或者 Re）。有些组织机构规定了额外的行，例如，优先（Priority）或者常规（Routing）。在字处理软件中可以使用格式化工具将一列中的首部标签和另一列中对应的文本对齐。

（3）将日期拼写出来

日期的格式取决于所在地区。例如，在美国 6/5/15 是 May 6，2015，在许多其他国家则是 June 5，2015。为了避免混淆，可以将月份的名字拼写出来并包含 4 位数的年份。

（4）使用名字或头衔来称呼读者

可以为一个人或者一群人准备备忘录。如果要将备忘录仅发送给几个人，在收信人（To）行中列出他们的名字即可。否则，使用职位头衔或者对群组的描述。

（5）省略敬语和签名块

在首部发件人（From）那一行，在名字的右面签上名字的首字母，而不是使用敬语来开始一个传统的备忘录（就像电子邮件那样）。这表明笔者已检查过这个备忘录，并且对其内容负责。不需要用结尾敬语或者签名来结束备忘录。

Part 3

Listening and Speaking

Dialogue：Talking about Operating Systems

(*Henry would like to know more about operating systems. Then he* **asks** *Mark and Sophie about it after class.*)

Henry： Exactly what are the functions of an operating system?

Sophie： Well, it controls key elements of the user interface, which includes the visual experience **as well as** the keyboard, mouse, microphone, or touchscreen that collects user commands.

Mark： And **behind the scenes**, the operating system is busy supervising critical operations that take place within a device.

Henry： Ok. Basically I'm familiar with operating systems such as Windows and iOS, but I think there are several others in widespread use.

Sophie: You are right. Operating systems can be categorized by the devices on which they are used.

Mark: Yes. A desktop operating system is designed for a desktop or laptop computer. The computer you use at home, at school, or at work is most likely [1] configured with a desktop operating system, such as Microsoft Windows, macOS, or Chrome OS.

[1] Replace with:
1. possibly
2. Probably

Sophie: In addition, operating systems such as iOS and Android are classified as mobile operating systems because they are designed for use on smartphones, tablet computers, and e-book readers.

Henry: Any others?[2]

[2] Replace with:
1. What else?
2. Anything else?

Sophie: Sure. Computers that are deployed as Web servers, or as servers for files, applications, databases, or email, generally use a server operating system designed for distributed networks accessed by many simultaneous users.

Mark: And Linux, UNIX, Windows Server, and macOS Server are examples of popular server operating systems.

Henry: Great. Where exactly is the operating system?

Mark: Well, in some digital devices, such as smartphones and e-book readers, the entire operating system is small enough to be stored in ROM. For most other computers, the operating system program is quite large, so most of it is stored on a hard disk or SSD.

Sophie: Right. During the boot process, the operating system kernel is loaded into RAM. A kernel provides essential operating system services, such as memory management and file access. The kernel stays in RAM the entire time your computer is on. Other parts of the operating system, such as customization utilities, are loaded into RAM as they are needed.

Henry: Ok, I've got it! Thank you very much.

Mark & Sophie: My pleasure.

 Exercises

Work in a group, and make up a similar conversation by replacing the statements with other expressions on the right side.

 Words

configure[kən'fɪgə] v. (尤指对计算机设备进行)配置,对(设备或软件进行)设定

kernel['kɜːn(ə)l] n. 内核

utility[juː'tɪləti] n. (用于帮助查故障的)工具,实用程序(= utility program),公用事业,公用事业公司

 Phrases

as well as 也,和……一样,不但……而且
behind the scenes 在幕后,秘密地
be classified as 被归类为……

 Abbreviations

ROM　Read Only Memory　只读存储器
SSD　Solid State Drive　固态硬盘
RAM　Random Access Memory　随机存取存储器

Listening Comprehension: Android

Listen to the article and answer the following 3 questions based on it. After you hear a question, there will be a break of 15 seconds. During the break, you will decide which one is the best answer among the four choices marked (A), (B), (C) and (D).

Questions

1. Android is Which kind of platform according to this article?

（A）Close

（B）Open

（C）Obsolete

（D）Old

2. Do hardware manufacturers have to adhere to certain specifications in order to be called "Android compatible" according to this article?

（A）Yes

（B）No

（C）Not necessary

（D）None of the above

3. Which kind of operating system is a Samsung smartphone using according to this article?

（A）iOS

（B）Windows 10

（C）Android

（D）macOS

 Words

impairment[imˈpɛəmənt] *n*. 损伤,损害

 Phrases

up with 比得上,接近
in mind 记住,考虑到
adhere to 遵守,坚持

Dictation: Linus Torvalds and the Software Nobody Knows

This article will be played three times. Listen carefully, and fill in the numbered spaces with the appropriate words you have heard.

Unit 4 Operating Systems

　　Torvalds, a 21-year-old student at the University of Helsinki in Finland, ___1___ his work on Minix, a scaled-down textbook ___2___ of the powerful UNIX operating system designed to run on PC hardware. Little by little, he cobbled together pieces of a ___3___, the part of the system where the real processing and control work is done.

　　When he mentioned his project on an Internet discussion group, a member ___4___ him space to post it on a university server. Others ___5___ it, tinkered with it, and sent the changes back to Torvalds. The communal work-in-progress ___6___ became known as Linux (pronounced "Linn-uks" by its creator). Within a couple of years, it was good enough to ___7___ as a product.

　　___8___ of copyrighting and selling Linux, Torvalds made it ___9___ available under the GNU General Public License (GPL) developed by the Free Software Foundation.

　　According to the GPL, anyone can give away, ___10___, or even sell Linux, as long as the source code—the program instructions—remain freely available for others to improve. Linux is the best ___11___ example of open-source software and now it spearheads the ___12___ open-source software movement.

　　Today Torvalds is an Internet folk hero. Web pages pay homage to him, his ___13___, and Tux, his stuffed ___14___ that has become the Linux mascot. In 1996 he completed his master's degree in computer science and went to work for Transmeta Corp., a chip design company in ___15___. In 2003 he moved to the Open Source Development Labs, which ___16___ with the Free Standards Group to become the Linux Foundation. He has become ___17___ thanks to stock options ___18___ by ___19___ companies that built their products on Linux. He ___20___ a relatively low profile, but still champions the open-source cause.

◆ Words

scaled-down 缩小比例的
textbook ['tekstbuk] adj. 经典的，合乎规范的
post [pəust] v. 张贴
communal [kə'mju:nəl, 'kɔmjə-] adj. 共有的，共用的
work-in-progress 半成品（价值），在制品（完成部分生产程序）
copyright ['kɔpirait] v. 获得……的版权

spearhead ['spiəˌhed] v. 当……的先锋，带头
folk [fəuk] adj. 民间的，普通平民的
stuffed [stʌft] adj. 充满的，饱的
mascot ['mæskət, -kɔt] n. 吉祥物，福神
champion ['tʃæmpjən] v. 捍卫，为……而斗争，声援
cause [kɔ:z] n. 事业，运动，(奋斗的)目标

Phrases

cobble together 胡乱拼凑,匆匆制作
tinker with 胡乱地修补,鼓捣
give away 赠送,捐赠
pay homage to 向……表示敬意
thanks to 幸亏,多亏,由于
stock options 职工优先认股权,在指定时期内定价定额购股权(stock option 的名词复数),购股选择权
low profile 不引人注目的形象

Unit 5

Computer Programing

Part 1

Reading and Translating

Section A: Web Application Development

Three technologies form the foundation for many Web applications: HTML5[1] specifies the structure of content displayed on a Web page; **CSS**[2] (Cascading Style Sheets) describes the design and appearance of information on a Webpage; and JavaScript[3] allows users to interact with a page's content. Many Web applications also access applications running on a server, connect to a database, or access third-party content from online sources. Together, these technologies enable developers to create browser-independent Web applications that run on a variety of devices (Figure 5-1).

Figure 5-1　Web application development

The **W3C** (World Wide Web Consortium) is an international organization that sets the standards for the technologies and operation of the Web. In addition, it defines the standards for HTML5 and CSS.

HTML5

HTML5 is the standard technology for creating Websites and applications. Recall that **HTML** uses a set of codes called tags to instruct a browser how to structure a Webpage's content. HTML tags specify how content is structured on a page, such as headings, hyperlinks, images, or paragraphs. This latest version of HTML has evolved to include new tags for playing audio and video files without relying on the use of third party **plug-ins**, or modules, to perform these tasks. For example, Silverlight is a free plug-in for creating engaging, interactive user experiences for Web and mobile applications. Some mobile devices, such as Apple's iPhone and iPad, do not support displaying media content that requires Silverlight. Instead, they rely on HTML5-**compliant** browsers, which are capable of interpreting HTML5 tags, to handle these tasks. Additional HTML5 features include recognizing gestures popular on mobile devices, such as swipe, or drag and drop; allowing applications to function in some limited fashion when no Internet connection is available; dynamically creating graphics, such as progress bars, charts, and animations; and geolocation (determining a user's location based on a device's GPS or connection to a cell tower).[4]

These HTML5 features allow Web developers to build applications that address the needs of how people use the Web today and provide richer user experiences. Each browser implements the HTML5 specification differently and may not support all of its features.

CSS

While HTML describes the structure of a Webpage's content as a collection of elements such as headings, paragraphs, images, and links, CSS allows Web designers to separate the code that specifies a page's content from the code that specifies the page's appearance.[5] For example, a Webpage may contain two paragraphs of text that are presented using a variety of fonts and sizes, styles, colors, borders, thicknesses, columns, or backgrounds. CSS provides Web designers with precise control over a Webpage's layout and allows the designers to apply different layouts to the same information for printing or for viewing in browsers on smartphones, tablets, or computers with varying screen sizes. The current version of CSS is known as CSS3 (Cascading Style Sheets, version 3).

JavaScript

JavaScript is a programming language that adds interactivity to Webpages. It often is used to check for appropriate values on Web forms, display alert messages, display menus on Webpages, control the appearance of a browser window, read and write cookies, display alert boxes, and detect the browser version in order to display a page especially designed for that browser. JavaScript code is loaded with a Webpage and runs in the browser.

Building Applications with HTML5, CSS, and JavaScript

Angry Birds is a popular game built using HTML5, CSS, and JavaScript in which players control a slingshot to launch birds at pigs located on a playing field. HTML5 creates the background screens dynamically; CSS helps control the appearance and position of the birds, pigs, blocks, and other on-screen game elements; JavaScript performs some of the calculations needed to model the physics for flight and other events in the game.

Words

plug-in 插件程序
compliant[kəmˈplaiənt] adj. （与系列规则相）符合的，一致的
animation[ˌæniˈmeiʃn] n. （指电影、录像、计算机游戏的）动画制作；动画片

geolocation[ˌdʒiəlouˈkeiʃn] n. 地理定位
address[əˈdres] v. 处理（问题）
layout[ˈleiaut] n. 布局,布置,设计
cookie[ˈkuki] n. 小型文本文件
slingshot[ˈsliŋʃɔt] n. 弹弓

block[blɔk] *n.* 障碍物
physics['fiziks] *n.* 物理成分,物理现象,物理学

 Phrases

cell tower 蜂窝基站,手机基站
a collection of 很多,一批

 Abbreviations

CSS　Cascading Style Sheets　级联样式表
W3C　World Wide Web Consortium　万维网联合会
HTML　Hypertext Markup Language　超文本标记语言

 Notes

[1]　HTML5 是万维网的核心语言、标准通用标记语言下的一个应用,超文本标记语言(HTML)的第五次重大修改。2014 年 10 月 29 日,万维网联盟宣布,经过接近 8 年的艰苦努力,该标准规范终于制定完成。

[2]　级联样式表(Cascading Style Sheets,CSS)是一种用来表现 HTML(标准通用标记语言的一个应用)或 XML(标准通用标记语言的一个子集)等文件样式的计算机语言。CSS 目前的最新版本为 CSS3,是能够真正做到网页表现与内容分离的一种样式设计语言。相对于传统 HTML 的表现而言,CSS 能够对网页中的对象的位置排版进行像素级的精确控制,支持几乎所有的字体字号样式,拥有对网页对象和模型样式编辑的能力,并能够进行初步交互设计,是目前基于文本展示最优秀的表现设计语言。CSS 能够根据不同使用者的理解能力,简化或者优化写法,针对各类人群,有较强的易读性。

[3]　JavaScript 是一种直译式脚本语言,是一种动态类型、弱类型、基于原型的语言,内置支持类型。它的解释器被称为 JavaScript 引擎,为浏览器的一部分,广泛用于客户端的脚本语言,最早是在 HTML(标准通用标记语言下的一个应用)网页上使用,用来给 HTML 网页增加动态功能。

[4]　**Original**:Additional HTML5 features include recognizing gestures popular on mobile devices, such as swipe, or drag and drop; allowing applications to function in some limited fashion when no Internet connection is available; dynamically creating graphics, such as progress bars, charts, and animations; and geolocation (determining a user's location based on a device's GPS or connection to a cell tower).

Translation:其他的一些 HTML5 特色包括识别在移动设备上常用的一些手势,例如猛击、拖放等;当没有互联网的时候,允许应用程序以某种限制的样式实现一些功能;动态

地创建图形，如进度条、图表和动画；还有地理定位的功能（根据设备的 GPS 或者对基站的连接确定用户的地理位置）。

［5］ **Original**：While HTML describes the structure of a Webpage's content as a collection of elements such as headings，paragraphs，images，and links，CSS allows Web designers to separate the code that specifies a page's content from the code that specifies the page's appearance.

Translation：虽然 HTML 能够将网页的内容描述为一系列元素的集合，如标题、段落、图片和链接，但是 CSS 能够让网页设计人员将确定网页内容的代码和确定网页外观的代码分离开来。

 Exercises

Ⅰ. Read the following statements carefully，and decide whether they are true（T）or false（F）according to the text.

　　____ 1. The W3C（World Wide Web Consortium）defines the standards for HTML5 and CSS.
　　____ 2. CSS is a programming language that adds interactivity to Webpages.
　　____ 3. HTML5，CSS，and JavaScript enable developers to create browser-dependent Web applications that run on a variety of devices.
　　____ 4. Angry Birds is a technology like HTML5，CSS，or JavaScript.
　　____ 5. JavaScript code is loaded with a Webpage and runs in the server.

Ⅱ. Choose the best answer to each of the following questions according to the text.

1. Which of the following is wrong about the Web development?
　　A. JavaScript is a programming language that adds interactivity to Webpages
　　B. HTML5 is the standard technology for creating Websites and applications
　　C. CSS allows Web designers to separate the code that specifies a page's content from the code that specifies the page's appearance
　　D. The current version of CSS is known as CSS5

2. How many technologies are mentioned forming the foundation for many Web applications?
　　A. One
　　B. Two
　　C. Three
　　D. Four

3. Which of the following technology is used for developing the popular game Angry Bird?

A. CSS
B. JavaScript
C. HTML5
D. All of the above

Ⅲ. Identify the letter of the choice that best matches the phrase or definition.

a. debugging
b. flowchart
c. object code
d. coding
e. syntax error

____ 1. A programming error that occurs when the programmer has not followed the rules of the programming language.

____ 2. A program design tool that graphically shows step-by-step how a computer program will process data.

____ 3. The machine language version of a computer program generated when the program's source code is compiled.

____ 4. The process of ensuring a program is free of errors.

____ 5. The process of writing the programming language statements to create a computer program.

Ⅳ. Fill in the numbered spaces with the words or phrases chosen from the box. Change the forms where necessary.

> program   create   text   describe   require
> reuse   full   acquire   senior   found

Student Entrepreneurs Create a New App in Five Days with "Premade Programming Lego Blocks"

52apps is a small software start-up ____1____ in 2012 by two 22 years-old ____2____ at the University of South Carolina whose business plan is to produce 52 apps in a year for iPhones and iPads by ____3____ an app within five days, and to sell the software through iTunes. Sometimes the apps are based on ideas ____4____ from members of the general public, with whom the firm shares royalties.

According to the founders, Christopher Thibault and Brendan Lee, the basis for ____5____ an app in less than a week—far less time than is usually ____6____ —is a proprietary module framework—what has been ____7____ figuratively as "premade programming Lego blocks."

"There's a lot of grunt work in creating apps," says Lee. "For example, it can take three to five hours to ___8___ implement all features in a device's GPS system. So we developed a bunch of ___9___ modules that we can plug into any app we write."

One of the 52app products is Canary, a smartphone app that can send an alarm to parents when their teens are doing dangerous things while driving, such as ___10___ .

Ⅴ. Translate the following passage into Chinese.

Programming Smartphones

Software for hand-held, mobile and embedded devices is often developed using the same general-purpose programming languages that are used in other contexts. With a larger keyboard and extra patience, some smartphone applications can be written using the smartphone itself. However, in most cases smartphone software is developed on desktop computers using special software systems that provide tools for editing, translating, and testing smartphone software. Simple apps are often written in Java, C++, and C#. However, writing more complex apps or core system software may require additional support for concurrent and event-driven programming.

Section B: Mobile App Development

Developers and technology managers should evaluate several possible approaches for creating mobile apps, and make a decision based on both technical and business considerations. Should they invest the time and money it takes to develop **high-performing** native apps [1] for many different mobile operating systems?

Would they be **better off** creating mobile Web apps, written using standard Web technologies, to run in a mobile browser? Or should they use a hybrid, or mixed, approach that can simplify the development process and lower development costs **at the expense of** a possible inconsistent user experience across platforms?

Native Apps

A native app is written for mobile devices running a particular mobile phone operating system, such as Google's Android or Apple's iOS. They offer fast performance and can store data for offline use. Native apps can access all of a device's content, including its contacts, calendar, and photos, and can interact with its hardware, including the microphone, camera, or accelerometer to measure movement and motion. For example, the native Instagram app can access the devices camera to take photos (Figure 5-2).

Apps developed for a specific mobile platform or device generally will not work on another without significant modification. Creating native apps requires programming languages, presentation technologies, and development tools particular to each platform.

After testing to be sure it works properly, developers **deploy**, or submit, a native

Figure 5-2 The native Instagram app can access the devices camera to take photos

app to an app store for approval and distribution. When deploying native apps to Google Play, Apple's App Store, or the Windows Store, developers must ensure that their apps follow rules and conditions that their publishers issue. For example, apps must run properly, may not contain offensive content, and should notify the user when requesting the current location or access to information stored on the device.

Developers pay an annual fee to publish apps in an app store. The store retains a percentage of the sales price of any apps sold as a commission.

Mobile Web Apps

Mobile Web apps are actually Websites that provide a user experience similar to native apps. Developers write them using standard Web technologies including HTML5, CSS, and JavaScript. Mobile Web apps are not deployed to an app store; rather, they are deployed to a Web server and users access them in a mobile browser. Users, therefore, always have access to the most recent version of an app. Creating a shortcut to the app's Website and saving it as an icon or tile on a device's home screen provides easy access to the mobile Web app. Many mobile Web apps have a responsive Web design, so that they will be displayed properly on devices with screens of different sizes.

Some companies choose to develop mobile Web apps so that they can write one app that works on all devices that is not subject to the rules of an app store. Mobile Web apps can access a limited set of device features, such as basic gestures, working offline, tap-to-call, and GPS, but do not have access to native features, such as the camera, microphone, accelerometer, and device notifications. For example, the Instagram mobile Web app runs in a browser and only displays photos, but does not allow you to take photos using your device's camera.

Hybrid Apps [2]

A hybrid app combines features of native and mobile Web apps. Like native apps, hybrid apps are developed for specific platforms and deployed to an app store. They can access many of a device's hardware features, such as its camera. Like mobile Web apps, they are built with HTML5, CSS, and JavaScript. Developers use development tools to package this code with a browser and prepare it as a native app to deploy to popular app stores. In this way, hybrid apps are cross-platform, meaning the same code can run on many mobile platforms. This approach often saves development time and costs, but may not provide a consistent user experience or fast performance on all devices.

Words

high-performing 高效的
deploy[di'plɔi] v. 部署
distribution[ˌdistri'bju:ʃən] n.（商品的）
　经销，推销，销售
offensive[ə'fensiv] adj. 无礼的，冒犯的
commission[kə'miʃən] n. 佣金，手续费，
　任命

shortcut['ʃɔ:tkʌt] n. 快捷方式，捷径
responsive[ri'spɔnsiv] adj. 反应迅速的，
　积极响应的
tap-to-call 点击呼叫

Phrases

better off 境况（尤指经济性）较好的，比较富裕
at the expense of 以……为代价，以牺牲……的利益为代价
be subject to 受……管制，使服从

Notes

[1] Native App（原生应用）是一种基于智能手机本地操作系统如 iOS、Android 并使用原生程式编写运行的第三方应用程序，也叫本地 App。

[2] Native App、Web App、Hybrid App 对比

比 较 项 目	Native App （原生应用）	Web App （网页应用）	Hybrid App （混合应用）
开发成本	高	低	中
维护更新	复杂	简单	简单

续表

比 较 项 目	Native App （原生应用）	Web App （网页应用）	Hybrid App （混合应用）
体验	优	差	优
应用商店或应用市场是否认可	认可	不认可	认可
安装	需要	不需要	需要
跨平台	差	优	优

 Exercises

Ⅰ. Read the following statements carefully, and decide whether they are true（T）or false（F）according to the text.

　　____ 1. Hybrid apps are deployed to an app store.
　　____ 2. HTML5，CSS，and JavaScript enable developers to write Hybrid apps.
　　____ 3. HTML5，CSS，and JavaScript enable developers to write mobile Web apps.
　　____ 4. Native apps are deployed to a Web server and users access them in a mobile browser.
　　____ 5. Apps developed for iOS generally will work on Android without significant modification.

Ⅱ. Choose the best answer to each of the following questions according to the text.

　　1. Which of the following is wrong about the mobile app development?
　　　A. Hybrid apps are deployed to an app store
　　　B. Mobile Web apps are deployed to an app store
　　　C. Native apps are deployed to an app store
　　　D. None of the above

　　2. How many technologies are mentioned writing mobile Web apps or hybrid apps?
　　　A. One
　　　B. Two
　　　C. Three
　　　D. Four

　　3. Which of the following technology is used for developing mobile Web apps?
　　　A. CSS
　　　B. JavaScript
　　　C. HTML5
　　　D. All of the above

Unit 5 Computer Programing

Ⅲ. Identify the letter of the choice that best matches the phrase or definition.

  a. compiler
  b. logic error
  c. object-oriented programming (OOP)
  d. software development kit (SDK)
  e. source code

  ____ 1. A computer program before it is compiled.
  ____ 2. A language translator that converts an entire program into machine language before executing it.
  ____ 3. An approach to program design in which a program consists of objects that contain data (attributes) and processes (methods) to be used with those objects.
  ____ 4. A programming package designed for a particular platform that enables programmers to develop applications for that platform more quickly and easily.
  ____ 5. A programming error that occurs when running a program produces incorrect results.

Ⅳ. Fill in the numbered spaces with the words or phrases chosen from the box. Change the forms where necessary.

> make   apply   submit   go   do
> lose   change   plumb   look   task

Who Decides When Programs Are Okay to Go?

  The title is release engineer, and he or she is the person "__1__ with gathering up all the code written by a company's many [software] engineers and __2__ sure it works together as a whole," according to one description. At Facebook in Menlo Park, California, the release engineer, Chuck Rossi, __3__ over code for bugs, talks to the engineers about their work, and decides which features are kept for the final product that goes up on the Facebook Website. His work comes after several software tools have been __4__ in a first round of checks.

  "It's like __5__," Rossi says about his job "It's not the most glamorous thing in the world, but I realized that if you're good at it, you could go to any software company in the world and they would say: 'When can you start?'"

  Rossi is able to pull up a profile of each engineer to see what code that person __6__. Everyone starts with four stars, but if Rossi has an issue with someone's work, he can take them down half a star. If engineers drop to two stars, they're not allowed to make ___7___ in programs until they've completed a review and retraining process. On the other hand, if they catch an error before the program ___8___ up on the Website, they can earn a half-star back.

"People here are pretty freaked out about ___9___ their stars," says Rossi, "but not in a bad way. It's all ___10___ in good fun."

Ⅴ. **Translate the following passage into Chinese.**
Programming Language Cultures

As with natural languages, users of different programming languages tend to develop cultural differences and often debate the merits of their perspectives. Sometimes these differences are significant as, for instance, when different programming paradigms are involved. In other cases, the distinctions are subtle. For example, whereas the text distinguishes between procedures and functions, C programmers refer to both as functions. This is because a procedure in a C program is thought of as a function that does not return a value. A similar example is that C++ programmers refer to a procedure within an object as a member function, whereas the generic term for this is method. This discrepancy can be traced to the fact that C++ was developed as an extension of C. Another cultural difference is that programs in Ada are normally typeset with reserved words in either uppercase or bold—a tradition that is not widely practiced by users of C, C++, C♯, FORTRAN, or Java.

Part 2

Simulated Writing: Communicating with Social Media

在科技交流方面,社交媒体可成为广泛的信息来源,其功能包括保持同事间的联系、从技术专家那里获取信息、了解顾客的喜好、与顾客分享最新的信息,以及在专业领域内进行广泛的联系。这里介绍几种常用的社交媒体(如博客、微博、社交网络站点、QQ和微信)进行交流的方式。

1. 博客

一个博客(Blog)就是一个网页,它通常是由简短且经常更新的文章构成;这些张贴的文章都按照年份和日期排列,也称为网络日志。博客的内容和目的有很大的不同,从对其他网站的超级链接和评论,有关公司、个人、构想的新闻到日记、照片、诗歌、散文,甚至科幻小说的发表或张贴等都有。许多博客都是作者个人心中所想的发表,另一些博客则是一群人基于某个特定主题或共同利益领域的集体创作。

随着博客的快速扩张,它的目的与最初的浏览网页心得已相去甚远。网络上数以千计的博主发表和张贴博客的目的有很大的差异。不过,由于沟通方式比电子邮件、讨论群组更简单和容易,博客已成为家庭、公司、部门和团队之间越来越盛行的沟通工具,它也逐渐被应用在企业内部网络(Intranet)中。

有些公司利用博客在雇员之间分享信息。这些仅在内部可访问的博客主要针对的是工程师、经理、行政人员和其他内部人员。公司所创建的内部博客可改进工作流程和提高士气。在大公司里，博客可作为电子邮件的一种替代方式，用于日常的内部交流。在网络上每个人都可上传消息，或对其他消息做出评论。在通过博客交流的环境里可以举行会议，不受面对面会议时间和场地的限制。还可以进行员工培训，传达公司发展的最新情况。博客对于协同工作特别有效。例如，公司软件部的人员可以创建论坛，讨论编程和测试的流程，然后部门人员可以加以衡量并提出建议。

公司所创建的外部博客可向客户提供对产品和服务的反馈渠道，改进营销和公共关系，提供及时的信息和更新，帮助大型组织的个性化。博客使公司有机会展示其人性和非正式的一面，对客户关注的问题做出亲切而快速的响应，让客户能提供想法和反馈。在公司的博客里语气十分关键，要表示友好、欢迎、真诚。博客应该邀请读者参与。

例如，迪士尼乐园(Disney Parks)创建了一个叫 Disney Parks Blog 的博客(如图 5-3 所示)，尽管迪士尼的品牌本质上针对的是小孩子，但是这个博客的内容对那些渴望获取一些旅行小贴士的父母来说是很有用的。与大多数的博客不同的是，迪士尼没有强调其社交的形象，它只是具有 RSS(聚合内容)和电子邮件订阅的链接。迪士尼也没有将每一个帖子底部的 Twitter 和 Facebook 的社交共享按钮包括进来。有关这个博客的参与度似乎有点低但比较稳定，每一个帖子都带有几个评论，并且每个帖子都在任意位置最多有 100 个赞(like)。此外，通常缺失的元素是要号召读者进行评论。还有一点就是，也许这个博客的目的就不是进行评论。

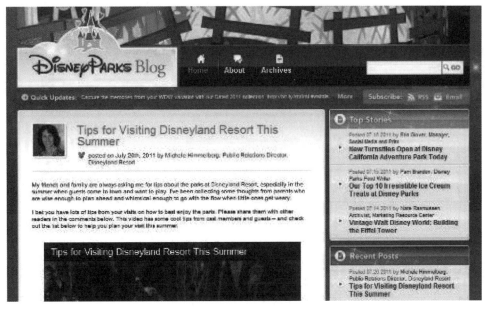

图 5-3　迪士尼乐园的博客

2. 推特

推特(Twitter)是美国的一个网站，它利用无线网络、有线网络的通信技术进行即时通信,是微博客(微博)的典型应用。它允许用户将自己的最新动态和想法以短信息的形式发送给手机和个性化的网站群,而不仅仅是发送给个人。

推特是一个可让你播报短消息给你的朋友或跟随者(followers)的在线服务,它也同样允许你指定你想跟随(follow)的推特用户,这样你就可以在一个页面上读取他们发布的信息。

推特提供以简洁形式进行实时发帖和更新的手段。个人以及公司、政府机构、其他组织通过推特简讯使朋友、商务关系人、顾客等获得信息并及时更新。推特被称为"小鸟叫声"(tweets),其写作方式简洁,每条消息限制在140个字符以内。

假如你在推特中输入一个项目,它们可以是私有的,只有当你的朋友获得你的允许才能查看,或者也可以是公开的,也就是说,所有知道你 Twitter ID 的人都可以读取或订阅你发布的消息。另外还有很重要的一点就是,推特是完全免费的。

推特可以用在很多地方,比如企业可以用它做客户服务。图 5-4 就是 JetBlue 公司所发布的推特。

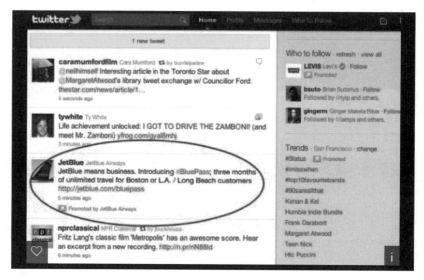

图 5-4　JetBlue 公司所发布的推特

也可以在中国最流行的新浪微博上进行撰写。

3. 社交网络站点

社交网络网站可将人们联系在一起,并将具有共同感兴趣的站点联系在一起。Facebook(脸书)是最流行的社交网之一。Facebook 最初是为大学生而开发的,现在被朋友、家庭、专业协会、政治组织、非营利机构、商业公司所使用。许多企业都有 Facebook 页面,用来强调或推销企业的一种特定产品或服务。例如招聘公司,可以创建 Facebook 页面进行招聘。非营利机构可以利用 Facebook 页面分享信息、提供照片、允许其他 Facebook 用户进行评论,与朋友分享信息。NASA(美国航空航天局)的火星探测器"好奇号"有一个 Facebook 页面,曾经受到 50 万人的喜爱。

Facebook 最流行的使用是在个人之间,人们可以用它保持与亲友的联系。虽然用户可能认为自己的个人 Facebook 页面与工作没有什么关系,但应记住,雇主会经常查看

Facebook 和其他社交网站，作为他们招聘面试的一部分。

图 5-5 为一个典型的 Facebook 页面。

图 5-5　一个典型的 Facebook 页面

4. QQ

QQ 是一款基于 Internet 的即时通信（IM）软件。QQ 支持在线聊天、视频通话、点对点断点续传文件、共享文件、网络硬盘、自定义面板、QQ 邮箱等多种功能，并可与多种通信终端相连。目前 QQ 已经覆盖 Microsoft Windows、macOS、Android、iOS 等多种主流平台。QQ 不仅仅是个人交流的平台，也是现代企业常用的推广工具。

图 5-6 是一个使用 QQ 进行交流的例子。

图 5-6　一个使用 QQ 进行交流的例子

5. 微信

微信（WeChat）是一个为智能终端提供即时通信服务的免费应用程序。微信支持跨通信运营商、跨操作系统平台，通过网络快速发送免费的（需消耗少量网络流量）语音短信、视频、图片和文字；微信提供公众平台、朋友圈、消息推送等功能，用户可以通过"摇一摇""搜索号码"、扫描二维码等方式添加好友和关注公众平台，也可将内容分享给好友或朋友圈。

其实微信相当于另一个QQ。但与QQ不同的是，它在交友方面的表现更具时效性，也更强大。不论是Android系统还是苹果系统的手机用户，只要安装了微信，就可以进行跨手机平台的畅通聊天。

图5-7是使用微信进行交流的一个例子。

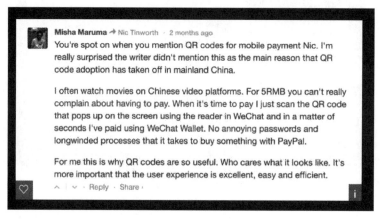

图5-7　使用微信进行交流的一个例子

Part 3

Listening and Speaking

Dialogue：Getting to Know Java Runtime Environment（JRE）and Java Virtual Machine（JVM）

（*Before the first lesson of Java programming，Mark downloaded a simple applet for a sample to learn，but he found that it wouldn't run.*）

Mark： Excuse me，Henry and Sophie. Could you help me？[1]

Henry： Sure. What's wrong？

Mark： Why won't this applet run？Its source code is correct.

[1] Replace with：
1. Can you give me a hand？
2. Could you please do me a favor？
3. Could you do me favor？

Unit 5 Computer Programing

Sophie: Has your computer installed Java Runtime Environment?

Mark: Not yet. What's Java Runtime Environment?

Henry: JRE for short, it is a software platform from Sun Microsystems that allows a computer to run applets and applications written in the Java programming language.

Sophie: It contains Java Virtual Machine, Java libraries and some other components.

Mark: What is Java Virtual Machine used for?

Sophie: A Java Virtual Machine, JVM for short, is a set of computer software programs and data structures which use a virtual machine model for the execution of other computer programs and scripts. It hides the details of the computer hardware on which their programs run.

Mark: What's the relationship between JVM and JRE?

Henry: The JVM, which is the instance of the JRE, comes into action when a Java program is executed. When execution is complete, this instance is garbage-collected. The JVM is distributed along with a set of standard class libraries which implement the Java API. The virtual machine and API have to be consistent with each other and are therefore bundled together as the JRE.

Sophie: So, this can be considered a virtual computer in which the virtual machine is the processor and the API is the user interface.

Henry: The JVM is a crucial component of the Java Platform. The use of the same bytecode for all platforms allows Java to be described as "compile once, run anywhere".

Mark: Bytecode?

Henry: Yes. JVM operates on a form of computer intermediate language commonly referred to as Java bytecode, which is normally but not necessarily generated from Java source code. Programs intended to run on a JVM must be compiled into this standardized portable binary format.

Mark: Is it visible for us or just an automatic temporary code?

Sophie: It typically comes in the form of .class files.

Mark: But a large program may consist of [2] many classes in different files.

[2] Replace with:
1. be composed of
2. be comprised of
3. be made up of

Sophie: Yes. For easier distribution of large programs, multiple class files may be packaged together in a .jar file, short for Java **archive**.

Henry: The JVM runtime executes .class or .jar files, emulating the JVM instruction set by interpreting it, or using a JIT compiler, **shortened form** of **just-in-time** compiler, such as Sun's HotSpot.

Sophie: JIT? I've heard a little of it before. What technology does JIT use?

Henry: JIT compiles parts of the bytecode that have similar functionality at the same time, and hence reduces the amount of time needed for compilation. It is used in most JVMs today to achieve greater speed.

Mark: So much knowledge I'm interested in! I'll do my best to learn. Thank you very much!

Exercises

Work in a group, and make up a similar conversation by replacing the statements with other expressions on the right side.

Unit 5 Computer Programing

 **Words**

applet [eplet] *n.* Java 小应用程序
　　（application let）
script [skript] *n.* 脚本
instance ['instəns] *n.* 实例,情况,建议
class [klɑːsɪ klæs] *n.* 类
bytecode ['baitkəud] *adj.* 字节码
archive ['ɑːkaiv] *n.* 档案,卷宗,案卷
just-in-time 及时,恰好

 Phrases

for short 简称,缩写
come into action 起作用,投入战斗
shortened form 简称,简写

Listening Comprehension: Writing the Code

Listen to the article and answer the following 3 questions based on it. After you hear a question, there will be a break of 15 seconds. During the break, you will decide which one is the best answer among the four choices marked (A), (B), (C) and (D).

Questions

1. Which point of view is not correct on the purpose of matching implementation to design?

　　(A) Easy to implement all the structures and relationships that are described with the charts and tables in the detailed design document as code directly

　　(B) Easy to trace the algorithms, functions, interfaces, and data structures from design to code and back again

　　(C) Easy to integrate all of the programmers' code into the whole system

　　(D) Easy for testing, maintenance, and configuration management over time

2. Which advantage of the design characteristics is not referred in this article?

　　(A) Low coupling

　　(B) Well-defined interfaces

　　(C) High cohesion

　　(D) Hierarchical building

3. Which technique is not mentioned in this article on coding with your team in mind?

　　(A) Standards

（B）Documents

（C）Common design techniques and strategies

（D）Information hiding

Words

daunt[dɔːnt] v. 沮丧，使气馁
construct[kənˈstrʌkt] n. 结构体
correspondence[ˌkɔrəˈspɔndəns] n. 通信
modularity[ˌmɔdjuˈlæriti] n. 模块性
couple[ˈkʌpl] v. 耦合

cohesion[kəuˈhiːʒn] n. 内聚
well-defined 定义明确的，清晰的
algorithm[ˈælgəriðəm] n. 算法
function[ˈfʌŋkʃn] n. 函数
invoke[inˈvəuk] v. 调用

Phrases

fit in with 适应，符合，与……一致
with... in mind 把……放在心上，以……为目的
work out 完成，得到（解决方法）

Dictation: Agile Software Development

This article will be played three times. Listen carefully, and fill in the numbered spaces with the appropriate words you have heard.

The modern business environment that **spawns** computer-based systems and software products is ___1___ and **ever-changing**. ___2___ conditions change rapidly, end-user needs ___3___, and new competitive threats ___4___ without warning. In many situations, we no longer are able to define requirements fully before the project begins. Software engineers must be agile ___5___ to respond to a **fluid** ___6___ environment.

The modern definition of agile software development evolved in the mid-1990s. ___7___, agile methods were called "___8___ methods" as part of a reaction against "heavyweight" methods. The aim of it is to create software in a lighter, faster, more ___9___ way. In 2001, several of the most **prominent proponents** of those "lightweight methodologies" started the Agile ___10___ and signed the "**Manifesto** for Agile Software Development.", a ___11___ of the values shared by them, for those **contemplating** new agile development processes, that is: individual and ___12___ over processes and tools, working software over comprehensive ___13___, ___14___ collaboration over contract negotiation, ___15___ to change over following a plan.

Actually, a number of methods similar to Agile were created ___16___ to 2000.

___17___ Programming (XP) is the most widely used agile process created by Kent Beck in 1996. An adaptive software development process was introduced in a paper by Edmonds in 1974. Other notable agile methods include Scrum, Crystal, ___18___ Software Development, ___19___ Driven Development, and ___20___ Systems Development Method.

 Words

spawn[spɔːn] v. 大量产生,造成,引发,引起
ever-changing 千变万化的,常变的
fluid['fluːid] adj. 变化的,流动的,液体的
prominent['prɒminənt] adj. 著名的

proponent[prə'pəunənt] n. 支持者,倡导者
manifesto[ˌmæni'festəu] n. 宣言,声明
contemplate['kɒntəmpleɪt] v. 思考,预期
adaptive[ə'dæptiv] adj. 适应的
notable['nəutəbl] adj. 著名的

Unit 6

Database

Part 1

Reading and Translating

Section A: Normalization: Ensuring Data Consistency

Normalization organizes a database into one of several normal forms to remove ambiguous relationships between data and minimize data **redundancy**. In zero normal form (ONF), the database is completely non-normalized, and all of the data **fields** are included in one relation or table. **Repeating groups** are listed within parentheses (Figure 6-1(a)). The table has large rows due to the repeating groups and wastes disk space when an order has only one item.

To normalize the data from ONF to 1NF (first normal form), you remove the repeating groups (fields 3 through 7 and 8 through 12) and place them in a second table (Figure 6-1(b)). You then assign a **primary key** to the second table (Line Item), by combining the primary key of the nonrepeating group (Order#) with the primary key of the repeating group (Product#), called a **composite key**. Primary keys are underlined to distinguish them from other fields.

To further normalize the database from 1NF to 2NF (second normal form), you remove partial dependencies. A partial dependency exists when fields in the table depend on only part of the primary key. In the Line Item table (Figure 6-1(b)), Product Name is dependent on Product#, which is only part of the primary key. Second normal form requires you to place the product information in a separate Product table to remove the partial dependency (Figure 6-1(c)).

To move from 2NF to 3NF (third normal form), you remove **transitive** dependencies. A transitive dependency exists when a non-primary key field depends on another non-primary key field. As shown in Figure 6-1(c), Vendor Name is dependent on Vendor#, both of which are non-primary key fields. If Vendor Name is left in the Line Item table, the database will store redundant data each time a product is ordered from the same vendor.

Third normal form requires Vendor Name to be placed in a separate Vendor table, with Vendor# as the primary key. The field that is the primary key in the new table in this case, Vendor#—also remains in the original table as a foreign key and is identified by a dotted underline (Figure 6-1(d)).[1] In 3NF, the database now is logically organized in four separate tables and is easier to maintain. For instance, to add, delete, or modify a Vendor or Product Name, you make the change in just one table.

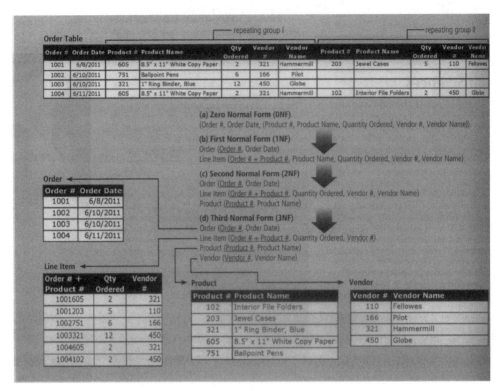

Figure 6-1　The process of normalizing a database

normalization [ˌnɔːməlaiˈzeiʃn] n. 规范化，正常化，标准化，正态化
redundancy [riˈdʌndənsi] n. 冗余，冗余度，过多，过剩，冗长
field [fiːld] n. 字段，信息组，栏
transitive [ˈtrænsətiv] adj. 传递的，过渡的，可传递的

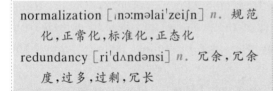

repeating group 重复组
primary key 主键，主（关）键（字）
composite key 组合键，复合关键字

[1]　**Original**：The field that is the primary key in the new table—in this case, Vendor＃—also remains in the original table as a foreign key and is identified by a dotted underline.

Translation: 在这种情况下，在这个新表中的主键 Vendor# 也要作为一个外键保留在原表中，它用点画线标识出。

 Exercises

Ⅰ. Read the following statements carefully, and decide whether they are true (T) or false (F) according to the text.

____ 1. Foreign keys are underlined to distinguish them from other fields.

____ 2. A partial dependency exists when a non-primary key field depends on another non-primary key field.

____ 3. A transitive dependency exists when fields in the table depend on only part of the primary key.

____ 4. A composite key is a combination of the primary key of the nonrepeating group with the primary key of the repeating group.

____ 5. In zero normal form (ONF), the database is completely normalized.

Ⅱ. Choose the best answer to each of the following questions according to the text.

1. Which of the following are underlined to distinguish them from other fields?

   A. Indices

   B. Primary Keys

   C. Stored Procedures

   D. Foreign Keys

2. Which of the following can be used to organize a database into one of several normal forms to remove ambiguous relationships between data and minimize data redundancy?

   A. Modernization

   B. Realization

   C. Normalization

   D. Confrontation

3. Which of the following exists when a non-primary key field depends on another non-primary key field?

   A. A transitive dependency

   B. Partial dependencies

   C. Full dependencies

   D. All of the above

Ⅲ. Identify the letter of the choice that best matches the phrase or definition.

   a. database
   b. index
   c. primary key
   d. query
   e. record

   _____ 1. A collection of related data that is stored in a manner enabling information to be retrieved as needed.
   _____ 2. A collection of related fields in a database and also called a row.
   _____ 3. A request to see information from a database that matches specific criteria.
   _____ 4. A small table containing a primary key and the location of the record belonging to that key; used to locate records in a database.
   _____ 5. A specific field in a database table that uniquely identifies the records in that table.

Ⅳ. Fill in the blanks with the words or phrases chosen from the box. Change the forms where necessary.

> analyze   call   launch   consist   library
> approximate   track   inventory   subscribe   complex

Database Everywhere

A database can be of any size and of any degree of ___1___. Traditional electronic databases include those that handle airline reservation systems, many library catalogs, magazine ___2___ for large publishing companies, patient tracking in large hospitals, and ___3___ for supermarkets and big-box stores such as Walmart. These databases typically use text- and numeric-based data. Newer types of databases include multimedia data and formulas for data ___4___.

Wikipedia (www.Wikipedia.org) is a Web-based, free-content, multilingual encyclopedia that anyone can log on to and add to or edit as he or she sees fit; it has more than 55 million articles in ___5___ 300 languages.

The National Geographic Society and IBM's Watson Research Labs ___6___ a massive database ___7___ the Genographic Project (https://genographic.nationalgeographic.com/genographic/index.htm) that is cataloging genetic markers and is capable of ___8___ the geographic origins of your and other people's ancestors back more than 10,000 years.

Google has created a database ___9___ of millions of digitally scanned books from several university ___10___ (http://books.google.com/).

Ⅴ. Translate the following passage into Chinese.

Database System for PCs

Personal computers are used in a variety of applications, ranging from elementary to sophisticated. In elementary "database" applications, such as storing Christmas card lists or maintaining bowling league records, spreadsheet systems are often used in lieu of database software since the application calls for little more than the ability to store, print, and sort data. There are, however, true database systems available for the PC market, one of which is Microsoft's Access. This is a complete relational database system, as well as chart- and report-generation software. Access provides an excellent example of how the principles presented in this text form the backbone of popular products on the market today.

Section B: NoSQL Databases

NoSQL, which stands for "not only SQL" is an approach to database design that provides flexible schemas for the storage and retrieval of data beyond the traditional table structures found in relational databases (Figure 6-2). While NoSQL databases have existed for many years, NoSQL databases have only recently become more popular in the era of cloud, big data and high-volume Web and mobile applications. They are chosen today for their attributes around scale, performance and ease of use. The most common types of NoSQL databases are key-value, document, column and graph databases.

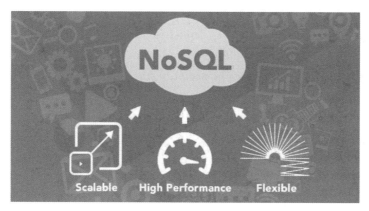

Figure 6-2 NoSQL Databases

It's important to emphasize that the "No" in "NoSQL" is an abbreviation for "not only" and not the actual word "No." This distinction is important not only because many NoSQL databases support SQL like queries, but because in a world of microservices [1] and polyglot persistence, NoSQL and relational databases are now commonly used together in a single application.

NoSQL databases do not follow all the rules of a relational database—specifically, it does use a traditional row/column/table database design and does not use structured query language (SQL) to query data.

To better understand, let's go back to the advent of the first databases designed for the masses, which appeared around 1960. Those databases included DataBase Management Systems (DBMS) to allow users to organize large quantities of data.

The original DBMSs were flat-file/comma-delimited, often proprietary to a particular application, and limited in the relationships they could uncover among data. DBMSs were also complex.

This eventually led to the development of Relational DataBase Management Systems (RDBMSs). Relational databases arranged data in tables that could be connected or related by common fields, separated from applications, and queried with SQL. In other words, the relational database placed data into tables, and SQL created an interface for interacting with it.

Relational databases and SQL work well for large servers and storage mediums. But as larger sets of frequently evolving, disparate data became more common for things like ecommerce applications, programmers needed something more flexible than SQL. NoSQL is that alternative.

NoSQL databases are built for specific data models and have flexible schemas that allow programmers to create and manage modern applications. NoSQL is also more agile because it's not built on the concept of tables and does not use SQL to manipulate or analyze data (although some NoSQL databases may have SQL-inspired query language).

NoSQL encompasses structured data (code in a specific format, written in such a way that search engines understand it), semi-structured data (data that contains tags or other markers to separate semantic elements and enforce hierarchies of records and fields within the data), unstructured data (information that either does not have a pre-defined data model or is not organized in a pre-defined manner), and polymorphic data (data that can be transformed to any distinct data type as required).

NoSQL enables you to be more agile, more flexible, and to iterate more quickly. NoSQL database enables simpler design, better control over availability and improved scalability.

A NoSQL database can manage information using any of four primary data models:

(1) Key-value store

In the key-value structure, the key is usually a simple string of characters, and the value is a series of uninterrupted bytes that are opaque to the database. The data itself is usually some primitive data type (string, integer, array) or a more complex object that an application needs to persist and access directly.

This replaces the rigidity of relational schemas (schemas are basically a blueprint of how tables work) with a more flexible data model that allows developers to easily modify fields and object structures as their applications evolve. In general, key-value stores have no query language. They simply provide a way to store, retrieve, and update data using simple GET, PUT and DELETE commands. The simplicity of this model makes a key-value store fast, easy to use, scalable, portable, and flexible.

(2) Document-based

A document is an object and keys (strings) that have values of recognizable types, including numbers, Booleans, and strings, as well as nested arrays and dictionaries. Document databases are designed for flexibility. They aren't typically forced to have a schema and are therefore easy to modify. If an application requires the ability to store varying attributes along with large amounts of data, document databases are a good option. MongoDB and Apache CouchDB are examples of popular document-based databases.

(3) Column-based

Column-based (also called "wide column") models enable very quick data access using a row key, column name, and cell timestamp [2]. The flexible schema of these types of databases means that the columns don't have to be consistent across records, and you can add a column to specific rows without having to add them to every single record. The wide, *columnar* stores data model, like that found in Apache Cassandra, are derived from Google's BigTable paper.

(4) Graph-based

The modern graph database is a data storage and processing engine that makes the persistence and exploration of data and relationships more efficient. In graph theory, structures are composed of *vertices* and edges (data and connections), or what would later be called "data relationships." Graphs behave similarly to how people think—in specific relationships between discrete units of data. This database type is particularly useful for visualizing, analyzing, or helping you find connections between different pieces of data. As a result, businesses *leverage* graph technologies for recommendation engines, fraud analytics, and network analysis. Examples of graph-based NoSQL databases include Neo4j and JanusGraph.

Many NoSQL databases were designed by young technology companies like Google, Amazon, Yahoo, and Facebook to provide more effective ways to store content or process data for huge Websites. Some of the most popular NoSQL databases include the following:

- Apache CouchDB, an open source, JSON [3] document-based database that uses JavaScript as its query language.
- Apache Cassandra, an open source, wide-column store database designed to manage large amounts of data across multiple servers and clustering that spans multiple data centers.
- MongoDB, an open source document-based database that uses JSON-like documents and schema, and is the database component of the MEAN stack [4].
- Redis, a powerful in-memory key value store used for session caching, message

queues, and other specific applications.

- Elasticsearch, a document-based database that includes a full-text search engine.

Relational databases have been around for over 40 years, and technology has changed dramatically since then. A relational database uses SQL to perform tasks like updating data in a database or to retrieve data from a database. Some common relational database management systems that use SQL include Oracle, DB2, and Microsoft SQL Server. Maintaining **high-end**, commercial relational database management systems are expensive because they require purchasing licenses, trained manpower to manage and **tune** them, and powerful hardware.

NoSQL enables faster, more agile storage and processing, which means NoSQL databases are generally a better fit for modern, complex applications like ecommerce sites or mobile applications.

NoSQL database's horizontal scaling and flexible data model means they can address large volumes of rapidly changing data, making them great for agile development, quick iterations, and frequent code pushes [5].

In a nutshell, the difference between relational databases and NoSQL databases are performance, availability, and scalability.

Some specific cases when NoSQL databases are a better choice than RDBMS include the following:

- When you need to store large amounts of unstructured data with changing schemas. NoSQL databases usually have horizontal scaling properties that allow them to store and process large amounts of data. And NoSQL enables **ad-hoc** schema changes. (In contrast, with a relational database, an engineer designs the data schema **up front**, and SQL queries are then run against the database; if subsequent schema changes are required, they're often difficult and complex to carry out.)

- When you're using cloud computing and storage. Most NoSQL databases are designed to be scaled across multiple data centers and run as distributed systems, which enables them to take advantage of cloud computing infrastructure—and its higher availability—**out of the box**.

- When you need to develop rapidly. NoSQL is often the data store of choice for Agile software development methods, which require very short sprint cycles. With NoSQL, you don't have to prepare data like you do if you're using a relational database, and instead of having to migrate structured data every time the application design changes, a dynamic NoSQL schema can evolve with the application.

- When a hybrid data environment makes sense. NoSQL is sometimes taken to mean not only SQL, which means that it can complement or sit alongside a relational database and provide the flexibility to choose the best tool for the job.

For example，Craigslist[6] hosts its active listings in a relational database，but manages its archives in a lower-overhead document-based NoSQL store．

Words

schema[ˈskiːmə] n. 模式
advent[ˈædvent] n. （重要事件、人物、发明等的）出现
mass[mæs] n. 民众，大量
comma-delimited 逗号分界
proprietary[prəˈpraiətri] adj. 专有的
medium[ˈmiːdiəm] n. 介质，媒介
disparate[ˈdispərət] adj. 不同的，不相干的，全异的
semantic[siˈmæntik] adj. 语义的
polymorphic[ˌpɒliˈmɔːfik] adj. 多态的
iterate[ˈitəreit] v. 迭代（数学或计算过程，或一系列指令）
opaque[əuˈpeik] adj. 不透明的，难懂的

rigidity[riˈdʒidəti] n. 严格
columnar[kəˈlʌmnə] adj. 印（排）成栏的，柱状的
vertices[ˈvɜːtisiːz] n. （三角形或锥形的）角顶，顶点，制高点（vertex 的复数）
leverage[ˈliːvəridʒ] v. 发挥杠杆作用，施加影响
high-end 高端的，价高质优的
tune[tjuːn] v. （使）协调
ad-hoc 特设的，特定目的的
sprint[sprint] n. 冲刺
overhead[ˌəuvəˈhed, ˈəuvəhed] n. 经常费用，经常开支

Phrases

stand for 代表
polyglot persistence 多语言持久性
in a nutshell 概括地说，简言之
up front 在前面
out of the box 能够满足一定需求的

Notes

［1］ 微服务（microservice）是一种云原生架构方法，其中单个应用程序由许多松散耦合且可独立部署的较小组件或服务组成。

［2］ 时间戳（timestamp）是使用数字签名技术产生的数据，签名的对象包括了原始文件信息、签名参数、签名时间等信息。时间戳系统用来产生和管理时间戳，对签名对象进行数字签名产生时间戳，以证明原始文件在签名时间之前已经存在。

［3］ JSON（JavaScript Object Notation，JS 对象简谱）是一种轻量级的数据交换格式。它基于 ECMAScript（欧洲计算机协会制定的 JS 规范）的一个子集，采用完全独立于编程语言的文本格式来存储和表示数据。简洁和清晰的层次结构使得 JSON 成为理想的数据

交换语言。易于人阅读和编写，同时也易于机器解析和生成，并能有效地提升网络传输效率。

［4］ MEAN（MongoDB，Express，AngularJS，Node.js）stack（MEAN 堆栈）是长期流行的 LAMP 堆栈的现代挑战者，用于使用开源软件构建专业网站。MEAN 代表了体系结构和思维模型的重大转变——从关系数据库到 NoSQL，从服务器端的 Model-View-Controller 到客户端的单页应用程序。

［5］ 代码推送（code push）是一种云服务，它能够使 Cordova 和 React Native 的开发者将移动 App 更新直接部署到其用户的设备上。

［6］ Craigslist 是由创始人 Craig Newmark 于 1995 年在美国加利福尼亚州的旧金山湾区地带创立的一个网上大型免费分类广告网站。

 Exercises

Ⅰ. Read the following statements carefully, and decide whether they are true（T）or false（F）according to the text.

　　____ 1. NoSQL stands for "No SQL".
　　____ 2. NoSQL databases follow all the rules of a relational database.
　　____ 3. The original DBMSs appeared around 1960.
　　____ 4. NoSQL is not built on the concept of tables and does not use SQL to manipulate or analyze data.
　　____ 5. NoSQL encompasses structured data, semi-structured data, unstructured data, and polymorphic data.

Ⅱ. Choose the best answer to each of the following questions according to the text.

1. Which of the following is a specific case when NoSQL databases are a better choice than RDBMS?
　　A. When you're using cloud computing and storage
　　B. When you need to develop rapidly
　　C. When you need to store large amounts of unstructured data with changing schemas
　　D. All of the above

2. Which of the following is the most common type of NoSQL databases?
　　A. Graph databases
　　B. Document databases
　　C. Key-value databases
　　D. All of the above

3. Which of the following is not NoSQL database?
　　A. MongoDB

Unit 6 Database

B. DB2
C. Apache CouchDB
D. Neo4j

Ⅲ. **Identify the letter of the choice that best matches the phrase or definition.**

a. data dictionary
b. data validation
c. middleware
d. relational database management system (RDBMS)
e. table

_____ 1. A type of database system in which data is stored in tables related by common fields; the most widely used database mode today.

_____ 2. In a relational database, a collection of related records (rows).

_____ 3. Software used to connect two otherwise separate applications, such as a Web server and a database management system.

_____ 4. The process of ensuring that data entered into a database matches the data definition.

_____ 5. The repository of all data definitions in a database.

Ⅳ. **Fill in the numbered spaces with the words or phrases chosen from the box. Change the forms where necessary.**

> mine   target   change   compete   concern
> buy   cost   pinpoint   inconsistent   design

The Uses of Data Mining

In government, the Internal Revenue Service has a program ___1___ to catch tax cheaters by locating ___2___ between mortgage payments and income. Counterterrorism experts analyze records "on travel habits, calling patterns, email use, financial transactions, and other data to ___3___ possible terrorist activity," according to one report.

In professional sports, Toronto Raptors management has used data mining to "rack and stack" the team to try to make it more ___4___ against other National Basketball Association (NBA) teams. NBA executives at the Miami Heat have used data mining to find more effective means of ___5___ an audience than traditional mass-media marketing.

In retailing, point-of-sale databases in department stores are ___6___ for sales data about thousands of products in hundreds of geographic areas to understand customer preferences and try to cater to individual ___7___ needs. Companies ___8___ that

115

opinion among users of social networks can make or break their products use data mining "sentiment analysis" tools to analyze what is being said online.

In medicine, data mining is used to see what subtle factors affect success and failure in back surgery, for example, or what groups are likely to experience health ___9___ increases or what treatment plans are most likely to be successful.

In science, DM techniques are used to find new patterns in genetic data, molecular structures, and global climate ___10___ and to catalog more than 50 million galaxies.

The accomplishments of data mining using conventional databases are truly impressive. But the field stands on the verge of a historic shift. The name for this shift: Big Data.

Ⅴ. **Translate the following passages into Chinese.**
Distributed Databases

With the advancement of networking capabilities, database systems have grown to encompass databases, known as distributed databases that consist of data residing on different machines. For instance, an international corporation might store and maintain local employee records at local sites yet link those records via a network to create a single distributed database.

A distributed database might contain fragmented and/or replicated data. The first case is exemplified by the previous employee-records example in which different fragments of the database are stored in different locations. In the second case, duplicates of the same database component are stored at different locations. Such replication might occur as a means of reducing information retrieval time. Both cases pose problems not present in more traditional centralized databases—how to disguise the distributed nature of the database so that it functions as a coherent system or how to ensure that replicated portions of a database remain duplicates of each other as updates occur. In turn, the study of distributed databases is a current area of research.

Part 2

Simulated Writing: Using Presentation Software to Write

使用 Microsoft PowerPoint(最常用)或其他软件,如 Apple Keynote 或 OpenOffice Impress,能很快、很容易地创建形象化元素,并且可将图片、声音、电影、动画、视频的网上链接包括进来。一种新的软件 Prezi 可以提供更多的选择。

在充满图片、视频的电子通信世界里,PowerPoint 或类似的软件常被认为是企业不可或缺的工具。

使用演示软件可以做以下事情:

- 用不同的颜色、底纹、纹理创建幻灯片。
- 创建绘画或曲线图,导入剪贴图、照片或其他图片。
- 创建有动画效果的文本和图像。例如,每点击一次进入一个符号列表项,或者图形中的纵向条形和横向条形逐个加亮,强调数据中的某些特征。
- 创建幻灯片之间的动态过渡,例如,一张幻灯片向右侧退出,另一张从左侧进入。
- 将每张幻灯片放大。
- 将幻灯片按不同顺序排列。.
- 精确设定演讲时间。
- 在计算机屏幕上、大型投影仪上、网页上、投影机上演示,或打印出来作为讲义分发。

下面以 PowerPoint 为例,具体介绍如何制作幻灯片。

1. 简介

PowerPoint 演示文稿(PPT)和海报演示很类似,唯一不同的是 PPT 是在计算机上用幻灯片来演示,而不是用真正的海报。这种形式往往用来配合口头报告,可以使报告更具说服力。我们还可以加入声音和视觉媒体。幻灯片演示通常用于与一个大的群体分享信息,如专业会议、课堂演示和会议等。幻灯片演示应该更像是报告的提纲。在幻灯片演示中有 3 个主要元素:文本、图片和表格。文本用于突出主要观点以及关键术语和概念。

2. 一些准备工作

在开始做 PPT 之前,应该先考虑清楚演示的几个关键部分:受众、目的(说服性、增长知识性等)、主题以及陈述。因为一个好的 PPT 设计应该适合用于演示的场合,因此在开始制作 PPT 之前,尽量搞清使用何种措辞有助于成功演示。

3. 主要组成部分

PPT 的幻灯片应该更像一个提纲。文字通常都是将主要内容列出来,而不是完整的句子。以下是几个可以在幻灯片中展示的内容:

- 图表和/或表格。
- 解释。
- 列表。
- 基本事实。
- 必要的图片。

4. 内容安排

PPT 内容的顺序应该取决于受众所需。无论做什么,都要谨慎地组织 PPT 并条理清晰地陈述论点,这样受众才会信服我们的论点。以下是一些可以参照的格式。

- 概述、主体和结论(此类格式通常用于帮助受众弄清演示内容,否则受众可能会被复杂的论点搞糊涂);
- 轶事、内容和结论(此类格式主要为了防止受众在开始演示之前就已经厌烦);
- 计划、好处和轶事(此类格式主要用于介绍一些新鲜事物,而且所面对的受众要求我们的演示简短且切题)。

5. 其他有用的信息

提倡的内容:

- 为整个 PPT 选择一个统一背景;

- 使用简单清晰的字体；
- 保证字体足够大，使后排的受众也能看到；
- 在列表中使用项目符号和一致的短语结构；
- 列出基本信息即可，运用关键词来引导读者或观众贯穿整个演示过程；
- 使用直接、简洁的语言，将文字数量减到最少；
- 必要时提供相关的解释；
- 使用空格来隔开文本或图表之类的可视组件；
- 保证每张幻灯片之间的联系符合逻辑；
- 为每张幻灯片加上标题。

避免的内容：
- 在幻灯片中堆满了图表；
- 使用复杂的字体；
- 添加不相干的信息；
- 写下所有要说的话；
- 使用分散观众注意力的图片；
- 颜色搭配难以阅读，如在蓝色背景上使用黑色的字体，尽量使用对比度高的组合。

使用 PowerPoint 展示的一个例子如下：

Introduction to Extreme Programming (XP)

Source: ExtremeProgramming.org_home

1

What is XP

- Extreme Programming (XP) is actually a deliberate and disciplined approach to software development. It was based on observations of what made computer programming faster and what made it slower. About eight years old, it has already been proven at many companies of all different sizes and industries world wide.
- XP is an important new methodology for two reasons:
  - it is a re-examination of software development practices that have become standard operating procedures.
  - It is one of several new lightweight software methodologies created to reduce the cost of software.
- XP is successful because it emphasizes:
  - Customer involvement and satisfaction
  - Team work
- XP improves a software project in four essential ways:
  - Communication
  - Simplicity
  - Feedback
  - Courage

2

When to use XP

- Dynamic requirements
- High project risks
- Small groups of programmers
- Testability
- Productivity

The Rules and Practices of XP

- Planning
    - User stories are written.
    - Release planning creates the schedule.
    - Make frequent small releases.
    - The Project Velocity is measured.
    - The project is divided into iterations.
    - Iteration planning starts each iteration.
    - Move people around.
    - A stand-up meeting starts each day.
    - Fix XP when it breaks.
- Designing
    - Simplicity.
    - Choose a system metaphor.
    - Use CRC cards for design sessions.
    - Create spike solutions to reduce risk.
    - No functionality is added early.
    - Refactor whenever and wherever possible.

The Rules and Practices of XP *(cont.)*

- Coding
    - The customer is always available.
    - Code must be written to agreed standards.
    - Code the unit test first.
    - All production code is pair programmed.
    - Only one pair integrates code at a time.
    - Integrate often.
    - Use collective code ownership.
    - Leave optimization till last.
    - No overtime.
- Testing
    - All code must have unit tests.
    - All code must pass all unit tests before it can be released.
    - When a bug is found tests are created.
    - Acceptance tests are run often and the score is published.

XP Map

- The XP Map shows how they work together to form a development methodology. Unproductive activities have been trimmed to reduce costs and frustration.

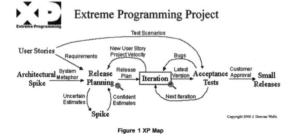

Figure 1 XP Map

Unit 6   Database

What We Have Learned About XP

- Release Planning
- Simplicity
- System Metaphor
- Pair Programming
- Integrate Often
- Optimize Last
- Unit Tests
- Acceptance Tests

7

More Information

- Web Sites
    - The Portland Pattern Repository
    - XProgramming.com
    - XP Developer
    - …
- Books
    - *Extreme Programming Explained: Embrace Change.* By Kent Beck
    - *Refactoring Improving the Design of Existing Code.* By Martin Fowler
    - *Extreme Programming Installed.* By Ron Jeffries, Chet Hendrickson, and Ann Anderson
    - …

8

Part 3

Listening and Speaking

Dialogue: Why is Big Data a Challenge

(*As big data is becoming more and more popular, Henry would like to know more about it.*)

Henry: Excuse me, Sophie and Mark. Could you tell me about big data? It is a **buzz** word nowadays.

121

Sophie: Sure. Big data **refers to** huge collections of data that are difficult to process, analyze, and manage using conventional database tools. Examples of big data include **user profiles** stored on social network sites, the archive of Google searches, medical records, astronomical data, and military surveillance data.

Mark: To my understanding,[1] analysts at International Data Corporation describe big data as a core component of an emerging computing platform that is likely to drive innovation and disruption through the next decade. The 3rd platform is based on cloud computing, mobile devices, social networking, and big data. This platform has massive scale, not only in cloud-based hardware technology, but also in the vast amount of data that will be generated, consumed, and analyzed.

[1] Replace with:
1. To what I know,
2. Based on my understanding,

Henry: Big data is a challenge?

Mark: Exactly! Big data is a relatively new phenomenon that businesses are just beginning to deal with[2]. The **sheer** volume of big data is difficult to handle, but additional factors further complicate its use.

[2] Replace with:
1. cope with
2. handle
3. solve
4. resolve
5. settle

Sophie: That is right. Big data was originally defined as having three Vs: volume, **velocity**, and variety. As big data evolved, however, additional V factors emerged. Today, big data is characterized as having high volume, high velocity, diversified variety, unknown **veracity**, and low-density value.

Henry: Could you please detail the 5Vs?

Sophie: Of course. First, let's talk about volume. Big data is high volume. It is measured in **petabytes**, **exabytes**, and even higher volumes. Storing such high volumes of data can be a challenge, as is making backups.

Mark: Right. Big data is typically distributed across many storage devices. For example, Facebook operates a cluster of 1,100 servers with about 12 petabytes of storage capacity just for its analytical activities.

Henry: How about the second V, velocity?

Sophie: Big data often needs to be handled quickly in order to be useful. As with Internet "speed," the velocity of big data is actually a measure of capacity and may be quantified in terabits per second (Tbps) or even petabits per second (Pbps).

Mark: Although a single Internet connection cannot handle such speeds, data may arrive simultaneously over multiple connections. The challenge is to organize the data as it arrives, process it if necessary, and store it where it can be easily retrieved.

Henry: Sounds very interesting.

Mark: Yes. Regarding the variety, big data commonly consists of multiple data types such as text, images, video, numbers, and audio that is generated from transaction processing systems, sensors, social media, smartphones, and a diversity of other sources.

Sophie: However, some data may be structured, while other data is unstructured. Organizing this mix of data is challenging and may require database designers to seek solutions other than the rigid structures of relational databases.

Henry: How about veracity?

Mark: Big data can contain an unknown amount of inaccurate data that is counter-productive to accurate analytics and decision making. Data verification can require cross checks, which in turn depend on even more data.

Henry: And the final V?

Sophie: In the context of big data, value does not necessarily **equate** to money, but rather to the usefulness of data. Big data typically includes a high proportion of low-density data that is not relevant to processing or analysis.

Mark: Low-density data refers to large volumes of very detailed data in which many of the details are not important. The opposite is high-density data, which is packed with lots of useful information.

Henry: I see! Anyway, thanks for your time.

 Exercises

Work in a group, and make up a similar conversation by replacing the statements with other expressions on the right side.

 Words

buzz[bʌz] *n.* 时髦的(词语、想法或活动)
sheer[ʃiə] *adj.* 绝对的,完全的,透明的
velocity[viˈlɔsiti] *n.* 速率,迅速,周转率
veracity[vəˈræsəti] *n.* 精确性,诚实
petabyte[ˈpetəbait] *n.* 2^{50} 字节
exabyte[igzəˈbait] *n.* 2^{60} 字节

cluster[ˈklʌstə] *n.* 集群,簇
terabit[ˈterəbit] *n.* 兆兆位,万亿比特
counter-productive 产生相反效果的
equate[iˈkweit] *v.* 等同,使相等,视为平等

 Phrases

refer to 指的是,参考,涉及
user profile (在网络或布告牌环境下的)用户简介

Listening Comprehension: Data Mining

Listen to the article and answer the following 3 questions based on it. After you hear a question, there will be a break of 15 seconds. During the break, you will decide which one is the best answer among the four choices marked (A), (B), (C) and (D).

Unit 6　Database

Questions

1. Where does data mining derive its name from?
   （A）Data analyzing
   （B）Mountain excavating
   （C）Knowledge discovery
   （D）Consumer focus

2. What is the ultimate purpose of data mining?
   （A）Analyzing enormous sets of data
   （B）Calculating an immense amount of value
   （C）Predicting behaviors and future trend
   （D）Producing market research reports

3. What measures did the retailer take after analyzing local buying patterns using data mining?
   （A）Move the beer display closer to the diaper display
   （B）Sell beer at a discount
   （C）Move the beer display away from the diaper display
   （D）Sell diapers at a discount

 Words

proactive[ˌprəuˈæktiv] adj. 主动的,先发制人的	loyalty[ˈlɔiəlti] n. 忠诚,忠实
vein[vein] n. 矿脉;特色,风格	grocery[ˈgrəusəri] n. 杂货店
ore[ɔː(r)] n. 矿石	diaper[ˈdaiəpə] n. 尿布
probe[prəub] v. 探查,查明	genetics[dʒiˈnetiks] n. 遗传学
spot[spɔt] v. 发现,准确地定出……的位置	

 Phrases

sift through 筛选,通过

Dictation：Data Warehouse

This article will be played three times. Listen carefully，and fill in the numbered spaces with the appropriate words you have heard.

125

The term "Data Warehouse" was coined by W.H. Inmon, who is ____1____ recognized as the "father of the data warehouse" in 1990, while IBM sometimes uses the term "information warehouse". However, the concept of data warehousing can ____2____ to the late-1980s when IBM researchers Barry Devlin and Paul Murphy developed the "business data warehouse".

Based on analogies with ____3____ warehouses, data warehouses were intended as large-scale ____4____/storage/staging areas for corporate data. Data could be retrieved from one ____5____ point or data could be ____6____ to "retail stores" or "data marts" which were tailored for ready ____7____ by users.

Data warehouses are designed to ____8____ reporting and analysis. An expanded ____9____ for data warehousing includes business intelligence tools, tools to extract, ____10____, and load data into the repository, and tools to manage and retrieve metadata. In essence, it was intended to provide an ____11____ model for the flow of data from ____12____ systems to ____13____ environments, with attempt to ____14____ the various problems associated with this flow—mainly, the ____15____ associated with it.

The term data warehouse also generally refers to the combination of many different ____16____ across an entire ____17____. It contains a wide variety of data that ____18____ a coherent picture of business conditions at a single point in time. Today, data warehouse has emerged as an important way for an organization to use data to come up with facts, ____19____ or relationships that can help them make effective decisions or create effective strategies to ____20____ their goals.

Words

repository [ri'pɔzitəri] n. 仓库
metadata ['metə'deitə] n. 元数据

coherent [kəu'hiərənt] adj. 一致的,连贯的

Phrases

staging area 临时数据交换区
data mart 数据集市,专用数据栈

Unit 7

Computer Network

Part 1

Reading and Translating

Section A: OSI Reference Model: The Driving Force behind Network Communications

Every message sent over a network—even the simplest email message—must be divided into **discrete** packages of data and **routed** via transmission media such as telephone lines. While **traveling** from the sending computer to the receiving computer, each data package can take a different path over the network. How do these messages get to their destination, **intact** and accurate?

The Open Systems Interconnection(OSI)**reference model**, a communications standard developed by the International Organization for Standardization (**ISO**), offers an answer. The OSI reference model describes the flow of data in a network through seven layers, from the user's application to the physical transmission media.

A simple way to understand the OSI reference model is to think of it as an elevator (Figure 7-1). On the sending end, data enters at the top floor (the application layer) and travels to the bottom floor (the physical layer). Each layer communicates with the layers immediately above and below it. When a layer receives data, it performs specific functions, adds control information to the data, and passes it to the next layer. The control information contains error-checking, routing, and other information needed to ensure proper transmission along the network.

The top layer, the application layer, **serves as** the interface between the user and the network. Using application software, such as an email program, a user can type a message and specify a recipient. The application then prepares the message for delivery by converting the message data into bits and attaching a header identifying the sending and receiving computers.

The presentation layer translates the converted message data into a language the receiving computer can process (from **ASCII** to **EBCDIC**, for example) and also may compress or **encrypt** the data. Finally, the layer attaches another header specifying the language, compression, and encryption **schemes**.

The next layer, called the **session** layer, establishes and maintains communications sessions. A session is the period between establishment of a connection, transmission of the data, and termination of the connection.

The transport layer, also called the end-to-end layer, ensures that data arrives

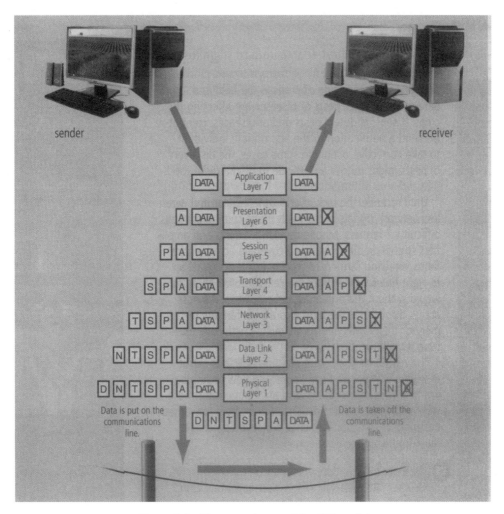

Figure 7-1 The seven layers of the OSI model

correctly and in proper sequence. The transport layer, divides the data into segments and creates a **checksum**, a mathematical sum based on the data, and puts this information in the transport header. The checksum later is used to determine if the data was **scrambled** during transmission.

The network layer routes the message from sender to receiver. This layer splits the data segments from the transport layer into smaller groups of bits called **packets**. Next, it adds a header containing the packet sequence, the receiving computer address, and routing information. The network layer also manages network problems by rerouting packets to avoid network congestion.

The data **link** layer supervises the transmission of the message to the next network node by specifying the network technology (such as **Ethernet** or **token ring**) and grouping data **accordingly**. The data link layer also calculates the checksum and keeps a copy of each packet until it receives confirmation that the packet arrived undamaged at the next node.

Finally, the physical layer encodes the packets into a signal recognized by the medium that will carry them—such as an analog signal to be sent over a telephone line—and sends the packets along that medium to receiving computer.

At the receiving computer, the process is reversed and the data moves back through the seven layers from the physical layer to the application layer, which identifies the recipient, converts the bits into readable data, removes some of the error-checking and control information from the data, and directs it to the appropriate application.[1] A modified 5-layer model is used for data sent using the Transmission Control Protocol (TCP) and/or the Internet Protocol (IP). This model includes the physical, data link, network, transport, and application layers. The next time you send an email message to a friend, consider the network communications processes described by the OSI reference model, which ensure that your message travels safely over many network to your friend's computer.[2]

  Words

discrete [di'skri:t] adj. 离散的,不连续的	scramble ['skræmbl] v. 把……搅乱,使混杂
route [ru:t] v. 按某路线发送,给……规定路线(次序,程序)	packet ['pækit] n. 包,束,分组,小包
travel ['trævl] v. 传送,移动,旅行	link [liŋk] n. 链路,链接,关联,关系
intact [in'tækt] adj. 完整无缺的,未经触动的,未受损伤的	Ethernet ['i:θənet] n. 以太网
	accordingly [ə'kɔ:diŋli] adv. 相应地,因此,依据
encrypt [in'kript] v. 加密,将……译成密码	encode [in'kəud] v. (将文字材料)译成密码,编码
scheme [ski:m] n. 方案,计划,设计图	identify [ai'dentifai] v. 辨认,识别,认出,确定
session ['seʃn] n. 会话,会议	
checksum ['tʃeksʌm] n. 校验和,检查和	

  Phrases

reference model 参考模型
serve as 充当,担任,为
token ring 令牌环

Unit 7　Computer Network

 Abbreviations

OSI　Open Systems Interconnection　开放系统互连
ISO　International Organization for Standardization　国际标准化组织
ASCII　American Standard Code for Information Interchange　美国信息交换标准代码
EBCDIC　Extended Binary-Coded Decimal Interchange Code　扩充的二进制编码的十进制交换码
TCP　Transmission Control Protocol　传输控制协议
IP　Internet Protocol　互联网协议

 Notes

〔1〕　**Original**：At the receiving computer, the process is reversed and the data moves back through the seven layers from the physical layer to the application layer, which identifies the recipient, converts the bits into readable data, removes some of the error-checking and control information from the data, and directs it to the appropriate application.

Translation：在接收计算机端,过程是相反的:数据从物理层到应用层这 7 层结构传送回来,这个过程可确定接收者,将比特值转换成可读的数据,删除一些来自数据的错误检查和控制信息,并将数据分配给合适的应用程序。

〔2〕　**Original**：The next time you send an email message to a friend, consider the network communications processes described by the OSI reference model, which ensure that your message travels safely over many network to your friend's computer.

Translation：下一次当你发送一封电子邮件消息给朋友时,考虑一下由 OSI 参考模型所描述的网络通信过程,它能够确保你的消息通过许多网络安全地传送到你朋友的计算机上。

 Exercises

Ⅰ. Read the following statements carefully, and decide whether they are true (T) or false (F) according to the text.

　　____ 1. It's not necessary for a message to be divided into discrete packages of data when travelling over a network.

　　____ 2. Each data package must take the same path over the network while traveling from the sending computer to the receiving computer.

　　____ 3. The transport layer makes sure that data arrives correctly and in proper sequence.

　　____ 4. A modified 5-layer model includes the physical, data link, network, transport, and session layers.

_____ 5. The network layer splits the data segments from the transport layer into smaller groups of bits called routers.

Ⅱ. **Choose the best answer to each of the following questions according to the text.**

1. Which of the following serves as the interface between the user and the network?
   A. The application layer
   B. The transport layer
   C. The data link layer
   D. The network layer

2. Which of the following is not included in a modified 5-layer model?
   A. The application layer
   B. The transport layer
   C. The network layer
   D. The presentation layer

3. Which of the following developed OSI reference model, a communications standard?
   A. TCP
   B. IP
   C. ISO
   D. ASCII

Ⅲ. **Identify the letter of the choice that best matches the phrase or definition.**

a. antenna
b. Bluetooth
c. computer network
d. mesh network
e. switch

_____ 1. A collection of computers and other hardware devices that are connected together to share hardware, software, and data, as well as to communicate electronically with one another.

_____ 2. A device used for receiving or sending radio signals; often used to increase the range of a network.

_____ 3. A device used to connect multiple devices on a single (typically wired) network; forwards packets to only the intended recipient.

_____ 4. A networking standard for very short-range wireless connections; the devices are automatically connected once they get within the allowable range.

_____ 5. A network in which there are multiple connections between the devices on the network so that messages can take any of several possible paths.

Ⅳ. Fill in the blanks with the words or phrases chosen from the box. Change the forms where necessary.

> receive build transmit call break
> use carry proper govern connect

Protocols

A protocol, or communications protocol, is a set of conventions ___1___ the exchange of data between hardware and/or software components in a communications network. Every device ___2___ to a network has an Internet Protocol (IP) address so that other computers on the network can ___3___ route data to that address. Sending and ___4___ devices must follow the same set of protocols.

Protocols are ___5___ into the hardware or software you are using. The protocol in your communications software, for example, will specify how receiver devices will acknowledge sending devices, a matter ___6___ handshaking. Handshaking establishes the fact that the circuit is available and operational. It also establishes the level of device compatibility and the speed of ___7___. In addition, protocols specify the type of electronic connections ___8___ the timing of message exchanges, and error-detection techniques.

Each packet, or electronic message, ___9___ four types of information that will help it get to its destination: (1) the sender's address (the IP), (2) the intended receiver's address, (3) how many packets the complete message has been ___10___ into, and (4) the number of this particular packet. The packets carry the data in the protocols that the Internet uses—that is, TCP/IP.

Ⅴ. Translate the following passage into Chinese.

Ethernet

Ethernet is a set of standards implementing a LAN with a bus topology. Its name is derived from the original Ethernet design in which machines were connected by a coaxial cable called the ether. Original developed in the 1970s and now standardized by IEEE as a part of the IEEE 802 family of standards, Ethernet is one of the most common methods of networking PCs. Indeed, Ethernet controllers have become a standard component in the PCs available in the current retail market.

Today there are actually several versions of Ethernet, reflecting advances in technology and higher transfer rates. All, however, share common traits that characterize the Ethernet family. Among these are the format in which data are packaged for transmission, the use of Manchester encoding (a method of representing 0s and 1s in which a 0 is represented by a descending signal and a 1 is represented by an ascending signal) for the actual transmission of bits, and the use of CSMA/CD for controlling the right to transmit.

Section B: Ethernet (802.3)

Ethernet (802.3) is the most widely used standard for wired networks. It is typically used with **LANs** that have a star topology (though it can also be used with **WANs** and **MANs**) and can be used in conjunction with **twisted-pair**, **coaxial**, or **fiber-optic** cabling. Ethernet was invented in the mid-1970s and has continued to evolve over the years; about every three years the new approved amendments are incorporated into the existing **IEEE** 802.3 Ethernet standard to keep it **up to date**. Figure 7-2 summarizes the various Ethernet standards; of these, the most common today are Fast Ethernet, Gigabit Ethernet, and 10 Gigabit Ethernet. The 40 Gigabit Ethernet and 100 Gigabit Ethernet standards were **ratified** in 2010. Development of the even faster 400 Gigabit Ethernet and Terabit Ethernet standards are currently being explored; if ratified, they are expected to be used for connections between servers, as well as for delivering video, digital X-rays and other digital medical images, and other high-speed, **bandwidth-intensive** networking applications.

STANDARD	MAXIMUM SPEED
10BASE-T	10 Mbps
Fast Ethernet (100BASE-T or 100BASE-TX)	100 Mbps
Gigabit Ethernet (1000BASE-T)	1,000 Mbps (1 Gbps)
10 Gigabit Ethernet (10GBASE-T)	10 Gbps
40 Gigabit Ethernet	40 Gbps
100 Gigabit Ethernet	100 Gbps
400 Gigabit Ethernet*	400 Gbps
Terabit Ethernet*	1,000 Gbps (1 Tbps)
*Under consideration for development	

Figure 7-2 Ethernet standards

Devices connected to an Ethernet network need to have an Ethernet port either built in or added using an expansion card. Ethernet networks can contain devices using multiple Ethernet speeds, but the slower devices will only operate at their **respective** speeds.

A relatively new Ethernet development is Power over Ethernet (PoE)[1], which allows electrical power to be sent along the cables in an Ethernet network (often referred to as Ethernet cables) along with data. Consequently, PoE devices are not plugged into an electrical outlet. PoE is most often used in business networks with remote wired devices (such as outdoor networking hardware, security cameras, and other devices) that are not located near a power outlet. It can also be used to place networked devices near ceilings or other locations where a nearby power outlet may not be available, and in homes to connect wired devices (such as security cameras) to a home network without running new electrical wiring.[2] Regular Ethernet-enabled devices can be powered via PoE if a PoE adapter is used.

Ethernet is a network standard for linking all devices in a local area network that describes how data can be sent between computers and other networked devices usually in close proximity. Ethernet is a network standard that specifies no central computer or device on the network (nodes) should control when data can be transmitted. That is, each node attempts to transmit data when it determines the network is available to receive communications. If two computers or devices on an Ethernet network attempt to send data at the same time, a collision will occur. When this happens, the computers or devices resend their messages until data transfer is successful.

Ethernet uses cables to connect devices; its wireless counterpart is Wi-Fi. Other network standards exist (two being TCP/IP, and IBM's Token Ring). But Ethernet is the most popular LAN standard in the world, particularly on star networks. This is because of the way it describes how data can be sent between nodes and enables it to be used with almost any kind of computer and network device. It is also inexpensive and easy to install and maintain. This popularity is the reason why most new microcomputers come equipped with an Ethernet card and an Ethernet port. Ethernet connections are available in the guest rooms of many hotel chains, such as Hilton and Hyatt.

Words

twisted-pair 双绞线 coaxial[kəu'æksəl] adj. 同轴的 fiber-optic 光纤 ratify['rætifai] v. 批准,认可 bandwidth-intensive 带宽密集型的	respective[ris'pektiv] adj. 各自的,分别的 proximity[prɔk'simiti] n. 邻近,接近 chain[tʃein] n. 连锁店或旅馆系列的事物

Phrases

up to date 拥有(或包含)最新信息的
power outlet 电源(引)出口,电源插座
come equipped with 配备

Abbreviations

LAN　Local Area Network　　局域网,局部区域网,局域网路
WAN　Wide Area Network　　广域网
MAN　Metropolitan Area Network　　城域网
IEEE　Institute of Electrical and Electronic Engineers　　电器和电子工程师学会

 Notes

〔1〕　PoE(Power over Ethernet,有源以太网),有时也被简称为以太网供电,在现有的以太网 Cat.5 布线基础架构不做任何改动的情况下,在为一些基于 IP 的终端(如 IP 电话机、无线局域网接入点 AP、网络摄像机等)传输数据信号的同时,还能为此类设备提供直流供电的技术。PoE 技术能在确保现有结构化布线安全的同时保证现有网络的正常运作,最大限度地降低成本。

〔2〕　**Original**：It can also be used to place networked devices near ceilings or other locations where a nearby power outlet may not be available, and in homes to connect wired devices (such as security cameras) to a home network without running new electrical wiring.

Translation：它还可以用于将网络化的设备置于天花板或其他地点附近,在那里,附近的一个电源插座可能不可用,并且在家里能够将有线设备(如安全摄像头)连接到不用布置新的电线的家庭网络。

 Exercises

Ⅰ. Read the following statements carefully, and decide whether they are true (T) or false (F) according to the text.

　　____ 1. Wi-Fi is a MAN.
　　____ 2. Ethernet, token ring, and TCP/IP are all network standards.
　　____ 3. PoE devices are plugged into an electrical outlet.
　　____ 4. Ethernet describes how data can be sent between nodes and enables it to be used with almost any kind of computer and network device in a LAN.
　　____ 5. Ethernet (802.3) is the most widely used standard for wireless networks.

Ⅱ. Choose the best answer to each of the following questions according to the text.

　1. Which of the following is the network standard?
　　　A. TCP/IP
　　　B. Token Ring
　　　C. Ethernet

D. All of the above

2. Which of the following is the counterpart of Ethernet?
   A. MAN
   B. Wi-Fi
   C. WAN
   D. None of the above

3. Which of the following is the most popular LAN standard in the world?
   A. Wi-Fi
   B. MAN
   C. Ethernet
   D. WAN

III. Identify the letter of the choice that best matches the phrase or definition.
   a. node
   b. peer-to-peer
   c. protocols
   d. TCP/IP
   e. Tree network

   ____ 1. In this network, nodes have equal authority and can act as both clients and servers
   ____ 2. A widely used Internet protocol
   ____ 3. Rules for exchanging data between computers
   ____ 4. Any device that is connected to a network
   ____ 5. This network, also known as a hierarchical network, is often used to share corporate-wide data.

IV. Fill in the blanks with the words or phrases chosen from the box. Change the forms where necessary.

> watch   detect   direct   provide   refer
> determine   turn   enable   embed   call

Can Embedded Computers Use the Internet to Communicate with Other Computers and Devices?

Many already do, on a small scale. For example, a Smart TV ___1___ you to browse the Web, stream video from online media services, listen to Internet radio,

137

communicate with others on social media sites, play online games, and more—all while ___2___ a television show.

A trend, ___3___ the Internet of Things, describes an environment where processors are ___4___ in every product imaginable (things), and those "things" communicate with each other via the Internet (i.e. alarm clocks, coffeemakers, apps; vehicles, refrigerators, phones, washing machines, doorbells, streetlights, thermostats, navigation systems, etc.).

For example, when your refrigerator ___5___ the milk is low, it sends your phone a text message that you need milk and adds a buy milk task to your scheduling app. On the drive home, your phone ___6___ the closest grocery store that has the lowest milk price and sends the address of that grocery store to your vehicle's navigation system, which in ___7___ gives you directions to the store. In the store, your phone ___8___ you to the dairy aisle, where it receives an electronic coupon from the store for the milk. Because this type of environment ___9___ an efficient means to track or monitor status, inventory, behavior, and more — without human intervention — it sometimes is ___10___ to as machine-to-machine (M2M) communications.

Ⅴ. **Translate the following passage into Chinese.**

Virtual Private Network (VPN)

A Virtual Private Network (VPN) is a private, secure path across a public network (usually the Internet) that is set up to allow authorized users private, secure access to the company network. For instance, a VPN can allow a traveling employee, business partner, or employee located at a satellite office or public wireless hotspot to connect securely to the company network via the Internet. A process called tunneling is typically used to carry the data over the Internet; special encryption technology is used to protect the data so it cannot be understood if it is intercepted during transit. Essentially, VPNs allow an organization to provide secure, remote access to the company network without the cost of physically extending the private network.

Part 2

Simulated Writing: Writing Professional Letters (Ⅰ)

商务信函是一种有效的方式,被用来传递正式的或有说服力的信息。它能够建立永久性的记录,或者能够发送重要、敏感或机密的信息。尽管电子邮件已经成为最流行的交换书面信息的方式,但商务信函仍然是一个必要的通信工具。通常写信是为了与所处的组织之外的人进行沟通,当然,也可以通过写信给同事发送正式的消息。除了页面上所写的话,信的设计和格式也在向读者展示作者自己,作者对细节的关注,以及作者的专业水平。

Unit 7　Computer Network

1. 如何撰写商务信函

商务信函是一种在组织外传递信息的专业交流工具。虽然商务信函的使用频率远低于其他的交流媒介，如电子邮件和传真，但当需要与供应商、其他商家，最重要的是与客户交流时，商务信函是最合适的选择。图 7-3 显示了典型的商务信函的例子。

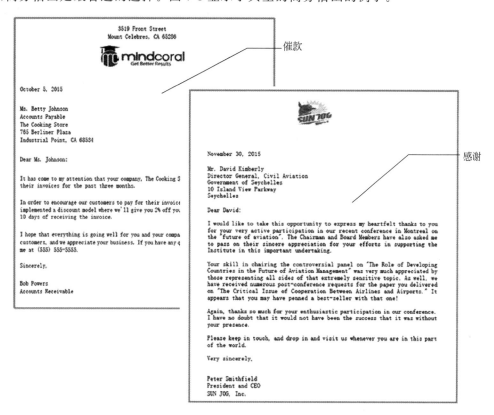

图 7-3　商务信函的例子

在以下情况下,可以写一封商务信函：

(1) 与不认识的人进行交流。如果需要和一个没见过或根本不认识的人进行交流,那么最好发一封商务信函来建立职业关系。虽然电子邮件很容易撰写,而且送达速度更快,但其非正式性及自发性会使邮件显得太自我或太大胆。

(2) 记录交流。如果需要保持与公司以外的人进行正式交流的书面记录,那么通常商务信函是最好的选择。商务信函可以提供一个永久的记录,尤其是在附有合同、协议条款或特别优惠时。

(3) 传达坏消息或讨论敏感的事情。打印在公司信纸上的商务信函会比其他渠道如电子邮件更正式,也更能表示尊重。撰写书面的信能够向读者展示作者对这个问题的认真态度。此外,商务信函可以保密,并且比一些数字通信的形式拥有更多的隐私。

(4) 表达善意。当想要表示感谢、祝贺、慰问或道歉时,书面信函是十分合适的。在每一种情况下,一封信,包括信纸、字体和签名,都会比一封非正式的信更加有效地表达作者的情感。

在以下情况下,可以打电话、亲自访问或发送电子邮件：

(1) 尽快发出信息。商务信函通常通过最好的邮递工具进行发送,这可能需要几天才能送达。隔夜快递服务是一个选项,虽然递送成本很高。

(2) 与有良好工作关系的人联系。用信件与认识的人进行日常交流有些过于正式,但当想表达善意或需要书面记录时就是例外了。

(3) 写一个常规的主题。电子邮件的流行是因为它的高效,而打电话和直接访问会比书面的信息更加个性化。对于常规的交流,如对于不需要创建永久性记录、保密、表示礼节,或提供有说服力的论据的请求和响应,请使用电子邮件或打电话。

2. 书写商业信函

在写一封商务信函之前,首先要确立沟通的目标或目的——是正在发出请求,响应查询,记录决策,还是确认一个行动？然后,可以考虑并预期读者对所写的信函的反应。当开始撰写的时候,可以遵循图7-4所示的商务信函的标准格式。作者应使用正确的格式,或者用齐头式来展示其专业性,并且简化任务。

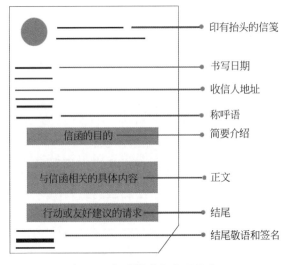

图7-4　标准的商务信函格式

1)印有抬头的信笺

大多数商务信函都是写在印有抬头的信笺上,上面含有公司的名称、地址、电话、传真号码及网址。通常还会有企业徽标来标志该组织。图 7-5 展示了 XETC 公司的信笺。

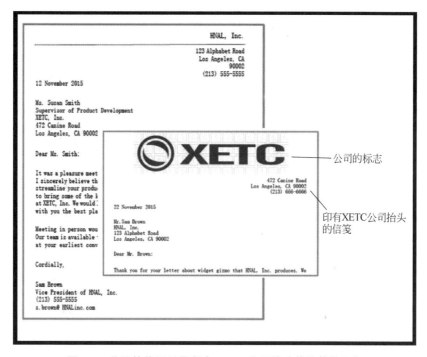

图 7-5　公司的信函以及印有 XETC 公司抬头的信笺的回复

2)书写日期

以今天的日期开头,再写上月份,并使用 4 位数表示年份。信最好使用当前的日期。不要提早或者推迟商务信函的日期。

3)(写在信笺左上角的)收信人地址

收信人地址包括有关收信人的基本信息:姓名、头衔,以及组织机构名称和邮寄地址。

4)(书信等开头的)称呼语

商务信函是比较正式的交流工具,它常常应该以称呼语开始。通常会说 Dear,后面紧跟收信人的名字,比如 Dear Ms. Mary。

5)简要介绍

信函的第一段应该直接表达信函的目的。要解释为什么写这封信,以便收信人可以更好地了解信中的信息。要使用礼貌与对话的语气,避免千篇一律的介绍语言。

6)正文

大多数商务信函都应该包含一个或多个段落,这些段落能够为收信人提供信息、解释,或者与此信函相关的其他细节。所有这些段落都应该支持介绍部分所展示的主旨。

7)结尾

还需要结尾段优雅地结束这封信,切忌突兀地结束商务信函。相反,以善意的表达、礼貌的评论或意见,或要求采取具体行动的请求来结尾会赢得他人的好感。

8) 结尾敬语和签名

在信的结尾用敬语,如真诚地(Sincerely)、恭敬地(Respectfully)或亲切地(Cordially)。之后在结尾敬语下面的 4 行插入名字,这 4 行为手写签名留够了空间。

3. 称呼语的使用

当撰写一封商务信函时,也是在建立一个你自己的以及你所代表的组织的形象。通常,信函决定了第一次和你接触的人对你的持久的印象。以用适当的称呼语和介绍开始商务信函可以建立这封信件友好的基调,而且可使收信人留下深刻的印象,如图 7-6 所示。

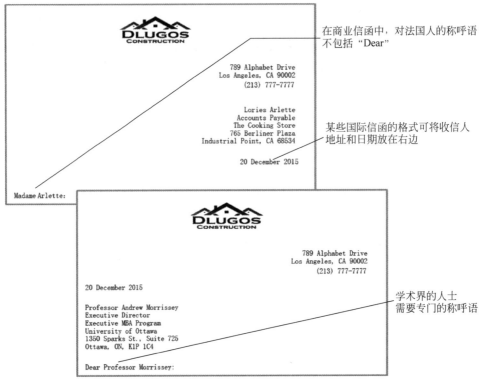

图 7-6　称呼语中常用的头衔

1) 称呼格式

尊敬的 + 头衔 + 姓名(Dear Title Name)的称呼格式在任何商务信函中都是正确的,应该用在所有的商务信函中。使用先生(Mr.)、女士(Ms.)的尊称,除非收信人是一个有着正式的头衔的人,如博士(Dr.)或牧师(Reverend)。

2) 标点符号

称呼语中的标点也代表着信的意图。商务信函在称呼语之后写一个冒号(:),而私人信件则用逗号(,)。

3) 名字

写一封正式的信件时,称呼中不能使用收信人的名字,如尊敬的路易莎·琼斯女士(Dear Ms. Louisa Jones)或尊敬的卡尔·罗伯茨先生(Dear Mr. Carl Roberts)。然而,如果你和收信人关系比较友好,则可以使用名字,如尊敬的鲍勃(Dear Bob)。

4) 非个人称呼

如果你并不知道收信人的名字,那就使用一个非个人称呼,如收信人的头衔,如尊敬的运营经理(Dear Operations Manager)的名称或使用其所在部门或单位的名称,如尊敬的人力资源部(Dear Human Resources Department)。

5) 等级和荣誉头衔

在撰写特别正式的商务信函时,你可能需要在称呼中加入工作头衔、等级或荣誉称号,如尊敬的坎宁安总统(Dear President Cunningham)、尊敬的史密斯博士(Dear Dr. Smith)或者尊敬的华顿大使(Dear Ambassador Wharton)。送到政要处的信件的称呼中可以加入尊敬的(Honorable)或阁下(Excellency)。图 7-7 中列出了一些常用的称呼语。

图 7-7 称呼语中常用的头衔

6) 撰写国际信件

在一些国家,看待信件的头衔和称呼可能要比在其他一些国家更加认真,当然,使用的规则也是因地而异。如果你使用了错误的形式也会很尴尬。如果收信人在国外,最安全的方法是使用传统的名称,即尊敬的 + 头衔 + 姓名(Dear Title Name),并使用正式的语气去撰写信函。表 7-1 总结了在写称呼语时的注意事项。

表 7-1 称呼语的注意事项

称呼语	适合提到	尽量避免
格式	• 使用尊敬的 + 头衔 + 姓名(Dear Title Name)的称呼格式 • 在商务信函的称呼后接一个冒号(:)	• 省略"尊敬的"(Dear) • 在结尾处使用逗号,除了私人信函之外
姓名	• 使用收信人的姓 • 仅使用收信人的名字(用于私人信函)	• 用"女士"(Miss)或"夫人"(Mrs)作为收信人头衔 • 在正式信函中使用收信人的名字
国际收信人	• 熟悉收信人国家的写信习俗 • 使用正式的称呼语	• 信函以个人为中心 • 你与收信人有着友好的关系,使用非正式的称呼语

转 163 页

Part 3

Listening and Speaking

Dialogue: Setting up Wireless Network

(Sophie currently has her computer connected directly to a modem in her home. Now she wants to replace the current wired modem with a wireless network, and asks Henry and Mark for help.)

Henry: Take it easy, Sophie. It's easier to install than you think, I promise. There are only 4 steps in brief.

Sophie: Really? What are they?

Mark: The first step is to make sure that you have the equipment needed. The list generally includes **broadband** Internet connection, a wireless router and a computer with built-in wireless network support or a wireless network adapter.

Sophie: Let me see. Ok, I think they are all ready now. And what [1] next?

Mark: The next step is to connect your wireless router. After turning your modem off, unplug the network cable from the back of your computer, and plug it into the **port** labeled Internet, WAN or **WLAN** on the back of your router. Meanwhile[2], the other end of the network cable should be plugged into your modem.

Sophie: Well, how can I know whether they have been connected correctly?

Henry: It's easy. To check this, plug in and turn on your modem. Wait a few minutes to give it time to connect to the Internet, and then plug in and turn on your wireless router. After a minute, the Internet, WAN or WLAN light on your wireless router should **light up**, indicating that it has successfully connected to your modem.

[1] Replace with:
1. what about
2. what do you think of

[2] Replace with:
1. At the same time
2. Meantime

Unit 7   Computer Network

Sophie: Ok, so what else?

Henry: Then, configure your wireless router. You should temporarily connect your computer to one of the open network ports on your wireless router which isn't labeled Internet, WAN or WLAN. Next, open a browser and type in the address and the password to configure your router.

Sophie: How can I get the address and password?

Henry: You can find them in the instructions **included with** your router.

Mark: Specially, in the process of configuration, Sophie, you should **find** three things: your wireless network name which is known as the Service Set Identifier, wireless encryption or Wi-Fi Protected Access, and your administrative password which controls your wireless network. **By the way**, disconnect the network cable from your computer after the configuration is completed.

Sophie: Yes, I've got it.

Henry: Now, we come into the final step, connecting your computers. Windows 10 should show a wireless network icon which includes a list of available wireless networks. View the available wireless networks list, choose your network and click Connect. Type the encryption key and then click Connect. Windows 10 will show its progress as it connects to your network. After you're connected, you can now close the Wireless Network Connection window. You're done for now.

Mark: Then you can use your laptop to surf the Web while you're sitting on your **couch** or in your **yard**.

145

Sophie: Thanks a lot! I can't wait. Shall we start right now?

Henry & Mark: No problem.

 Exercises

Work in a group, and make up a similar conversation by replacing the statements with other expressions on the right side.

 Words

broadband['brɔːdbænd] n. 宽带
port[pɔːt] n. 端口
find[faind] v. 知道，得知，获悉

couch[kautʃ] n. 睡椅，沙发
yard [jaːd] n. 院子

 Phrases

light up 照亮，点燃
be included with 包括在
by the way 顺便提一句

Listening Comprehension：IPv6

Listen to the article and answer the following 3 questions based on it. After you hear a question, there will be a break of 15 seconds. During the break, you will decide which one is the best answer among the four choices marked (A), (B), (C) and (D).

Questions

1. What is the most direct and powerful driving force behind the development of IPv6?

　　(A) The explosive growth of networks
　　(B) An increasing demand for IP addresses
　　(C) An escalating demand for wireless devices
　　(D) A mature technique of network address translation

2. How many unique IP addresses can be supported by IPv6 at most?
　　(A) 32

(B) 2^{32}
(C) 128
(D) 2^{128}

3. Why does IPv4 need to use the technique of network address translation?
   (A) Providing interoperability between IPv4 and IPv6 hosts
   (B) Avoiding running out of the available address space
   (C) Extending the amount of available address space
   (D) Providing control information to route packets

Words

packet-switched 包交换
deem[di:m] v. 认为, 视为, 相信

escalate['eskəleit] v. 逐步增强

Phrases

run out of 用光, 用完

Dictation: Router

This article will be played three times. Listen carefully, and fill in the numbered spaces with the appropriate words you have heard.

A router consists of a computer with at least two network ___1___ cards supporting the IP ___2___, whose software and hardware are usually tailored to the tasks of ___3___ and forwarding information. It may be used to connect two or more wired or ___4___ IP networks, or an IP network to an Internet connection. ___5___, a router is a "Layer 3 ___6___" which operates at the network layer of the OSI reference ___7___.

The router receives ___8___ from each interface via a network interface and ___9___ the received packets to an appropriate ___10___ network interface. By maintaining ___11___ information in a piece of storage called the "routing table", it also has the ability to filter ___12___ to ensure that ___13___ packets are discarded.

The very first device that had ___14___ the same ___15___ as a router does today, was the Interface Message Processor (IMP). IMPs were the devices that made up the ARPANET, the first packet ___16___ network. The idea for a router (although they were called "gateways" at the time) ___17___ came about through an international group of computer networking researchers called the International Network Working Group (INWG).

Many engineers believe that the use of a router provides better ___18___ against **hacking** than a software ___19___, because no computer IP addresses are ___20___ exposed to the Internet.

Words

discard [disˈkɑːd] v. 丢弃，抛弃   hack [hæk] v. 非法侵入（他人计算机系统）

Phrases

make up 组成，构成
come about 发生，出现

Abbreviations

IMP   Interface Message Processor   接口报文处理器
INWG   International Network Working Group   国际互联网工作组

Unit 8

The Internet and World Wide Web

Part 1

Reading and Translating

Section A: Social Networking

Social networking has developed to become one among the most influential elements of the Web(Figure 8-1). However, despite how **viral** it is within the Western part of the globe, (particularly among the young adults), not every individual uses it **or else** understands it. Social networking is the practice of expanding one's social contacts or business through creating connections via persons, often via social media sites, for instance, LinkedIn, Facebook, and Twitter **among others**. Accordingly, the following concentrates on **shedding light on** the advantages and disadvantages of social networking.

Figure 8-1　Social Networking

Advantages of Social Networking

One **pro** of social networking is the **aptitude** to connect to different individuals internationally. One can utilize Facebook to stay connected with old friends who have moved in different parts of the world, **get on** Google+ to keep in touch with family members who stay halfway around the globe. Also, one can meet new persons on Twitter from towns or regions that one has never heard of before.

Another pro is easy as well as **prompt** communication. Now that a person is connected wherever he goes, he does not have to depend on his answering machines, **snail** mail or **landlines** to contact somebody. One can easily use a computer or a smartphone and instantly begin communicating with any person on social platforms, such as, Facebook, or one among the diverse social messaging applications accessible.

Real-time news as well as information discovery is another advantage. Gone are the times of **sticking around** for the seven o'clock news to be aired on television or else for the delivery person to bring the daily paper in the morning. On the off chance that one needs to realize what is happening around the globe, one should simply use social networking media. A special reward is that one can customize his/her news as well as information discovery encounters through following precisely what one desires.

A great opportunity for entrepreneurs is another pro of social networking. Entrepreneurs and different sorts of professional associations may connect with current clients, sell their items and extend their reach utilizing online networking. Actually, there are numerous business owners as well as businesses out there which flourish completely on social networking and would not be in a position to work without it.

In addition, another advantage is general fun and satisfaction. One need to concede that social networking is simply fun once in a while. Many individuals find refuge in social networking when they get a break at job or simply need to relax while at home. Since individuals are normally social beings, it is frequently very fulfilling to see remarks and likes appear on one's own posts, and it is helpful to have the capacity to see precisely what our pals are doing without asking them straightforwardly.

Disadvantages of Social Networking

One disadvantage is backlash. A joke amid pals is one thing; however, a joke with rest of the universe is another thing. If potentially aggressive contents are posted online, the degree of feedback may be excessive, besides, is normally brutal. This is especially valid with profoundly opinionated topics, such as, religion and politics. Likewise, this backlash has a long-term effect upon an individual's future, principally in a globe, which is greatly involved in over-sharing. Actually, even schools are realizing that comments they post via social media may impact whether a university accepts their admission application. During a time where selfies are currently the norm, over-sharing might be modifying our perspective through making a more opinionated outlook.

Crimes and cyber bullying against kids is a con of social networking. Utilization of social networks might expose individuals to diverse forms of harassment and wrong connection. This may be predominantly valid for teenagers. Unless parents diligently control online content accessible to their kids, children may be exposed towards explicit content, such as pornography. Other than releasing age-improper content, the computerized age additionally brought forth a social phenomenon, known as cyberbullying. Cyberbullying may occur 24 hours on a daily basis. Adding to this domain of cyberbullying are the independent social networking sites which may raise the seriousness of the crime, following false warranty of privacy. The negative consequences include depression, stress and anxiety.

Another disadvantage is risks of fraud and identity theft. Regardless, the information one post online is available to any person who is smart to retrieve it. Most criminals need a few basic bits of a person's information towards making one's life a living hell. If they successfully acquire a person's identity, it can cost one dearly. Studies have shown that Millennials[1] are among the quickest developing population to be targets. This is connected towards the population's **solace** with sharing almost everything on the Web—including individual information.

Time consuming. Social networking is both time consuming as well as addictive. Simply keeping up to do the most recent updates consumes time that could be better used elsewhere. It is never more genuine than in a job situation where a ton of profitable time is lost since workers communicate online, download music, play online games and so on.

Social networking causes serious relationship problems. Online interactions have not only started relationships, but they have also played a greater part in ending countless others. It is easy to communicate as well as share pictures with persons on social media **plus** keep them **under wraps**. This temptation causes complications in people's life, offline relationship, frequently ending some for good. Further, social networking results to trust issues.

Sedentary lifestyle behaviors and sleep disruption. Finally, because social networking is done on either smartphone or computer, it can **at times** promote excessively sitting down for a really long time. Likewise, staring the phone screen or computer screen at night may adversely affect one's ability to get a good sleep.

Conclusion

Social networking is the practice of expanding one's social contacts or business through creating connections via persons, often via social media sites, for instance, LinkedIn, Facebook, and Twitter among others. Some advantages of social networking include aptitude to connect to different individuals internationally, easy as well as prompt communication, real-time news as well as information discovery, a great opportunity for entrepreneurs, and general fun and satisfaction. Disadvantages of social networking include backlash, crimes and cyber bullying against kids, is risks of fraud and identity theft, time consuming, causes serious relationship problems and sedentary lifestyle behaviors and sleep disruption. **As with** any innovation, there are both advantages and disadvantages. Thus, it is solely in the user's part to acquire the utmost possible advantage. Accordingly, one should be very careful on what he/she posts.

 **Words**

viral['vairəl] *adj.* 病毒的,病毒性的,病毒引起的	landline['lænd,lain] *n.* 座机电话
pro[prəu] *n.* 赞成的论点	encounter[in'kauntə(r)] *n.* 偶遇
aptitude['æptitju:d] *n.* 天生的才能,天赋	concede[kən'si:d] *v.* 承认(某事属实、合乎逻辑等)
prompt[prɔmpt] *adj.* 迅速的,及时的	fulfilling[ful'filiŋ] *adj.* 让人感觉有意义的,令人满足的
snail[sneil] *n.* 蜗牛,行动迟缓的人或物	

Unit 8 The Internet and World Wide Web

pal[pæl] n. 好友,伙伴
backlash['bæklæʃ] n. 激烈反应
aggressive[ə'gresiv] adj. 好斗的,挑衅的,富于攻击性的
opinionated[ə'pinjəneitid] adj. 固执己见的,顽固的
selfie['selfi] n. 自拍照(尤指那些自拍后上传到社交网站的照片)
norm[nɔːm] n. 常态,标准
con[kɔn] n. 反对,反对的理由
bully['buli] v. 恐吓,伤害,胁迫
explicit[ik'splisit] adj. 清楚明白的,易于理解的

pornography[pɔː'nɔgrəfi] n. 淫秽作品,色情书刊(或音像制品等)
depression[di'preʃn] n. 抑郁症,精神忧郁
regardless[ri'gɑːdləs] adv. 不管怎样,无论如何
dearly['diəli] adv. 高价地,昂贵地
solace['sɔləs] n. 慰藉,给以安慰的人(或事物)
plus[plʌs] conj. 而且,此外
sedentary['sedntri] adj. 需要久坐的,惯于久坐不动的

  Phrases

or else (表示另外一种可能性)或者
among others 其中,包括
shed light on 阐明,解释
get on 继续做,开始做
stick around 待在原处(等待)
on the off chance 说不定,看能不能,希望
out there 在那里,存在
once in a while 偶尔,间或
bring forth 提出(建议、证据等)
living hell 活地狱,活受罪
under wraps 保密,秘而不宣(常指待日后宣布)
at times 有时,间或
as with 如同,和……一样

  Notes

[1] 千禧世代(millennials)是 millennial generation 的缩写,是人口统计学家用来描述出生于1980—2000年的一代年轻人,媒体称他们为"Y世代"。

  Exercises

Ⅰ. Read the following statements carefully, and decide whether they are true (T) or false (F) according to the text.

　　　1. One con of social networking is the aptitude to connect to different

153

individuals internationally.

____ 2. Real-time news as well as information discovery is a disadvantage of social networking.

____ 3. General fun and satisfaction is a pro of social networking.

____ 4. Backlash is a con of social networking.

____ 5. If criminals successfully acquire a person's identity, it can cost one dearly.

II. Choose the best answer to each of the following questions according to the text.

1. Which of the following is not a pro of social networking?
   A. General fun and satisfaction
   B. A great opportunity for entrepreneurs
   C. Time consuming
   D. The aptitude to connect to different individuals internationally

2. Which of the following is not a con of social networking?
   A. Crimes and cyber bullying against kids
   B. Real-time news as well as information discovery
   C. Backlash
   D. Sedentary lifestyle behaviors and sleep disruption

3. Which of the following is not social networking related?
   A. Twitter
   B. Lenovo
   C. Facebook
   D. LinkedIn

III. Identify the letter of the choice that best matches the phrase or definition.
   a. social media
   b. World Wide Web (WWW)
   c. Internet
   d. keyword
   e. podcast

____ 1. A recorded audio or video file that can be played or downloaded via the Web.

____ 2. A word typed in a search box on a search site to locate information on the Internet.

____ 3. The collection of social networking sites and other communications channels used to transmit or share information with a broad audience.

____ 4. The collection of Web pages available through the Internet.

____ 5. The largest and most well-known computer network, linking millions of computers all over the world.

Ⅳ. **Fill in the numbered spaces with the words or phrases chosen from the box. Change the forms where necessary.**

> designate   post   follow   contact   activity
> celebrity   professional   confirm   online   common

How do Facebook, Twitter, and LinkedIn differ?

People you know through personal and professional circles form your social networks. You share ___1___ interests, work or spend leisure time together, and know many of one another's friends. Social networking sites allow you to manage your social networks ___2___.

Your account on a social networking site includes profile information, such as your name, location, photos, and personal and professional interests. You might create accounts on a variety of social networking sites to better separate your personal and professional ___3___. Social networking sites allow you to view the profiles of other users and ___4___ them as your friends or contacts. Some social networking sites, such as Facebook and LinkedIn, require friends to confirm a friendship, while others, such as Twitter and Google+ allow users to follow one another without ___5___.

With Facebook, you share messages, interests, activities, events, photos, and other personal information—called ___6___—with family and friends. You also can 'like' pages of ___7___, companies, products, etc. so that posts on these pages appear on your Facebook page. With Twitter, you 'follow' people, companies, and organizations in which you have an interest. Twitter enables you to stay current with the daily activities of those you are following via their Tweets, which are short posts (messages) that Tweeters broadcast for all their ___8___.

On LinkedIn, you share professional interests, education, and employment history, and add colleagues or coworkers to your list of ___9___. You can include recommendations from people who know you ___10___. Many employers post jobs using LinkedIn and consider information in your profile as your online resume.

Ⅴ. **Translate the following passage into Chinese.**

Online Social Network

An online social network, also called a social networking Web site, is a Web site that encourages members in its online community to share their interests, ideas, stories, photos, music, and videos with other registered users. Most include chat rooms, newsgroups, and other communications services. Popular social networking Web sites include LinkedIn and Facebook, with Facebook alone boasting more than 2.5 billion active users. In some social networking Web sites, such as Second Life, users assume an imaginary identity and interact with other users in a role-playing type of environment.

A media sharing Web site is a specific type of online social network that enables members to share media such as photos, music, and videos. Flickr, Fotki, and Webshots are popular photo sharing communities; PixelFish and YouTube are popular video sharing communities.

Section B: 5G Internet: Transforming the Global Business Landscape

Every generation of wireless standard — 1G, 2G, 3G, 4G, or 5G — has come with advanced data-carrying capacity, improved latency, and another transformation for our global landscape. When 1G was introduced to the world in 1973, technology paved the way for wireless communication. However, 1G **was riddled with** flaws due to its lack of **roaming** support among a **multitude** of operators, lack of encryption, poor coverage, and sound quality.

That's when we felt the need for a better version of the mobile network. And beginning from 1991, we witnessed a cultural revolution with 2G as it delivered improved digital call quality with less static and call encryption while introducing us to text messages (SMS), picture messages, and multimedia messages (MMS) on our mobile phones.

However, we required much faster data transfer speeds, and 3G fulfilled that requirement as it offered four times faster data transfer than 2G. 3G also aimed to standardize the network protocol employed by every vendor, which made international roaming possible.

In 2009, 4G came with much faster speeds, making **HD** video streaming, gaming, and high-quality video conferencing a norm. Despite being there for more than a decade, most regions of the world still experience low 4G penetration.

Yet 5G has gathered quite a lot of buzz in the past few years as it is expected to revolutionize the digital landscape of every other industry, from banking to healthcare, **like never before**.

As our mobile phones have **metamorphosed** into smartphones with each successive generation of mobile networks, the demand for mobile data and network coverage has **multiplied** and always exceeded the network's capability. With the Internet of Things (IoT) gaining momentum, we **desperately** require a network capable of seamless data sharing across the globe. 5G may just make it possible with its significantly faster speeds of 1 Gigabyte per second.

As you expand your business abroad, the differing geography and infrastructure can wreak havoc on a stable Internet connection, which is essential for every business in this era.

Whether you are communicating from or with the international regions, the limitations of previous wireless connectivity networks with smooth video or voice conversations can greatly impede your business progress. Sluggish and fluctuating Internet connectivity can affect the downloading and uploading of large and complex files, accessing your data and assets on the cloud, and even inhibit customer service.

Though wired broadband like fiber-optic can provide Gig speeds to power business operations, they are limited by the heavy and expensive network infrastructure. One of the advantages mobile networks have over wired broadband networks is that they can provide extensive coverage across the country and continents while delivering speeds faster than a satellite connection.

5G towers can easily surpass fiber-optic, DSL [1], cable, or satellite Internet, in terms of being the primary method of going online, especially with the ubiquity of mobile phones. It hasn't been long since 5G was launched in the U.S., yet only a few players i.e. T-Mobile, AT&T, and Spectrum have already ensured 5G coverage to millions of U.S. residents across thousands of cities.

Until 5G becomes a reliable and stable form of connectivity for businesses and homes, you can rely on fiber-powered AT&T Internet Plans, which are not only affordable but deliver superfast and powerful connectivity to enable hard-core gaming, streaming, international communication, and even power IoT devices around you.

5G is poised to revolutionize the way we communicate, entertain, or conduct our businesses(Figure 8-2). It won't be long before 5G has penetrated every market with its superior network coverage. So here's what to expect as 5G becomes mainstream.

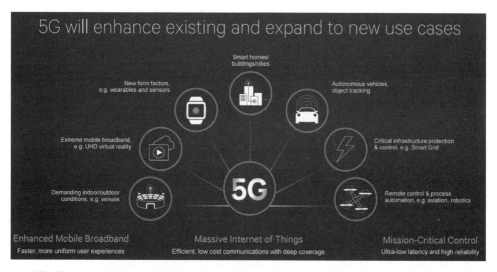

Figure 8-2　5G is poised to revolutionize the way we communicate, entertain, or conduct our businesses

Sales

Whatever your business is selling, whether it is a digital or tangible good. To ensure growth, online and international sales must become an indelible business component. For that, you need to not only strategize online storefront management but require adequate digital paraphernalia to support those strategies, including uploading of high-resolutions pictures and videos of your product.

On the other hand, customers in every international market will demand equal support and service that you provide to local customers. To alleviate the cost of communications required for international services, businesses are switching from traditional phones to Skype or other digital avenues. Even communications and transactions across the supply chain are conducted via software and apps. These operations not only need fast and stable connectivity. But flexible systems that can aid mobility without restricting operations to a physical location of the business.

Investment

A steady and stalwart infrastructure is a cardinal part of any business. Investors look for such reliability before they invest in any business. If your business gives even a hint of unreliability and inflexibility to adapt to constant and contemporary changes, your investment may be impacted.

According to forecast reports by CITA, U.S. telecoms are set to invest a whopping $275 billion in 5G technology, including small cells, fiber-optic network, and other 5G infrastructure. 5G trials started in 2018 and 2019 with its mass usage increasing in 2020 across major urban centers.

Productivity

It may seem like a tiny issue, but unstable Internet can drastically affect your business's productivity and revenue. As per a study from the memory and storage specialist at Sandisk, an average employee wastes one week per year waiting for the snail-paced Internet connection to download or upload their files, send emails, and conduct other online activities, bringing down the company's productivity.

Moreover, it affects employees' morale as the unstable Internet contributes to their frustrations. A poll conducted by Deloitte Australia determined that slow and unstable Internet is the number one cause of frustration among users. Plus, it could result in a loss of business revenue as your business responds slowly to customers online.

Stable and faster connectivity can be the panacea to many business problems. 5G is the answer as it seamlessly loads media-laden Web pages and download large and complex files quickly. Besides, 5G clears the air for the emergence of new startups, especially of the online variety. Which will mushroom the job market, introduce more flexible working schedules and settings, and transform the way we do business.

With 5G gaining popularity in usage across urban centers, it is a matter of time before entire regions succumb to the latest technological revolution. The 5G will give rise to exponential business growth as it permits small-scale entrepreneurs to easily erect their businesses from scratch, employ flexibility while remaining productive, which will consequently spur sales and growth.

Words

roam[rəum] v. 漫游	storefront['stɔ:frʌnt] n. 网上店铺,虚拟店面
multitude['mʌltitju:d] n. 众多,大量	paraphernalia[ˌpærəfə'neiliə] n. (尤指某活动所需的)装备
metamorphose[ˌmetə'mɔ:fəuz] v. 变化,发生质变	avenue['ævənju:] n. 途径,手段
multiply['mʌltiplai] v. 成倍增加,迅速增加	stalwart['stɔ:lwət] adj. 健壮的,强壮的
desperately['despəritli] adv. 不顾一切地,绝望地	cardinal['kɑ:dinl] adj. 最重要的,基本的
inhibit[in'hibit] v. 阻止,阻碍	whopping['wɔpiŋ] adj. 巨大的,很大的
cable['keibl] n. 有线电视(= cable TV)	morale[mə'rɑ:l] n. 士气
ubiquity[ju:'bkwəti] n. 无所不在,随处可见	panacea[ˌpænə'si:ə] n. 万灵药,万能之计
hard-core 铁杆的,骨干的	laden['leidn] adj. 载满的,装满的
good[gud] n. 好东西	mushroom['mʌʃrum] v. 快速生长,迅速增长
indelible[in'deləbl] adj. 无法忘记的	spur[spə:(r)] v. 促进,加速

Phrases

be riddled with 布满,充满
like never before 前所未有
wreak havoc 给……造成混乱(或破坏)
be poised to do 准备做
be set to do 准备做某事
as per 按照,根据
succumb to 屈服于,屈从于
give rise to 引起,导致
from scratch 从头做起,白手起家

Abbreviations

HD   High Definition   高分辨率
Gig   Gigabyte   千兆字节(GB)

159

Notes

[1] DSL(Digital Subscriber Line,数字用户线路)是以电话线为传输介质的传输技术组合。DSL 包括 ADSL（Asymmetric Digital Subscriber Line,非对称数字用户线）、RADSL、HDSL 和 VDSL 等。DSL 技术在传递公用电话网络的用户环路上支持对称和非对称传输模式,解决了经常发生在网络服务供应商和最终用户间的"最后一公里"的传输瓶颈问题。由于 DSL 接入方案无须对电话线路进行改造,可以充分利用已大量铺设的电话用户环路,大大降低了额外的开销。因此,利用铜缆电话线提供更高速率的因特网接入,更受用户的欢迎,在一些国家和地区得到大量应用。

 Exercises

Ⅰ. Read the following statements carefully, and decide whether they are true（T）or false（F）according to the text.

____ 1. 1G was introduced to the world in 2009.

____ 2. 3G made international roaming possible.

____ 3. Wireless broadband can provide Gig speeds to power business operations.

____ 4. One of the advantages wired broadband networks have over mobile networks is that they can provide extensive coverage across the country.

____ 5. 5G may just make it possible with its significantly faster speeds of 1 Gigabyte per second.

Ⅱ. Choose the best answer to each of the following questions according to the text.

1. Which of the following made international roaming possible?

    A. 1G

    B. 2G

    C. 3G

    D. None of the above

2. Which of the following is right about 5G?

    A. 5G is poised to revolutionize the way we communicate, entertain, or conduct our businesses

    B. 5G may just make it possible with its significantly faster speeds of 1 Gigabyte per second

    C. 5G clears the air for the emergence of new startups, especially of the online variety

    D. All of the above

3. Which of the following made HD video streaming, gaming, and high-quality video conferencing a norm?

    A. 1G

    B. 2G

    C. 3G

    D. 4G

Ⅲ. Identify the letter of the choice that best matches the phrase or definition.

    a. smartphone

    b. tablet

    c. laptop

    d. Wi-Fi

    e. hotspot

    ____ 1. Broadband Internet connection that uses radio signals to provide connections to computers and devices with build-in Wi-Fi capability or a communications device that enables Wi-Fi connectivity

    ____ 2. Thin, lightweight mobile computer with a screen in its lid and a keyboard in its base, designed to fit on your lap

    ____ 3. A wireless network that provides Internet connections to mobile computers devices

    ____ 4. An Internet-capable phone that usually also includes a calendar, an appoint book, an address book, a calculator, a notepad, game, browser, and numerous other apps

    ____ 5. Thin, lighter weight mobile computer that has a touch screen, usually smaller than a laptop but larger than a phone

Ⅳ. Fill in the numbered spaces with the words or phrases chosen from the box. Change the forms where necessary.

use	design	associate	upgrade	result
fast	equal	allow	call	tremendous

Mobile Data Caps

    Mobile data use has increased ___1___ recently as individuals are watching TV and videos, downloading music and movies, playing online multiplayer games, participating in video phone calls, and otherwise performing high-bandwidth activities ___2___ their smartphones and media tablets. This has created the issue of wireless carriers potentially running out of bandwidth available for customers, ___3___ in outages or delays. In response, many wireless carriers have implemented data caps and have eliminated unlimited data plans (though many plans still have unlimited talk and texts). With a data cap, customers either temporarily lose high-speed Internet access (such as being slowed down from 4G to 2G speeds— __4__ data throttling) or are charged an additional fee if they exceed their download limit (often 2 GB per month).

One explanation for the increased data usage is speed—4G data speeds are significantly __5__ than 3G service and the results (such as faster Web pages and smoother streaming videos) make it easier for users to go through a large amount of bandwidth in a relatively short period of time. One potential solution under consideration by wireless carriers is __6__ content providers or app developers to pay carriers so that their services don't count against a customer's monthly data limit—essentially buying traffic for their content. However, the Internet is designed for all content and services to be treated __7__ . Because this solution would give larger companies an unfair advantage over upstarts, it is viewed by some as a net neutrality issue.

So how do you avoid the expensive or annoying ramifications __8__ with going over your data cap? The best way is to not go over your limit in the first place. To help with this, use Wi-Fi for large downloads instead of your cellular connection. It is also prudent to monitor your data usage to make sure you stay under your data cap (you can also use this information to decide if you need to consider __9__ to a higher plan if your usage is typical but still over your data cap). Some smartphones have an option for viewing your total data usage for the current billing period, as well as usage per app or Web site to help you see where you are using the most data.

Another useful tool is third-party apps __10__ to help you monitor your bandwidth usage. One such app is Onavo Extend. It gives you a breakdown of consumption by app, so you know your worst bandwidth offenders. As a bonus, it compresses your incoming data by up to 500% so you can do up to five times more with your data plan without going over. Five times more data for free? It's about time!

Ⅴ. **Translate the following passage into Chinese.**

Internet2

Now that the Internet has shifted from a research project to a household commodity, the research community has moved on to a project called Internet2. Internet2 is intended as an academic-only system and involves numerous universities working in partnership with industry and government. The goal is to conduct research in Internet applications requiring high bandwidth communication, such as remote access and control of costly state-of-the-art equipment such as telescopes and medical diagnostic devices. An example of current research involves remote surgery performed by robot hands that mimic the hands of a distant surgeon who views the patient by video. You can learn more about Internet2 at http：//www.internet2.org．

Part 2

Simulated Writing：Writing Professional Letters（II）

接 143 页

4．结束商业信函

　　结束商务信函的方式会影响收信人对信件的理解、对请求的意愿以及他们对你的印象。商务信函的最后总是以谦称结尾，如真诚地（Sincerely）。签名档应该出现在商务信函的结尾，由签名、打印的名字和头衔（如果你正在写一封正式信函）组成。图 8-3 即为正式的商务信函的结尾例子。

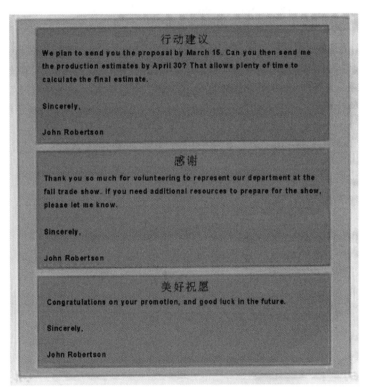

图 8-3　结尾的例子

1）结束时呼吁行动

　　收信人通常会浏览信函的最后一段以寻找行动要求、期限和你要求他们完成的工作。截止日期特别有用。记得在要求时要有礼貌，因为人们在受到尊重时，反应会更为亲切，表 8-1 总结了商务信函的结尾和签名档的注意事项。

表 8-1 结尾和签名档的注意事项

结尾元素	适合提到	尽量避免
结尾段	• 在提出请求时要具体而有礼貌 • 包括截止日期 • 通过提供联系方式使回复更容易	• 命令读者尽快回复 • 以"感谢您关注此事"(Thank you for your attention to this matter)这样老套的语言结尾
谦称结尾	• 大部分商务信函使用传统的"真诚的"(Sincerely)结尾 • 一些个人信函可以使用替换词"亲切的"(Cordially) • 在跨国信函中使用"恭敬的"(Respectfully)来表达敬意	• 以消极的情绪结尾,比如"愤怒的"(Angrily)或"失望的"(Disappointedly) • 省略正式信件之后的结尾和逗号
签名档	• 在正式信函中,手写并打印你的全名 • 如果收信人地址写明了收信人的头衔,那你也要写清你的头衔 • 如果代表公司,那么写上公司的全名	• 在正式信函中,只写你的名字 • 签缩写名字 • 使用计算机合成的名字

2) 表示感谢

在要求某事的同时要表示感谢。可以在请求中直接感谢,如"若能在 6 月 15 日前完成这个报告,我将不胜感激。"(I appreciate your help in completing this report by June 15.)

3) 包含善意

如果不做具体要求,则以积极的陈述、观察,或追求一个持续的关系来结尾。即使写的是一个消极的主题,也要试图以积极、专业的方式结束这封信函。

4) 正式的商务信函使用传统的结尾

商务信函中最常见的谦称结尾是"真诚的"(Sincerely)。其他的都可以基于此进行变化,如"你真诚的"(Sincerely yours)。使用"恭敬的"(Respectfully)这个词结尾可以表达你对收信人的敬意,所以在敬意这种情况下使用这样的结尾。

5) 非正式信件使用个性化结尾

对于写给朋友和熟人的个人或非正式的信函,可以使用如"亲切的"(Cordially)、"热情的问候"(Warm regards)和"最美好的祝愿"(Best wishes)这类结束语。

6) 在签名档中写明职位

在正式的商务信函中,需要在名字旁写上头衔或职位。一个好的经验法则是如果你给收信人加了头衔或职位,那么也要列出你的职位。

7) 在签名档中写明公司

如果你是公司的代理,比如提交一个方案或合同,在谦称结尾和 4 行之后的签名下面要写明公司的法定名称。这表明你代表的是公司,不是代表个人。

8) 提供其他描述

在适当的时候,包括"附件"(Enclosure 或 Enc)表明你随函寄了一些材料。如果是你写的信,但是是别人打的字,还要包括证明人的姓名首字母。例如,KL:MCD 表明 KL 写信,MCD 打字。

5. 日常信函撰写

虽然使用分块的方式来撰写正式的商务信函，但也可以使用一个简化的信函格式来撰写日常信函，使用这样更直接、不那么正式的方式可以方便地发送大量信函，如销售信函，以及将通知发送给客户、股东、供应商或员工。这样简化的信函格式省略了称呼、结尾谦称和签名，更专注于第一行和信的正文，如图 8-4 和图 8-5 所示。

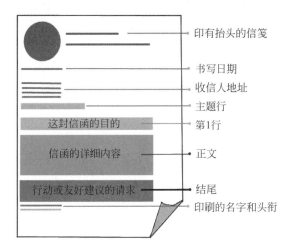

图 8-4　简化的信函格式的大纲

图 8-5　简化了格式的 Quest 公司的信函

1) 用主题行替换称呼语

信的开始就要说明这封信的主题，强调目的，这样收信人才能立即预测和了解其余部分。

2）第一行说明目的

提出提议、请求、应答、要解决的问题，或正在采取行动的明确的声明。

3）正文中详细描述

在正文部分可以阐述能够支持在第一行陈述的目的的一些细节。这些细节可以提供有关的提议或请求，列出想法的优势，或提供相关的事实。按照逻辑来安排这些信息，如按时间顺序或按照重要程度排序。直接称呼收信人为"你"（you），并且关注于如何使信的内容能够让收信人受益。

4）调整正文段落的格式增加可读性

使用尽可能少的段落。取而代之的是，编号或项目符号、表格、图形可以使信函更容易阅读。

5）省略敬意的结尾

简化的信函格式并不适用于正式的信函，也就不需要一个结尾。取而代之的是，应该写一个结尾段来进行总结。

6．放弃签名

在简化的信函格式中手写签名是不需要的。在许多情况下，可能会发送很多份信函，那样在每一封上签名会很麻烦。如果使用彩色打印机来打印信件，可以选择蓝色的墨水来打印签名项。

Part 3

Listening and Speaking

Dialogue：Knowing the Myths about the Internet

（Because the Internet is so unique in the history of the world—and its content and applications keep evolving—several widespread *myths* about it have surfaced. Henry, Mark and Sophie are having a discussion about it.）

Henry: I have found that there are three myths about the Internet.

Mark: Sure. The first one is the Internet is free. This myth **stems from** the fact that there has traditionally been no cost associated with[1] accessing online content such as news and product information with email exchange, **other than** what the Internet users pay their **ISPs** for Internet access.

[1] Replace with：
1. linked with
2. connected

Sophie: And many people—such as students, employees, and consumers who opt for free Internet service or use free access available at public libraries or other public locations—pay nothing for Internet access. Yet it should also be obvious that someone, somewhere, has to pay to keep the Internet up and running.

Henry: However, businesses, schools, public libraries, and most home users pay Internet service providers flat monthly fees to connect to the Internet. In addition, businesses, schools, libraries, and other large organizations might have to lease high-capacity communications lines (such as from a telephone company) to support their high level of Internet traffic.

Mark: I agree with you. Mobile users that want Internet access while on the go typically pay hotspot providers or wireless providers for this access. ISPs, phone companies, cable companies, and other organizations that own part of the Internet infrastructure pay to keep their parts of the Internet running smoothly.

Sophie: And ISPs also pay software and hardware companies for the resources they need to support their subscribers. Eventually,[2] most of these costs are passed along to end users through ISP fees. ISPs that offer free Internet access typically obtain revenue by selling on-screen ads that display on the screen when the service is being used.

[2] Replace with:
1. In the end,
2. At last,
3. Finally,

Mark: Another reason the idea that the Internet is free is a myth is the growing trend of subscription or per-use fees to access Web-based resources. For instance, downloadable music and movies are very common today and some journal or newspaper articles require a fee to view them online.

Henry: In fact,[3] many newspapers and magazines have moved entirely online and most charge a subscription fee to view the level of content that was previously published in a print version. **In lieu of** a **mandatory** fee, some Web sites request a donation for use of the site. Many experts expect the use of fee-based Internet content to continue to grow at a rapid pace.

[3] Replace with:
1. Actually,
2. As a matter of fact,
3. In reality,
4. De facto,
5. In truth,

Mark: Ok. Let's talk about the second myth which is someone controls the Internet. Actually, no single group or organization controls the Internet. Governments in each country have the power to regulate the content and use of the Internet within their borders, as allowed by their laws.

Sophie: Regarding this issue, I think it's a little bit complicated. I suggest we discuss it sometime later. Now it's better for us to talk about the third myth which is that the Internet and the World Wide Web are identical.

Henry: Well, because you can now use a Web browser to access most of the Internet's resources, many people think the Internet and the Web are the same thing.

Mark: Not really. Even though in everyday use many people use the terms Internet and Web interchangeably, they are not the same thing. Technically, the Internet is the physical network, and the Web is the collection of Web pages accessible over the Internet.

Henry: As a matter of fact, a majority of Internet activities today take place **via** Web pages, but there are Internet resources other than the Web that are not accessed via a Web browser. For instance, files can be uploaded and downloaded using an **FTP** (File Transfer Protocol) program and conventional email can be accessed using an email program.

Unit 8 The Internet and World Wide Web

Sophie: Ah, these myths seem true. However, if we analyze them carefully, we can find there are some **misconceptions**.

Henry & Mark: That's right!

Exercises

Work in a group, and make up a similar conversation by replacing the statements with other expressions on the right side.

Words

myth[miθ] *n.* 神话,虚构的人,虚构的事
flat[flæt] *adj.* (费率等)一律的,稳定的
smooth[smuːð] *adj.* 顺利的,光滑的,平稳的
subscriber[səbˈskraɪbə] *n.* 订户,签署者;捐献者

mandatory[ˈmændətəri] *adj.* 强迫性的,强制的,义务的
via[ˈvaɪə] *prep.* 经由,经过,取道
misconception[ˌmɪskənˈsepʃən] *n.* 误解,错觉,错误想法

Phrases

stem from 出自,来源于,发生于
other than 不同于,除了
opt for 选择
keep up 保持,继续(做某事)
in lieu of (以……)替代,作为(……的)替代

Abbreviations

ISP   Internet Service Provider   因特网服务商
FTP   File Transfer Protocol   文件传输协议

Listening Comprehension: How a World-Shaking Technology Came About: Tim Berners-Lee Invents the World Wide Web

Listen to the article and answer the following 3 questions based on it. After you hear a question, there will be a break of 15 seconds. During the break, you will decide which one is the best answer among the four choices marked (A), (B), (C) and (D).

Questions

1. From which university did Tim Berners-Lee graduate?
   (A) Massachusetts Institute of Technology
   (B) Harvard
   (C) Oxford University
   (D) Cambridge University

2. Where is the European Organization for Nuclear Research (CERN) located?
   (A) The United States
   (B) Switzerland
   (C) United Kingdom
   (D) Germany

3. When was the World Wide Web Consortium (W3C) founded by Berners-Lee?
   (A) 1994
   (B) 2000
   (C) 2004
   (D) 2009

 Words

hypertext[ˈhaipətekst] n. 超文本（含有指向其他文本文件链接的文本） facilitate[fəˈsiliteit] v. （指物体、过程等，不用于指人）使（更）容易，使便利	prototype[ˈprəutətaip] n. 原型，标准，模范 knight[nait] v. 授以爵位

 **Phrases**

soldering iron 烙铁，焊铁

Dictation: How Web Search Engines Work

This article will be played three times. Listen carefully, and fill in the numbered spaces with the appropriate words you have heard.

A Web search engine is a search engine designed to search for information on the

World Wide Web. Information may ___1___ of Web pages, images and other types of files. Unlike Web directories, which are maintained by human editors, search engines ___2___ **algorithmically** or are a ___3___ of algorithmic and human input.

Web search engines work by storing information about many Web pages in the following ___4___: Web crawling, indexing and searching. They ___5___ these pages from the WWW itself by sending out a **Web crawler** (sometimes also known as a ___6___)— an ___7___ Web browser which follows every link it sees. Data about Web pages are collected, **parsed**, and stored by another program, called an indexer which creates an index based on the contents of each page. The purpose of storing an index is to ___8___ speed and performance in finding relevant pages for a search ___9___. Without an index, the search engine would scan every page in the **corpus**, which would require ___10___ time and computing power.

Some search engines, such as Google, store all or part of the ___11___ page, referred to as a ___12___, as well as information about the Web pages, whereas others, such as AltaVista, store every word of every page they find. This cached page always ___13___ the actual search text since it is the one that was actually indexed, so it can be very useful when the content of the current page has been ___14___ and the search ___15___ are no longer in it. This problem might be considered to be a mild form of **LinkRot**, and Google's handling of it increases usability by ___16___ user expectations that the search terms will be on the ___17___ Web page. This satisfies the principle of least astonishment ___18___ the user normally expects the search terms to be on the returned pages. Increased search ___19___ makes these cached pages very useful, even ___20___ the fact that they may contain data that may no longer be available elsewhere.

Words

algorithmic [ˌælɡəˈrɪðmɪk] *adj.* 算法的
parse [pɑːz] *v.* 分解,解析

corpus [ˈkɔːpəs] *n.* 文集,(事物的)主体
LinkRot 出错链接页面

Phrases

Web crawler 网络爬虫,爬网程序

Unit 9

Ecommerce

Part 1

Reading and Translating

Section A: How to Use Online AI—Artificial Intelligence for Ecommerce

I know, I know: we've all heard about the rise of "Artificial Intelligence" (AI) in practically all areas of business—but what exactly is it, anyway? What does it **have to do with** marketing and how to use AI for ecommerce?

If you're not familiar with AI, all you really need to know is that it's machines doing tasks that would normally require us to help. On top of that, many of these machines are able to actually learn how to improve the way in which they're doing the tasks too.

A lot of us in the marketing sphere probably think of AI as something only engineers are interested in. Maybe you've heard Elon Musk[1] or Tim Cook[2] talking about the exciting future of it, but that's not really relevant for us...is it?

The truth is, the development of AI is increasingly important for those of us in the marketing game! It all **boils down to** machines being able to tackle tasks that would normally require our input, freeing up time and energy for us.

The key for us is not only how quickly these machines handle the tasks, but how much more efficient they do them as well. With new developments happening all the time in the world of AI, machines are not only **conquering** projects, but they're learning while working!

This type of "machine learning" allows for exponential growth and automation of AI when implemented for marketing purposes, and there lies the key.

With the current status of the online marketplace, ecommerce has become more **saturated** and competitive meaning that for a business to succeed, it needs to be faster and smarter. Take building websites, for example. Whereas before, you would have to hire a Web designer and pay thousands of dollars to have a professional website, now you only need an AI website builder to produce your website for you within minutes. Customer and visitor data is all around us, constantly collected, and always important for businesses to analyze. But what if we could collect, organize, analyze, and then put that data to work for us in an even more efficient manner? Well that's exactly where AI comes in, and it's **changing up** the online marketing game in a big way.

There are five ways that ecommerce can use online AI.

1. Smart Technology

Are you familiar with the Internet of Things (IoT)? In today's world, the Internet is so much more than a bunch of computers and laptops connected together. Just like your smart phone (that you may be reading this on right now), so many other objects are connected to our modern day Internet. From printers to smartwatches and cars to fridges, everything can be connected to make life easier! Wait, did I just say fridges?

Yes! Let me introduce you to Samsung's Family Hub. This refrigerator (yes, you read that correctly—it's a fridge) uses a combination of AI and interior cameras to fully integrate this once old school icebox into a smart appliance that makes your family's life easier!

The fridge actually monitors what is stocked in the fridge with three cameras and can order more groceries as food levels get low. On top of that, the AI can even recommend recipes for upcoming meals based on what's stocked in the fridge: talk about convenient!

2. Chatbots

Have you ever used that handy "chat now" box when shopping online? Chances are, when you were chatting with someone online, you were actually talking to a bot programmed to help with any questions you may have; and honestly, it's getting difficult to even tell the difference! With new chatbots on the market, the chatting experience is becoming more personalized, branded, and intelligent.

Now ecommerce shops can offer 24/7 customer support to visitors, quickly collect valuable data, track behavior, and reach seamless brand continuity—all through AI's machine learning and advancement. With an effective, automated chatbot, ecommerce sites and retailers can further conversion rates by tailoring the online experience for the consumer without having to do any extra work(Figure 9-1).

Figure 9-1 Artificial Intelligence in eCommerce: Using Chatbots

3. Customer Relationship Management

Perhaps one of AI's most impressive features is its predictive nature. Customer

Relationship Management, or CRM, is now a thing of the past. What used to be collecting copious amounts of data to be tackled by someone when they finally had enough time to conquer the project for drawing conclusions and making future predictions, is now streamlined and far more efficient.

Don't have anyone in-house who's an expert at Excel Pivot Tables? Don't worry about it. Now all you need is your handy AI programmed to consume all the incoming data (which is a lot to sift through, believe me) and spit out important information about who is likely to buy from you, what they're going to buy, and what you can do to effectively engage with them to maximize conversion of visitors to customers—and even increase the spending habits of current customers.

With the help of AI, the days of aggressive re-marketing and focusing on amount of ad exposure will be long gone. The new marketing era will be able to focus on quality and directing more relevant advertising to the right visitors at the right time. On top of making things easier for you, these advances are also going to improve the overall experience of the customer too.

What's that I hear? I don't know about you, but that definitely sounds like higher conversions to me.

4. Inventory Management

Similarly, AI's predictive analytics are making big waves in the world of inventory management. If you're reading this and you've ever worked with the constant pain of keeping inventory up to date, shelves stocked, and keeping an accurate track of everything, you'll know how much an absolute nightmare inventory management can be. Traditionally, inventory management used a hindsight perspective; however, we all know that what was is not the best metric for determining what is in the dynamic ecommerce marketplace.

AI technology allows shop owners to get important information about factors driving demand and predictive analysis for what future demands are likely to come into the market. Based on how machine learning works, the longer you use your AI buddy, the smarter it will become for your business as it learns more about your company, customers, and visitors. Thanks to advances in AI, shop owners will be able to more accurately predict both real-time and future inventory needs for their business.

5. Image Classification

If you're anything like the rest of us online, you've inevitably had the experience of coming across something you loved and wanted to buy, but you didn't actually know what it was called or how you could find it. Luckily, that's another way AI is changing the game. With its ability to classify, interpret, and understand images, AI is making it easier to find what you didn't even know the name of.

The next time you're on Pinterest [3] and you find a room that you absolutely love, how about being directed to Visually Similar results on the side? Makes it a whole lot easier to find that chair, rug, or artwork, eh? Or maybe even quickly snapping a picture of the shoes you saw someone walking down the sidewalk in and then using an App to help you find and buy those exact shoes? Now shopping for that perfect item is not only easier, but can be done anytime, anywhere.

Want an example of AI already working for a business? If you weren't already familiar with this feature, you can open up the Amazon mobile app and point the camera on your phone at something and Amazon will identify it and pull it up for you to add it to your cart. Talk about using AI to make it as easy as possible for consumers to purchase products online!

So what does this all mean for us marketers?

Ultimately, this means that AI will help us to improve our ecommerce platforms to **cater to** the needs and interest of visitors. We can recommend products and services in an effective manner that are actually relevant to consumers (so the ads will **intrigue** them and catch their attention, rather than annoy and push away) and we can help visitors find new products in a relaxed, conversational manner in the same way they would speak with an actual person.

Retailers that have implemented personalization strategies have seen sales gains of 6%-10%, a rate two to three times faster than other retailers, according to a report by Boston Consulting Group (BCG). It could also boost profitability rates 59% in the wholesale and retail industries by 2035, according to Accenture[4].

AI is changing the name of the game with online retailers and ecommerce marketing. With all of the value being added to the marketplace, e-retailers cannot only advance their business practices, but free up their own time to focus on other important matters. So what are you waiting for? It's time to get smarter and faster with your business!

Words

conquer['kɒŋkə(r)] v. 攻克，征服	nightmare['naitmeə(r)] n. 难处理之事，噩梦
saturated['sætʃəreitid] adj. 饱和的，充满的	buddy['bʌdi] n. 朋友，同伴，伙伴
fridge[fridʒ] n. 冰箱	rug[rʌg] n. 小地毯，垫子
bot[bɒt] n.（能执行特定任务的）网上机器人程序（robot 的缩略）	eh[ei] int.（表示惊奇、疑问或没听清楚对方的话）啊，嗯，什么
brand[brænd] v. 使显得独一无二，表明……与众不同	snap[snæp] v. 给……拍快照，快摄（照片）
further['fɜːðə(r)] v. 促进，增进	intrigue[in'triːg, 'intriːg] v. 激起……的兴趣，引发……的好奇心
copious['kəʊpiəs] adj. 大量的，充裕的，丰富的	

Unit 9　Ecommerce

 Phrases

have to do with 和……有关系
boil down to 将……归结为，重点是
change up 加挡，换高速挡
a bunch of 大量，许多
old school 守旧派
spit out 吐出……，愤怒地说
long gone 已经过去
hindsight perspective 事后诸葛亮
a whole lot 非常多，多得不能再多了
cater to 满足……的需要

 Notes

　　[1]　埃隆·马斯克(Elon Musk)，1971年6月28日出生于南非的行政首都比勒陀利亚(现名：茨瓦内)，企业家、工程师、慈善家。他同时具有南非、加拿大和美国三重国籍。现任太空探索技术公司(SpaceX)CEO兼CTO、特斯拉公司CEO、太阳城公司(SolarCity)董事会主席。

　　[2]　蒂姆·库克(Tim Cook)，1960年11月1日出生于美国亚拉巴马州，现任苹果公司首席执行官。

　　[3]　Pinterest是一个图片社交平台。Pinterest采用的是瀑布流的形式展现图片内容，无须用户翻页，新的图片不断自动加载在页面底端，让用户不断地发现新的图片。

　　[4]　埃森哲(Accenture)注册成立于爱尔兰，是全球最大的上市咨询公司和《财富》世界500强公司之一，为客户提供战略、咨询、数字、技术和运营服务及解决方案。

 Exercises

Ⅰ. Read the following statements carefully, and decide whether they are true (T) or false (F) according to the text.

　　____ 1. There are three ways that ecommerce can use online AI.
　　____ 2. AI is changing the name of the game with online retailers and ecommerce marketing.
　　____ 3. It could also boost profitability rates 59% in the wholesale and retail industries by 2035, according to Boston Consulting Group (BCG).
　　____ 4. Shop owners will be able to more accurately predict both real-time and future inventory needs for their business via AI.
　　____ 5. Retailers that have implemented personalization strategies have seen sales gains of 6%-10%, a rate two to three times faster than other retailers,

according to a report by Accenture.

II. Choose the best answer to each of the following questions according to the text.

1. How many ways that ecommerce can use online AI?
   A. One
   B. Three
   C. Five
   D. Seven

2. Which of following is not mentioned?
   A. Accenture
   B. Tim Cook
   C. Elon Musk
   D. Bill Gate

3. What does CRM stand for?
   A. Control Real Matter
   B. Coast River Management
   C. Cost Reduction Management
   D. Customer Relationship Management

III. Identify the letter of the choice that best matches the phrase or definition.

a. ecommerce

b. e-tailer

c. m-commerce

d. meta tag

e. Web analytics

____ 1. An online retailer.

____ 2. Ecommerce carried out via smartphones and other mobile devices.

____ 3. Statistics about Web site traffic that can be used to help evaluate the effectiveness of a Web site or a Web site promotion strategy.

____ 4. A special HTML or XHTML tag containing information about the Web page that is added by the person creating a Web page and is used primarily by search sites.

____ 5. The act of doing business transactions over the Internet or similar technology.

Unit 9   Ecommerce

Ⅳ. Fill in the numbered spaces with the words or phrases chosen from the box. Change the forms where necessary.

| will | use | compare | visit | success |
| find | proud | make | fight | simple |

Changing Retail Practices: The Fight against "Showrooming"

Target has made it clear it's __1__ back. "What we aren't __2__ to do," its management says, "is let online-only retailers use our brick and mortar stores as a showroom for their products and undercut our prices without __3__ investments, as we do, to __4__ display our brands.

Mobile phones are indispensable to showroomers for __5__ prices. E-tailer Amazon even provides its users with a mobile app with "the ability to __6__ price lookups on its site by letting them scan product bar codes __7__ their smartphone cameras" according to one report. Bed Bath & Beyond, PetSmart, and Toys "R" Us were __8__ to be among the retailers __9__ most by Amazon showroomers.

What can traditional retailers do? One strategy, found to be __10__ at Target and Best Buy during the 2012 holiday shopping period, is for a retailer to announce that it will match an e-tailer's low prices. That practice is now a year-round policy.

Ⅴ. Translate the following passage into Chinese.

Is it Safe to Use My Credit Card Online?

Online shoppers are justifiably worried that personal information and credit card numbers supplied in the course of an ecommerce transaction might be hijacked and used inappropriately. Many shoppers worry that hackers might use packet sniffers to intercept credit card numbers traveling over the Internet.

To protect your credit card from packet sniffers, you should engage in electronic transactions only over a secure connection. A secure connection encrypts the data transmitted between your computer and a Web site. Even if a hacker can capture the packets containing payment data, your encrypted credit card number is virtually useless for illicit purposes. Technologies that create secure connections include SSL/TLS and HTTPS.

Section B: Ecommerce Lessons for Why Amazon is so Successful

Amazon has come a long way from its humble beginnings as an online bookseller. Since its launch in 1994, Amazon has grown to become an ecommerce behemoth. These days, it's one of the first places shoppers turn to buy anything from cleaning products to the latest tech gadgets.

And with over 564 million products sold in the U.S. alone, Amazon is the **uncontested** ecommerce leader and continues to grow and innovate.

This success took years to achieve and is due in part to Amazon's strategic approach to growth. Any ecommerce business, regardless of where they start, can learn from Amazon's example to grow their business and attract and retain more customers.

Here are six lessons that are at the center of why Amazon is so successful(Figure 9-2).

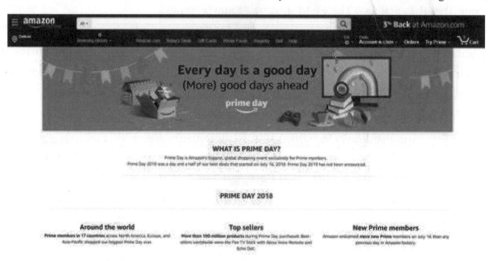

Figure 9-2 Why Amazon is so successful

1. **Meet the needs of your customers**

Part of the reason for Amazon's evolution from book retailer to "everything" retailer is its ability to **tap into** the power of **referrals**.

Jeff Bezos, Amazon CEO, **is quoted as saying**, "It used to be that if you made a customer happy, they would tell five friends. Now, with the **megaphone** of the Internet, whether online customer **reviews** or social media, they can tell 5,000 friends."

News travels at lightning speed across the Internet, so to Bezos' point, by offering customers a positive experience, Amazon grows when their customers share their experiences with their friends and family. This in turn drives new people to Amazon's store to browse the product pages, experience the benefits for themselves, and then share about it.

The key to sustaining long-term growth with this cycle is to take a customer-focused approach. Bezos explains it this way, "There are many ways to center a business. You can be competitor focused, you can be product focused, you can be technology focused, you can be business model focused, and there are more. But in my view, **obsessive** customer focus is by far the most protective of Day 1 **vitality**."

2. **Incorporate data analysis into your decision making**

Amazon prides itself on its commitment to innovation and testing. They test every aspect of their business—from pricing to product selection—so that decisions are based on customer needs and not what Amazon thinks customers might want.

As Bezos puts it, "Our customers are loyal to us **right up until** the second somebody offers them a better service. And I love that. It's super-motivating for us. "

In part, it's this constant threat of customers switching to the competition that drives Amazon's innovation. Even though it's the largest ecommerce retailer, with $280.05 billion in revenue in 2020 across all of its business segments, Amazon is constantly **in competition with** other businesses.

For example, smart home devices are gaining momentum in the market. More customers are choosing to equip their homes with devices that make modern day living more interactive and seamless. To compete with a smart speaker like Google Home, Amazon continues to upgrade its Echo to include more distinctive features.

In fact, Amazon Echo has grown to the point it makes up 75% of the global smart speaker market.

When it comes to features, Alexa on Amazon Echo was one of the first versions of voice-controlled tech. It was designed to make it easier for users to connect to the different devices they use. Amazon has gone further with its smart speaker tech to release the Amazon Echo Dot and the Amazon Echo Show to further cater to customers' need to be connected.

3. Get to know your customers

Amazon is constantly learning about its customers. For example, as customers search and add products to their cart, behavioral data shows trends that identify product preferences and buying behaviors.

Amazon takes this information and shows customers products related to items they've recently browsed and makes recommendations based on their search habits.

At the bottom of the homepage, customers can also see more recommendations based on recent purchases and a history of products they've recently viewed. All of this information serves to personalize customers' shopping experiences and guides them to buy more.

Amazon takes personalization further by confirming whether or not a selected product ships to the location entered in the customer profile. This is incredibly helpful because it avoids customers adding items to their cart only to find out at checkout that they can't receive it.

This tactic works because research shows that customers expect personalized experiences. When brands position themselves as partners in the shopping journey, it:

- reinforces the brand/customer relationship
- improves the customer experience
- improves conversions and boosts revenue
- promotes customer loyalty and

- increases retention

Product recommendations based on what Amazon knows about its customers are targeted and in line with what customers want to buy or are interested in.

4. Build a community for your customers

Research shows that 87% of customers prefer product feedback from people they know and trust vs. brands. In fact, 45% of shoppers read reviews before buying.

Add to this the fact that 82% of customers use their cell phones to conduct online research before they buy a product, and you have the perfect opportunity to build a community designed to educate shoppers and move them along the customer journey quicker.

Amazon uses a few different strategies to build its customer community. One way is it proactively asks recent customers to rate and review their experience.

This information is added to the list of customer reviews on the product page. These reviews also appear with a "verified purchase" flag, which adds to the trustworthiness of the review.

Amazon also offers a customer question-and-answer section at the bottom of its product pages to give shoppers the option to ask specific questions before they buy something. Past customers provide some of the answers.

Both of these options make it possible for shoppers to rely on other customers for information and not Amazon. Shoppers can read about honest experiences from other customers and base some of their purchase decisions on this.

5. Build a loyalty program to incentivize customers

Amazon launched Amazon Prime in 2005 and positioned it as a membership service that offered two-day free shipping and other benefits. Prime has evolved since then to also include exclusive offers at Whole Foods grocery stores, access to award-winning TV shows, access to their music streaming service called Amazon Music, and much more.

Then in 2015, the service gained even more attention when Amazon Prime Day was launched. For one day only, Amazon Prime members have access to deep discounts and exclusive offers.

This annual event, available globally, is a highlight for Prime members. In fact, there were over 100 billion products sold globally during the most recent Prime Day. This beat out sales from Cyber Monday, Black Friday, and the last Prime Day.

While Amazon Prime isn't like most loyalty programs that customers automatically qualify for—you have to pay to join Amazon Prime—it does a good job of driving traffic to the store and encouraging shoppers to buy something.

Customers want loyalty programs. In fact, 71% of customers choose to join loyalty programs because of the promise to save money on their purchases. 63% join because of the potential to receive products for free.

Amazon has been able to tap into these need customers have to save money instantly when they shop. By offering special discounts and reduced or free shipping rates, shoppers are naturally drawn to Amazon to meet their purchase needs.

6. Think of new ways to evolve

Amazon continues to grow as a result of its dedication to trying new things. Features like product reordering and returning damaged products aren't standard practice for all ecommerce retailers.

Tracking their orders of customers or managing their returns goes a long way to helping Amazon become a company that's constantly thinking of new ways to make the customer experience simple and seamless.

Plus, once Amazon has shoppers' attention, they think of new ways to keep their audience engaged. Whether it's by introducing new TV and movie programming as part of Prime membership or access to new audio content, Amazon is always looking for new opportunities to evolve.

Words

behemoth[bɪˈhiːməθ] n. 巨头（指规模庞大、实力雄厚的公司或机构）
uncontested [ˌʌnkənˈtestɪd] adj. 无争议的，无人反对的
referral[rɪˈfɜːrəl] n. 推荐，引荐来源（指给某个网站带来了流量的其他网站）
megaphone[ˈmeɡəfəʊn] n. 扩音器，传声筒

review[rɪˈvjuː] n. 评论
obsessive[əbˈsesɪv] adj. 着迷的，迷恋的；难以释怀的
vitality[vaɪˈtæləti] n. 生命力，活力，热情
incentivize[ɪnˈsentɪvaɪz] v. 以物质刺激鼓励

Phrases

come a long way 取得很大进展
tap into 利用，开发
be quoted as saying 用……的话说
as sb. put it 正如某人所说的那样
right up until 一直到
in competition with 与……竞争
in line with 和……一致，符合
add to this 而且，另外
beat out 打败，击败，战胜
for free 免费的
go a long way 对……大有帮助

Abbreviations

vs. versus 相对照，相对立

 Exercises

Ⅰ. Read the following statements carefully, and decide whether they are true (T) or false (F) according to the text.

　　____ 1. Amazon was founded in 2005.

　　____ 2. There are two lessons that are at the center of why Amazon is so successful.

　　____ 3. Jeff Bezos is a CEO of Google.

　　____ 4. Amazon is seldom learning about its customers.

　　____ 5. Amazon's long-term growth is to take a customer-focused approach.

Ⅱ. Choose the best answer to each of the following questions according to the text.

1. How many lessons that are at the center of why Amazon is so successful?

　　A. Two

　　B. Four

　　C. Six

　　D. Eight

2. Which of the following is not right for Amazon?

　　A. Build a community for your customers

　　B. Meet the needs of your customers

　　C. Rarely learn about its customers

　　D. Get to know your customers

3. Which of the following is right when brands position themselves as partners in the shopping journey?

　　A. It promotes customer loyalty

　　B. It improves the customer experience

　　C. It reinforces the brand/customer relationship

　　D. All of the above

Ⅲ. Identify the letter of the choice that best matches the phrase or definition.

　　a. brick-and-mortar store

　　b. business-to-business (B2B) model

c. business-to consumer (B2C) model

d. digital wallet

e. online payment service

___ 1. A conventional store with a physical presence.

___ 2. A type of payment service accessed via the Internet and used to make electronic payments to others, such as via deposited funds, a bank account, or a credit card.

___ 3. An ecommerce model in which a business provides goods or services to other businesses.

___ 4. An ecommerce model in which a business provides goods or services to consumers.

___ 5. An app or online service that stores information (such as credit, debit, and loyalty cards; digital coupons; and shipping information) and that can be used to speed up purchase transactions.

Ⅳ. **Fill in the blanks with the words or phrases chosen from the box. Change the forms where necessary.**

> popular   available   significant   ticket   converge
> purchase   custom   base   deliver   store

Mobile Commerce

Mobile commerce(m-commerce)—the use of smart phones, tablets, PDAs, laptops, and other portable electronic devices to conduct commerce while on the move—has been possible in one form or another for many years. But in recent years, mobile commerce has increased dramatically as a result of several ___1___ trends:

- The growing ___2___ of portable computers as a percentage of the total PC market.
- The widespread ___3___ of wireless Internet connections through Wi-Fi hotspots and 3G and 4G networks.
- The popularity of mobile phones with GPS technology and Web access.
- The development of smart phones with Web access and applications that aren't ___4___ compromised by size.

Here is a sampling of m-commerce applications that are becoming popular:

- Mobile ___5___. E-tickets can be sent directly to mobile phones and dashboard computers, which can in turn communicate wirelessly with ticket takers at entertainment events, parking facilities, toll roads, and so on.
- Mobile coupons. Electronic coupons and loyalty cards ___6___ in mobile

phones can replace their paper and plastic counterparts.
- Mobile ___7___ . Many mobile phones make it easy to buy music, news, and other digital data; some stores encourage their customers to buy physical goods on their mobile devices; the actual goods can then be picked up at the stores or ___8___ .
- Location-___9___ m-commerce. Mobile devices with GPS and other localization technology can ___10___ offers and ads based on location.

Ⅴ. **Translate the following passages into Chinese.**
What is the Impact of Social Media on Web Sites Today?

For a rapidly growing number of Web-based businesses, social media represents more than yet another sales channel. With customers leveraging their own online influence to elicit responses directly from businesses, social channels are now serving as real time customer service platforms. Businesses quick to acknowledge these customers can take advantage of this trend to build brand authenticity and customer loyalty. Similarly, businesses slow (or unable) to incorporate social media into their practices risk losing customers to more socially competent competitors.

As a result, social media empowers consumers by encouraging and incentivizing corporate transparency. Maintaining transparency will become an increasingly important component to corporate strategy as these social channels continue to mature. This is true today for customer service interactions, and it will be true tomorrow for additional company practices.

Part 2

Simulated Writing: Writing for Employment (I)

有效地搜寻就业机会是可以培养的最重要的职业技能之一。求职的时候需要使用所有的沟通技巧,其中大部分的早期步骤涉及书面交流。那些按时提交了专业文档并且在简历上看起来很不错的申请人往往是雇主邀请进行最后面试的人。

1. 了解求职

找到合适的工作的第一步是评估你的兴趣、目标和资历,然后确定相应的工作和雇主。求职将一直持续到最后一步——接到录用通知。研究表明,一般人会在一生中改变从业领域三到五次,并在每个从业领域都有数次工作机会,因此发展求职能力将会为你提供十分有价值的生存技能。求职的细节将会依照每份工作有所变化,但是如图9-3所示的一般步骤是保持不变的。

大多数求职过程都包括以下步骤:

1）确定就业目标

在完成第一份申请之前，对要寻找什么样的工作要有一个清晰的概念。可以问自己一些问题，比如说：你的专业技能是什么？天赋和兴趣点在哪里？你现在想要寻找什么样的职位？这个职位和你的长期职业目标契合吗？在你感兴趣的领域中求职市场的特性是什么？你想要生活在什么样的环境之下呢？参见图9-4，你的回答将帮助你制定专属于你的求职策略。

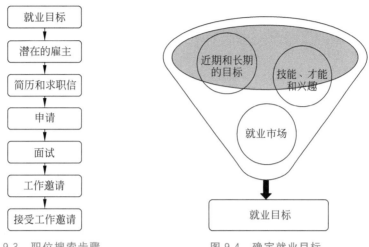

图9-3　职位搜索步骤　　　　　图9-4　确定就业目标

2）识别潜在的雇主

待选的工作数目取决于联系的雇主的数量。想要识别潜在的雇主，就要善于利用网站和平面媒体提供的就业信息和岗位空缺，并且要花费大量的时间与他人（朋友、熟人、老师和家人等）交谈就业机会。在个人通信的网络（包括社交网络）上进行交流，是找到工作机会以及发现潜在雇主的有价值信息的最有效方法。

3）撰写有针对性的简历和求职信

在申请特定职位时，简历和求职信将成为可以用来提升自己的营销工具。有效的简历和求职信就像是为想要申请的岗位特别定制的一般，并且它会突出相关的资历。有一些求职者会准备几份针对性不同的简历，并利用它们在不同的行业申请职位。

4）申请合适的职位

雇主需要一个可以从中找到能够填补空缺职位的申请者的候选群体。很大程度上他们会从符合条件和有资格的人当中来挑选，但还是由你来标明你的兴趣。有一些组织会要求填写一份申请表，还有一些组织会选择接受简历和求职信。应该确定每一份申请的流程，并且认真仔细地开展每一个步骤。

5）为面试做准备

递交简历和求职信的目的是得到面试的机会。面试是和招聘经理既要讨论工作机会又要讨论你的资历的一次会面。许多机构的初步面试是通过电话进行的，但基本不会在没有进行一个面对面的会面之前做出聘用的决定。最后得到这份工作的人往往是为面试做了最好的准备的人——并不总是一个最能胜任这个位置的人。

6)接受工作邀请

接受一个满足就业目标的就业邀请是实现终极目标的最后一步。得到工作邀请后,要对这个工作做个评估,看它是否符合你的需求和兴趣。最好的工作邀请是同时非常适合你和你的雇主的。仔细权衡得到的工作邀请的优劣,接受那些符合你的兴趣、天赋和求职目标的邀请。

2. 撰写有效的求职信

求职信(有时被称为申请信)是一封简短且个性化的、伴随着简历一起发送给你感兴趣的雇佣机会的信。一封写得很好的求职信应该能够吸引读者的注意力,标明想要申请的职位,突出简历中的关键资历,并请求进入面试。将求职信和简历发送给负责招聘决策的人,如果这个人的联系方式很难得到,就把求职信发送到这个组织的人力资源部门。表9-1列出了写求职信时的注意事项。

表9-1 撰写求职信的注意事项

求职信元素	适合提到	尽量避免
问候	• 用收信人的名字向他致辞	• 使用笼统的称呼来进行问候,比如"尊敬的人事部经理"(Dear Hiring Manager)
开头	• 明确表示要申请的职位 • 适当提到建议提出申请的那个人的名字 • 说明是从哪里看见工作招聘广告的	• 笼统地指向众多职位,例如"我想要申请一个贵公司现在空缺的职位"(I'm applying to fill the job vacancy at your company.)
资历	• 列举3~5个与职位直接相关的资历 • 描述可以为雇佣者做些什么 • 重点表现优势可以如何使雇主受益	• 列举所学课程或者之前的工作职责 • 包括不具备的技能和经历 • 描述资历中的各种细节或者重复简历上的细节
总结	• 自信地请求一次面试 • 如果没有提到简历,那么就在这部分提起 • 提供电话号码并说明最方便的联系时间	• 直接地要求获得这份工作 • 让求职信看起来不真诚、要求过高或者过分担忧
后续跟进	如果没有收到一个潜在雇佣者的回信,那么将求职信和简历重发一次	忽略来自雇佣者的关于后续跟进的建议和指导

1)用收信人的名字向他们致辞

在开始写求职信的时候,用收信人的名字向他们致辞。这会吸引他们的注意力,并且使申请显得更加人性化。避免使用通用的称呼,例如"尊敬的先生/女士,"(Dear Sir/Madam,)或"敬启者"(To Whom It May Concern.)。

2)确定申请职位

当进行申请的时候,目标单位可能有几个职位空缺,在求职信的第一段应该确定想要寻求的那个职位。如果时机适宜,可以提一下是谁建议提出申请或者是从哪里看到这个工作广告的。

3)突出最相关的技能

在求职信的第二段应简要介绍三到五个就职资格、所获成就或与这个空缺职位相关的技能。推销自己的长处来显示能为雇主做些什么,但不必细讲。目标是引起对方的兴趣,并鼓动他们认真阅读简历。当描述到资历的时候，可以建议其参考简历来获取更多的信息。

图9-5是一封求职信的开始部分。

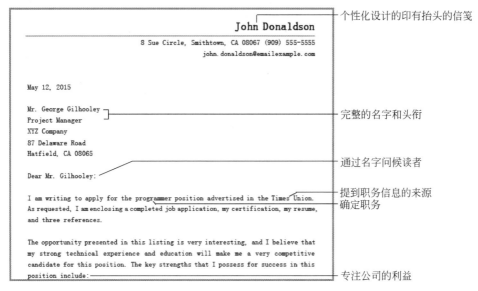

图9-5 修订过的求职信的开始部分

4）用请求行动来进行总结

求职信和简历的直接目标是让申请通过初步的筛选，并且能够得到面试机会，那么就可通过直接请求面试机会来结束求职信。

5）用令人关注的态度跟进

最初的申请并不总能在正确的时间被正确的人看到，如果在几周之内都没有收到任何回应就再发送一次信件。对申请状况进行持续跟进会向招聘经理显示主动性以及对这份工作机会的热情。

转 205 页

Part 3

Listening and Speaking

Dialogue：Protecting Buyers' Privacy with Online Payment Services

（Henry was excited to find a long-expected book in an online bookstore，but he hesitated when it required the payment via an account.）

Henry: Recently publicized accounts of credit card fraud on the Internet are no doubt alarming to us. It's not always easy to tell who's at the other end of your online transaction when you hand over[1] your credit card number.

[1] Replace with:
1. transmit
2. deliver
3. transfer

Mark: Maybe you can use a third-party payment service to make payments for things online a little easier and safer.

Henry: A third-party payment service?

Sophie: Yes. In brief,[2] when you use a third-party payment service, you transfer money into an online account and make payments from that account. That way, you never expose your real credit card or bank account information.

[2] Replace with:
1. In short,
2. In summary,
3. In a word,
4. All in all,
5. Anyhow,

Henry: Sounds much safer. Are any of them easily available?

Mark: Yes. One of the most popular of these services is PayPal, but there are others such as Amazon.com Payments. To take basic payments for instance, such as online auctions or simple Website sales, the merchant can simply provide buyers with their email address, and buyers can make the appropriate payments to the merchant's PayPal account.

Henry: Ok. I've got it.

Sophie: After you make a choice, it's recommended to be attentive to some details for choosing a more secure service.

Henry: What are they, please?

Sophie: First, read the privacy policy and make sure you agree with it; If you don't, go elsewhere. Besides, check for a stamp of approval from the authoritative organizations which certify that a Web site has met certain standards. People sometimes overlook those items but they are very important indeed.

Mark: When using a payment service, please remember, Henry, never respond to email messages from third-party payment services asking you to confirm account details, such as passwords or other personally identifiable information. These email messages could be an identity theft scam, such as phishing.

Henry: Then, how can I confirm or fix my account details more safely?

Sophie: If you need to confirm or update your account information or change your password, I suggest you visit the website by using your personal bookmark or by typing the URL of the payment service directly into your browser.

Henry: How can I verify further whether a seller providing this payment service is valid?

Mark: You can do it by checking if the seller has been a verified member of the payment service for a few months or more. Some sites also allow you to check the seller's rating. Although these ratings cannot be guaranteed, they can be helpful.

Sophie: Keep in mind, Henry, never use your account to transfer money for someone else that you don't know. This might be an advanced fee fraud. And be more careful when you purchase very expensive items, such as jewelry or computers, especially around the holidays and for items that are sold in stores.

Henry: Ok. Now I'm much more confident in safe online payments. Thanks a lot for your advice.

Exercises

Work in a group, and make up a similar conversation by replacing the statements with other expressions on the right side.

Words

long-expected 期待已久的
publicize['pʌblisaiz] v. 宣传,公布,引人注意
tell[tel] v. 辨别,断定
stamp[stæmp] n. 印章,戳记
scam[skæm] n. 阴谋,诡计,(尤指)欺诈,骗局
phish[fiʃ] v. 网络钓鱼
fix[fiks] v. 安排,决定
rate[reit] v. 评估,给……估价
advanced[əd'vɑːnst] adj. 价格高的,昂贵的

 Phrases

hand over 移交,交出
in brief 简单地说
be attentive to 注意,留心
keep in mind 记住

 Abbreviations

URL   Uniform Resource Locator   统一资源定位器

Listening Comprehension: Social Commerce

Listen to the article and answer the following 3 questions based on it. After you hear a question, there will be a break of 15 seconds. During the break, you will decide which one is the best answer among the four choices marked (A), (B), (C) and (D).

Questions

1. Which of the following is the impact of social media on ecommerce?
   (A) The term papers
   (B) The social aspect
   (C) The homework
   (D) The exams

2. Which of the following is the description of social commerce according to this article?
   (A) Amazon.com sells goods or services to individuals.
   (B) Lenovo sells computers to its distributors based on its own website.

Unit 9   Ecommerce

(C) Individuals sell directly to other individuals based on eBay.

(D) The use of social networking sites and other social media to promote online sales.

3. What do F-commerce and F-store mean according to this article?

(A) Businesses and individuals can sell real goods and real services inside factories.

(B) Businesses and individuals can sell real goods and real services in a flash.

(C) Businesses and individuals can sell real goods and real services inside Facebook.

(D) Businesses and individuals can sell real goods and real services in fountains.

 Words

| custom['kʌstəm] adj. 定制的,定做的 | word-of-mouth 口头的,口述的 |
| dub[dʌb] v. 授予称号 | profile['prəufail] n. 简介,传略 |

 Phrases

social aspect   社会要素,社会层面

Dictation: Mobile Payments

This article will be played three times. Listen carefully, and fill in the numbered spaces with the appropriate words you have heard.

Because most ___1___ carry a smartphone or another mobile device with them at all times in order to communicate with others and **look up** information, m-commerce (___2___) is a natural next step in ecommerce. You can use your smartphone in ___3___ with the **NFC** readers that are appearing in retail stores, train stations, and other locations to pay for purchases. You can also purchase ___4___ tickets, order and pay for meals at some restaurants, and perform other transactions ___5___ your smartphone and then have a **QR** code or other proof of purchase ___6___ on your phone to **finalize** the transaction at the ___7___ location. To send money to individuals (to **split a check**, **reimburse** someone for ___8___ tickets or gifts, or just pay back a ___9___, for instance), you can use your mobile ___10___ app or a mobile payment app such as PalPay or Google Wallet Mobile payment processing (collecting payment for goods and services via a mobile device) is another ___11___ m-commerce trend that is

193

growing rapidly. Mobile payments ___12___ utilize a credit card reader attached to a smartphone or media ___13___ that enables individuals as well as businesses to accept credit card payments. For instance, ___14___ workers such as repair technicians can easily collect payment as soon as the service is completed and ___15___ at craft shows can accept credit card payments to increase potential sales. It also enables ___16___ buying in retail stores, where sales ___17___ can process purchases on the sales floor instead of making the customer wait in line at a ___18___ counter. This can help the experience feel more personal to the customer as well as avoid walk-outs during busy periods ___19___ to long checkout lines. This concept is also being expanded to other businesses, such as hotels that offer check-in service in the lobby as soon as ___20___ enter the hotel.

Words

finalize['faɪnəlaɪz] v. 把（计划、旅行、项目等）最后定下来
reimburse[ˌriːɪm'bɜːs] v. 偿还，向……付还，报销（所花的费用）
craft[krɑːft] n. 工艺，手艺

walk-out 退席
check-in 签到，住宿登记手续
lobby['lɒbi] n.（公寓、旅馆、剧院等公共建筑物的）门厅，门廊，前厅，穿堂，休息室

Phrases

look up 查阅（词典或参考书），(在词典、参考书等中）查找
split a check 付账的时候几个人分账单

Abbreviations

NFC　Near Field Communication　近场通信
QR　　Quick Response　快速反应（QR code 是二维码的一种）

Unit 10

Computer Security and Privacy

Part 1

Reading and Translating

Section A: Ways to Protect Your Personal Information Online

The Internet has made our lives easier in so many ways over the years. Using the World Wide Web, we can get access to **unprecedented** amounts of information in just seconds and access all sorts of entertaining, **engaging**, and useful content.

However, the phenomenon has also opened us up to new dangers, as various malicious individuals **scour** the net looking for easy targets.

Some of the biggest threats we face online include the risk of identity and money theft. We use our personal information to **sign up** with almost any website out there, but the risk becomes even greater when we use our banking information online. For example, when using online casinos operating in the Philippines, users are often asked to share their banking info. While the sites themselves may be safe, there are potential threats from the outside to consider.

We take a look at the top five ways you can protect your personal and banking info while using the Internet and keep yourself safe while enjoying all the **perks** of the online world(Figure 10-1).

Figure 10-1 How to protect your personal information online

1. Careful What You Click

One of the main ways that hackers access private data of individual users is by using a method known as phishing. The hacker will send you an email or another type of message with a link or an attachment in it. Accessing the link or downloading the attachment will download some type of malicious software onto your device, **without you knowing**.

The best way to protect yourself against this kind of intrusion is to never click on links or even open emails from unknown senders. Promotional emails will be sent from email addresses that will clearly show the website they belong to, but if you have not signed up for offers from one company, you should probably just ignore their emails just the same.

2. Make Strong Passwords

When using the Internet, you will need to create passwords to protect your various accounts, whether you are just using email or social networks or accessing your banking accounts. In either case, using a strong password will prevent potential hacking attempts into that account.

More and more sites these days require users to use passwords with capital letters, numbers, and special symbols, but some will still let you use an extremely simple password. Using simple passwords is an invitation to hackers, so we recommend using more complicated ones and never using the same password for your sensitive accounts and less important ones.

3. Enable Two-Step Authentication

As the Internet is becoming more sophisticated, numerous companies are giving users an opportunity to further protect their accounts by using the two-step authentication process. This process makes it harder or nearly impossible for hackers to access your information as the password alone is not alone.

The two-step authentication requires that you choose a phone number along with your password. Once you enter the password, you will be sent an access code via SMS to that phone number. Only once you have entered that access code will you get logged in, adding a physical element of security to the mix, as you need to actually have access to the phone in question to get access to your accounts.

4. Install Antivirus Software

In this day and age, antivirus software is not as effective as it once was, or as necessary. The Internet is a lot safer today than it used to be some years ago and the chances of your device getting infected by random viruses are quite low. This is especially the case if you only visit sites you trust.

However, if you are surfing the Web, it is still always a good idea to have some protection in terms of antivirus software. For private users, getting a simple license from one of the major antivirus providers should be enough to protect against most threats.

5. Only Visit Trusted Websites

One of the most important things you can do while surfing the Internet is to pick and choose which websites you access. There are millions of websites out there today and many of them are either malicious or simply not safe.

For starters, you will want to always use websites whose address starts with https instead of http. This **signifies** that the site is secure and uses modern security measures like the **SSL** certificates to protect and encrypt any private data that you share on it. Using **big name** sites for everything you can will ensure that you are never in doubt **in regard to** the website's safety.

 Words

unprecedented[ʌn'presidentid] *adj.* 前所未有的,空前的,没有先例的	perk[pɜːk] *n.* (工资之外的)补贴,津贴,额外待遇
engaging[in'geidʒiŋ] *adj.* 有趣的,令人愉快的,迷人的	mix[miks] *n.* 混乱,迷惑
scour['skauə(r)] *v.* (彻底地)搜寻,搜查	starter['stɑːtə(r)] *n.* 起始者,初学者
	signify['signifai] *v.* 表示,说明

 Phrases

sign up 注册
without you knowing 在不了解你的情况下
just the same 仍然,依然,照样
in question 被提及的,讨论中的,相关的
in this day and age 当今
protect against 保护,保卫
big name 成功人士,知名人士
in regard to 在……方面,就……而论

 Abbreviations

SMS　Short Message Service　短信服务
SSL　Secure Sockets Layer　安全套接层

 Exercises

Ⅰ. Read the following statements carefully, and decide whether they are true (T) or false (F) according to the text.

　　____ 1. Identity and money theft risks are one of the biggest threats we face online.
　　____ 2. Many of websites are either malicious or simply not safe.
　　____ 3. If you are surfing the Web, it is not necessary to have some protection.
　　____ 4. The two-step authentication process makes it harder or nearly impossible for hackers to access your information as the password alone is not alone.

_____ 5. Phishing is a method that can be used by hackers who access private data of individual users.

II. **Choose the best answer to each of the following questions according to the text.**

1. How many ways are mentioned to protect your personal and banking info?
   A. One
   B. Three
   C. Five
   D. Seven

2. Which of the following is right?
   A. The two-step authentication process makes it harder or nearly impossible for hackers to access your information as the password alone is not alone.
   B. Phishing is a method that can be used by hackers who access private data of individual users.
   C. Identity and money theft risks are one of the biggest threats we face online.
   D. All of the above

3. Which of the following is needed to create a password?
   A. Social network
   B. Email
   C. Banking account
   D. All of the above

III. **Identify the letter of the choice that best matches the phrase or definition.**
   a. disaster recovery plan
   b. presence technology
   c. surge suppressor
   d. system failure
   e. uninterruptible power supply (UPS)

_____ 1. A device containing a built-in battery that provides continuous power to a computer and other connected when the electricity goes out.
_____ 2. A device that protects hardware from damage due to electrical fluctuations.
_____ 3. A written plan that describes the steps a company will take following the occurrence of a disaster.
_____ 4. Technology that enables one computing device (such as a computer or mobile device) to locate and identify the current status of another device on

the same network.

_____ 5. The complete malfunction of a computer system.

Ⅳ. **Fill in the blanks with the words or phrases chosen from the box. Change the forms where necessary.**

> discover   submit   vulnerable   depend   affect
> pay   adopt   proper   disclose   call

Microsoft Pays "Bug Bounties" to White-Hat Hackers

In 2013, Microsoft initiated a new policy—also-___1___ bug bounty program to pay white-hat (and gray-hat) hackers for their efforts in ___2___ security flaws in Microsoft software. Bug bounty programs, which have been around since 2004, encourage hackers to work with vendors to fix problems instead of simply publicly ___3___ software bugs (errors in a program that cause it not to work ___4___).

An early ___5___ of the policy, Mozilla, offered $500 to hackers ___6___ security flaws to them. Facebook followed suit, ___7___ $500 and sometimes a lot more, as did Google, which pays up to $20,000 for submitting bugs ___8___ its products.

Microsoft, says a company security strategist, hopes to "encourage the security research community"—meaning ethical hackers—"to report ___9___ in the latest browser and exploitation techniques across the latest platform to Microsoft as early as possible." Hackers can claim bounties of up to $100,000, ___10___ on the type of bug discovered.

Ⅴ. **Translate the following passage into Chinese.**

Why do Some Websites Allow Me to Use My Email Address as a Username?

No two users can have the same email address; that is, your email address is unique to you. This means you can use your email address and password from one website to validate your identity on another website. Facebook, Google, and Twitter, for example, are three popular websites that provide authentication services to other applications. By using your email address from one of these websites to access other websites, you do not have to create or remember separate user names and passwords for the various websites you visit.

Section B: Using Computer Forensics against Cybercrime

Conventional crimes, such as car theft, are often solved by using standard investigative techniques with information from computer databases. To solve cybercrimes, however, the special skills of computer forensic investigators are often required.

Computer forensics is the scientific examination and analysis of data located on computer storage media, which is conducted to offer evidence of computer crimes in court(Figure 10-2). Computer crimes can be separated into two categories. The first includes crimes that use computers, such as transmitting trade secrets to competitors, reproducing copyrighted material, and distributing child pornography. The second includes crimes targeted at computers, such as denial-of-service attacks[1] on servers, Web site vandalism, data theft, and destructive viruses. Computer forensics can be applied to both categories.

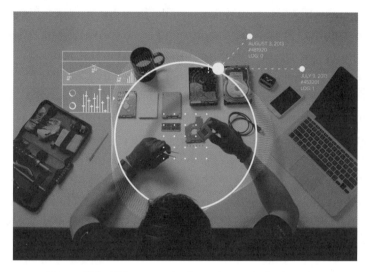

Figure 10-2　Using computer forensics against cybercrime

Whether investigators suspect that a digital device is the origin of a cyber-attack or contains evidence, the first step in the forensic process is to use disk imaging software to make an exact replica of the information stored on the hard disk or SSD drive. The disk image is collected on a write-once medium that cannot be altered with planted evidence, and the forensic scientist begins analyzing the disk image data with simple search software that looks through files for keywords related to the crime.

In the case of the Gap-Toothed Bandit, who was convicted for robbing nine banks, analysis of the disk image revealed word processing files containing notes he handed to tellers demanding money. In the case of the San Bernardino terrorist attack, investigators were able to use data from the shooter's iPhone to track the activities of the shooter and his accomplice prior to the attack.

Criminals might attempt to delete files with incriminating evidence, but a good forensic scientist can retrieve data from deleted files with undelete software or data recovery software. Cloud storage, temporary Internet files, and cache files can also yield evidence that points law enforcement officers to Web sites the suspect visited that might be fronts for illegal activity.

When a network is the target of a cyber-attack, forensic investigators use three techniques to track the source. The first option is to make an immediate image of the server's hard disk and look through its log files for evidence of activity coming from unauthorized IP addresses. The second technique is to monitor the intruder by watching login attempts, changes to log files, and file access requests. Sophisticated intruders might be able to detect such monitoring, however, and cover their tracks. The third technique is to create a "honeypot[2]"—an irresistible computer system or Web site containing fake information that allows investigators to monitor hackers until identification is possible.

Despite the many techniques and tools available to forensic investigators, they have three main constraints. First, they must adhere to privacy regulations and obtain warrants to set up **wiretaps** or gather information from ISPs about their customers. Second, they must **scrupulously** document their procedures so that the evidence they produce cannot be **discredited** in court as planted or fabricated. Third, forensic investigators must examine a wide range of alternatives pertaining to the crime, such as the chance that an IP address or email address used to commit a cybercrime might belong to an innocent **bystander** being **spoofed** by the real hacker.

Privacy, documentation, and **evidentiary** constraints cost forensic investigators time, and failure to adhere to strict standards can sometimes allow criminals to avoid **conviction** and penalties. But even within these constraints, careful forensic investigation is an important aspect of catching and convicting high-tech criminals.

Words

forensics [fə'rɛnsiks] n. 取证,网络法医学
vandalism ['vændəlizəm] n. 故意破坏公共财物的行为,恣意毁坏他人财产的行为
note [nəut] n. 便条
teller ['telə(r)] n. (银行的)出纳,出纳员
accomplice [ə'kʌmplis] n. 共犯,帮凶,同谋
incriminate [in'krimineit] v. 使负罪,连累
point [pɔint] v. 为(某人)指出

wiretap ['waiətæp] n. 窃听装置,窃听
scrupulous ['skru:pjələs] adj. 仔细的,细致的
discredit [dis'kredit] v. 使怀疑,使不可置信
bystander ['baistændə(r)] n. 旁观者
spoof [spu:f] v. 欺骗
evidentiary [ˌevi'denʃəri] adj. 作为证据的
conviction [kən'vikʃn] n. 定罪,证明有罪

Unit 10　Computer Security and Privacy

 Phrases

planted evidence 栽赃，伪造证据
look through 逐一查看，翻阅

 Notes

[1]　拒绝服务攻击(denial-of-service attacks)是攻击者想办法让目标机器停止提供服务，是黑客常用的攻击手段之一。攻击者进行拒绝服务攻击，实际上让服务器实现两种效果：一是迫使服务器的缓冲区满，不接收新的请求；二是使用 IP 欺骗，迫使服务器把非法用户的连接复位，影响合法用户的连接。

[2]　蜜罐技术(Honeypot)是一种对攻击方进行欺骗的技术，通过布置一些作为诱饵的主机、网络服务或者信息，诱使攻击方对它们实施攻击，从而可以对攻击行为进行捕获和分析，了解攻击方所使用的工具与方法，推测攻击意图和动机，能够让防御方清晰地了解他们所面对的安全威胁，并通过技术和管理手段来增强实际系统的安全防护能力。

 Exercises

Ⅰ. Read the following statements carefully，and decide whether they are true（T）or false（F）according to the text.

____ 1. When a network is the target of a cyber-attack，forensic investigators use two techniques to track the source.

____ 2. The special skills of computer forensic investigators are often required for solving cybercrimes.

____ 3. Computer crimes can be separated into three categories.

____ 4. A good forensic scientist can retrieve data from deleted files with undelete software or data recovery software.

____ 5. Forensic investigators have three main constraints despite the many techniques and tools available to them.

Ⅱ. Choose the best answer to each of the following questions according to the text.

1. How many techniques do forensic investigators use to track the source when a network is the target of a cyber-attack?

　　A. One
　　B. Two
　　C. Three
　　D. Four

2. Which of the following can cost forensic investigators time?

   A. Evidentiary constraints

   B. Privacy

   C. Documentation

   D. All of the above

3. Which of the following can yield evidence that points law enforcement officers to Web sites the suspect visited that might be fronts for illegal activity?

   A. Temporary Internet files

   B. Cache files

   C. Cloud storage

   D. All of the above

Ⅲ. Identify the letter of the choice that best matches the phrase or definition.

   a. digital counterfeiting

   b. full disk encryption（FDE）

   c. information piracy

   d. software piracy

   e. spam

   ____ 1. The rights of individuals and companies to control how information about them is collected and used.

   ____ 2. A technology that encrypts everything stored on a storage medium automatically without any user interaction.

   ____ 3. The unauthorized copying of a computer program.

   ____ 4. The use of computers or other types of digital equipment to make illegal copies of currency, checks, collectibles, and other items.

   ____ 5. Unsolicited, bulk email sent over the Internet.

Ⅳ. Fill in the blanks with the words or phrases chosen from the box. Change the forms where necessary.

```
teach    help    hack    acquire    know
gain    stop    deficiency    anonymity    take
```

Should College Teach Hacking?

____1____ the traditional admonition "know thy enemy" literally, some colleges offer courses that teach students how to write computer viruses and other malware. One instructor ____2____ students how to thwart antivirus software and how to generate

___3___ email spam. He claims that if college students easily bypass antivirus software, then the products clearly are ___4___. Proponents of such courses claim that these hacking skills enable the next generation of security experts to think like malicious hackers, thereby ___5___ to stop the spread of malware. They liken the ___6___ skills to physics students who learn how atomic weapons work, or biology students who learn how poisons work. Critics claim that this practice only encourages more virus authoring and ___7___. Others claim that ___8___ how to write malware does not make someone more capable of ___9___ malware. Questions remain about who is responsible legally, financially, and morally if one of the students in such a course releases malicious code to the Internet or uses the knowledge ___10___ in the course to infect other computers purposefully.

Ⅴ. **Translate the following passages into Chinese.**
How Popular are Biometric Devices?

Biometric devices are gaining popularity as a security precaution because they are a virtually foolproof method of identification and authentication. For example, some grocery stores, retail stores, and gas stations use biometric payment, where the customer's fingerprint is read by a fingerprint reader that is linked to a payment method such as a checking account or credit card. Users can forget their user names and passwords. Possessed objects can be lost, copied, duplicated, or stolen. Personal characteristics, by contrast, are unique and cannot be forgotten or misplaced.

Biometric devices do have disadvantages. If you cut your finger, a fingerprint reader might reject you as a legitimate user. Hand geometry readers can transmit germs. If you are nervous, a signature might not match the one on file. If you have a sore throat, a voice recognition system might reject you. Many people are uncomfortable with the thought of using an iris scanner.

Part 2

Simulated Writing: Writing for Employment (Ⅱ)

接189页

3. 策划简历

简历是学历、工作经历、技能和成就汇总而成的一至两页的总结。就像求职信一样,要为每一个潜在的雇主定制一份简历。一份好的简历介绍了申请人的背景、突出水平和成就,这些都是最有可能吸引目标雇主的东西。尽管简历很短,只是结构化的文档,但它们需要精心的策划、编辑和校对。为了让简历能够吸引雇主从而保障拿到每一个面试的机会,最好准备几个不同版本的简历。表10-1总结了制作简历的注意事项。

表 10-1　制作简历的注意事项

简历元素	适 合 提 到	尽 量 避 免
主标题	• 包括完整的名字和完整的地址 • 使用简单且专业的格式来凸显名字 • 提供私人邮箱地址来显得更加专业 • 在找工作的时候要定期查看信息和邮件	• 遗漏联系方式 • 列出无效的联系信息 • 包含工作邮箱 • 使用华而不实或标新立异的格式 • 显示年龄、婚姻状况和薪资要求
职业目标和资历概述	• 如果向某个职业做出了承诺就要包括一个职业目标 • 列出最重要的资历而不是一个目标	• 目标和工作描述不符就放进来 • 将职业目标确定为初级职位,而小看了自己的才能
教育经历总结	• 标明与职位相关的具体课程 • 在信息的多少之间找到一个平衡点 • 如果课程平均绩点大于或等于3.0就标注出来	• 上了大学还列出高中的信息 • 把所学的所有课程都列出来
工作经历	• 使用简单而准确的描述 • 量化成就 • 用列表将经历格式化	• 列出全部的工作职责或活动 • 使用被动词汇或者强调个人主义(如一直提到我)
技能、活动和荣誉	• 重点强调所拥有的适合这个职位的技能 • 提供书面需求证明的具体细节 • 使用行动动词来描述技能和活动	• 荣誉过少或很小还列出来 • 假设读者知道这个荣誉的意义,而没有提供一个简单的解释

1) 主标题

在简历的最开始,常常要标明姓名、地址和其他的联系信息,包括电话号码和电子邮件地址等。开通语音邮件、微信、QQ 等可以让招聘者或雇主更加方便地留言。

2) 职业目标和资历总结

如果给一个帖子或广告写回复,那么可以在主标题后面包括一个"目标"部分。我们的目标是给这个职位空缺定制一份简历,来展示你的职业目标与这个职位要求有多相符。比较接近的趋势是将目标和资历概述融合在一起。要想让招聘经理从可能会收到的数百人的简历中区分出你的那一份,就需要一个包括三到八条目标性很强并能够显示你是这个职位的理想人选的列表。图 10-3 显示了一份包括目标部分的简历。

3) 教育经历总结

如果你刚毕业,那么接下来可以总结你的教育程度。列出就读学校的名称和地点、主修课程或研究的领域、第二学位或者辅修课程,以及已经获得的所有学位的时间。当然如果你在课程中做得很好,还可包括课程平均绩点。

4) 工作经历

过去的工作经验和专业成就向招聘经理展现了你如何能够融入他们的组织。对于曾经经历过的每个职位,要列出单位的名称和地点、职务和职位、聘用期(按年份,如 2012—2014

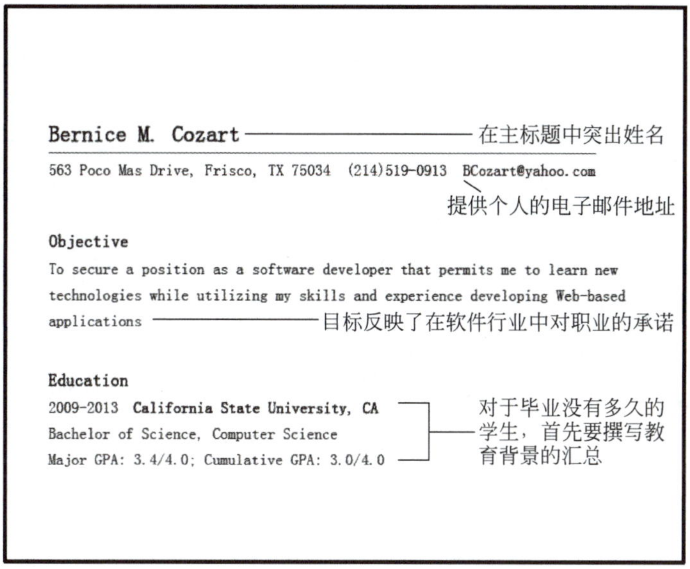

Unit 10　Computer Security and Privacy

```
Bernice M. Cozart ──────────── 在主标题中突出姓名
563 Poco Mas Drive, Frisco, TX 75034  (214)519-0913  BCozart@yahoo.com
                                      └── 提供个人的电子邮件地址

Objective
To secure a position as a software developer that permits me to learn new
technologies while utilizing my skills and experience developing Web-based
applications ──────────── 目标反映了在软件行业中对职业的承诺

Education
2009-2013  California State University, CA ┐  对于毕业没有多久的
Bachelor of Science, Computer Science      ├─ 学生，首先要撰写教
Major GPA: 3.4/4.0; Cumulative GPA: 3.0/4.0┘  育背景的汇总
```

图 10-3　带有目标部分的简历

年；按月，如 2012 年 10 月—2014 年 3 月），以及一个简短的、对职责和成就的描述。

5）技能、活动和荣誉

列出适合这个职位的特殊技能，如计算机水平、能讲的语言和行业认证等。也可以列出参加过的活动、加入的团体或曾获得的奖励，当然前提是有一些这样的经历。

4. 按时间顺序写简历

两种最流行的组织简历的方式是按时间展开和按功能展开。一份按时间顺序展开的简历，是按时间排序来呈现工作经历和教育经历，有时也被称为逆时间顺序的简历。从最近的工作经历或学习经历开始介绍，然后往前推进。尽量多包含近期的作品，少量谈及过去的经历。这种按时间顺序展开的风格是目前最受招聘人员和招聘主管欢迎的，因为它展现了你的就业经历的一个明确的时间线。如果曾有一个相对稳定的工作经历和几个相关的职位经历，那么按时间顺序排列的格式通常是你最好的选择。表 10-2 概括了按瞬间顺序写简历时该做的和不该做的注意事项。

表 10-2　按时间顺序写简历的注意事项

简历元素	适合提到	尽量避免
工作或教育经历	• 如果是一个刚毕业的大学生，就先列出教育经历 • 如果工作业绩很显著，就先列出工作经历	• 如果工作经验很多，全部列出来
格式	• 按照大纲的格式来，用列表的方式列出细节 • 尽量保证顺序清晰且阅读体验好	• 列出一大段文字 • 使用未经修改的标准模板，这对招聘人员来说太熟悉了

续表

简历元素	适合提到	尽量避免
标题	• 每个部分都以标题开头 • 使用标准的文本，例如资历、经验和教育的总结	• 使用带有幽默口吻或者另类的标题 • 在校对的时候对标题一带而过
写作	• 使用简洁但准确的语言 • 要检查拼写和语法错误 • 描述性语言以动词开头	• 包括含糊不清或冗长的描述 • 有任何一个错字或者错误 • 使用被动动词
长度	• 如果经历有限，简历只需一页 • 如果经历很丰富，或者想要申请的职位不止一个，那么就将简历拓展至两页	• 使简历过长或过短 • 为了让简历只有一页或者有两页而刻意改变两边的界限

1）确定是先列出教育经历还是工作经验

如果你现在是一名学生或是一个刚刚毕业没有太多工作经历的大学生，那么就先列出你的教育经历。如果已经经历了三个或以上与你目前申请的工作前景有关的工作职位，那么对读者来说你的工作经历会更加有趣。随着工作经历的增多，你应该适当减少教育经历部分的内容，用一个简单的列表列出上学的学校和获得的学位。

2）格式化简历使其更具可读性

通常情况下，招聘人员和经理会快速扫视简历来寻找重要亮点，并跳过难以阅读的简历。用一两行总结工作经历和教育程度，并用（加在文字下面表示强调的）着重号来呈现工作和成就（参见图10-4）。使用标题、行、空格（没有文字或图形的区域）、颜色、粗体和斜体字体来布局页面，将注意力集中到具有清晰整洁的格式的部分。

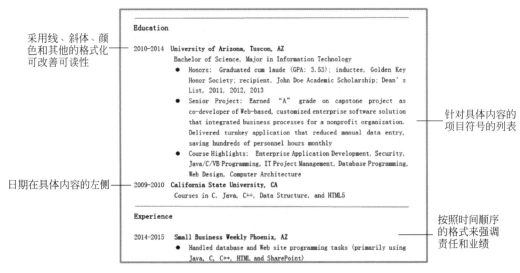

图10-4 按照时间顺序撰写的简历

3）标题左对齐

将标题左对齐（不是中心）来组织页面，这就缩短了每行的长度，使文字更易于阅读。左边统一的留白会将读者的目光吸引到页面上，只在标题做短暂的停留。

Unit 10　Computer Security and Privacy

4）用明确有效的文字来写

认真编辑你的简历,使每一个句子都简短、准确并且积极向上。用一些积极向上的动词来展开你的句子,如"明确了"(clarified)、"改进了"(improved)、"解决了"(resolved)等,而不是"做了"(did)、"是"(was)、"具有"(had)等。用现在时态的动词来描述你目前的工作,用过去时态描述你过去的工作。

5）限定长度

如果工作经历少于3个职位,则可将简历限定到一页。招聘人员自称他们更喜欢这种简短的格式,因为这样他们可以快速概览多份简历。当然,随着工作经验的增长,简历也可以扩展到两页。

5. 书写功能型简历

功能型简历也称为技能简历,突出的是技术和能力,而不是工作经历。功能型简历由几个部分组成,分别展示才华、责任感和在大学课程中学习到的技能,还包括志愿者工作、实习、爱好或者其他方面。书写功能型简历适用于工作经历有限的学生、经常跳槽或者没有固定工作经历的人。功能型简历也在某些行业很流行,如艺术、平面设计和网页制作等行业。表10-3 对时间顺序型和功能型简历进行了比较。除了写一份修改版的时间顺序简历,还可以写一份功能型的简历来突出你的技能。

表 10-3　选择按时间顺序或功能型的方案

方　　案	按时间顺序	功　能　型
工作经历有很多的空白		●
频繁地更换工作		●
很多经历都是在一个领域内	●	
工作经历遵循了一个清晰的职业道路	●	
想要进入一个新的职业领域		●
新领域通常不接受功能型简历	●	
是一个所在选择领域中没有工作经验的大学生		●
计划给一个在线工作平台或招聘公司提交简历	●	

1）分成3～5个类别

确定几个类别来描述经验或能力,并且为每个类别创建一个标题。选择最能反映你的能力的类别,如客户服务能力和技术能力,然后每个类别讲述一个例子。请你信任的人仔细阅读你的简历,并让他们向你分享这份简历给他们留下了关于你的哪些印象。

2）按重要性列出类别

按照对未来上司的重要性,给功能类别排序,组织各类别中的项目符号,先展示最相关的技术和能力。为了形成职位定制的简历,要改变类别的顺序以满足每个职位的要求。

3）用动词作为每个条目的开始

在每一个列表中的条目都要简短、精炼,并且让人印象深刻。用行为动词作为每一个条目的开始,使它们更有趣,更易于阅读。在互联网上搜索"简历行为动词"(resume action verbs)来寻找可以使用的例子。

4）提供工作经验简介

尽管你试图在技术和能力的基础上推销自己，招聘人员和招聘经理还是想知道你在哪里工作过。不推荐省略与工作经历相关的证明人。相反，应该在简历的最后总结性地简要列出工作经历，并标出每次工作经历的用人单位、时间段和职位，参见图 10-5。

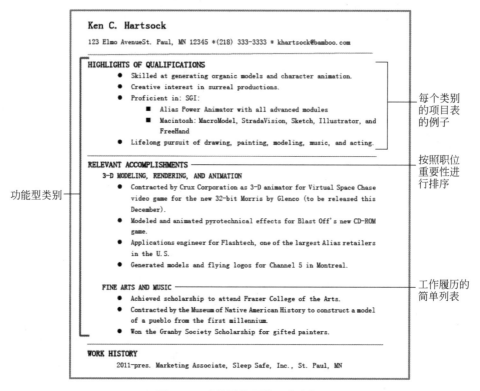

图 10-5　功能型简历的工作大纲

Part 3

Listening and Speaking

Dialogue：Using Antivirus Software

（Sophie's computer is unfortunately infected by a malicious email attachment. Now she is trying to find some measures to cure and protect her computer from virus infections effectively.）

Mark： I think antivirus software is one of the main defenses against online problems.

Henry: Yes, I agree. Antivirus software is a type of utility software that looks for and eliminates viruses, Trojans, worms, and malware. It is available for all types of computers and data storage devices, including smartphones, tablets, personal computers, USB flash drives, servers, PCs, and Macs.

Sophie: Could you suggest any reputable antivirus software for me to use?

Mark: Sure. Popular antivirus software includes Norton AntiVirus, Kapspersky Anti-Virus, F-Secure Anti-Virus, Windows Defender, and Avast.

Sophie: How does antivirus work?

Henry: Modern antivirus software runs as a background process and attempts to identify malware that exists on a device as a download, email message, attachment, or Web page. The process of searching for malware is sometimes referred to as scanning or performing virus scan. To identify malware, antivirus software can look for a virus signature or perform heuristic analyses.

Sophie: What happens when malware is detected?

Mark: When antivirus software detects malware, it can try to remove the infection, put the file into quarantine, or simply delete the file.

Sophie: How dependable is antivirus software?

Henry: Today's antivirus software is quite dependable but not infallible. A fast-spreading worm can reach your digital device before a virus definition update arrives, and cloaking software can hide some viral exploits.

Mark: Despite[1] occasional misses, however, antivirus software and other security software modules are constantly **weeding out** malware that would otherwise infect your device. It is essential to use security software, but it is also important to take additional precautions, such as making regular backups of your data and avoiding untrustworthy software distribution **outlets**.

[1] Replace with:
1. Although
2. In spite of
3. Though
4. Regardless of
5. Whereas

Sophie: How do I ensure[2] that my antivirus software is running?

[2] Replace with:
1. make sure
2. guarantee
3. assure

Mark: Antivirus software is an aspect of our digital life that we tend to **take for granted**. We assume that it is installed and carrying out its work.

Henry: However, antivirus software can be **inadvertently** disabled. Its configuration can be changed by malware that manages to **infiltrate** a device. It can expire at the end of a trial period or subscription. Ensuring that antivirus software is performing correctly may require periodic intervention from users.

Mark: And many antivirus products display an icon in the taskbar or notification area. The icon may offer a visual clue to indicate when the antivirus utility is active, scanning, or updating. Glancing at the icon can assure you that the software is running properly.

Henry: Some targeted malware attacks may alter the icons, however, leading you to believe that the antivirus software is active when, in fact, it has been disabled by a malware attack. Opening the antivirus software periodically to view its status is a good practice.

Sophie: Ok, I've got it. Thank you very much!

Henry & Mark: Not at all. Good luck, Sophie!

Unit 10 Computer Security and Privacy

 Exercises

Work in a group, and make up a similar conversation by replacing the statements with other expressions on the right side.

 Words

cure[kjuə] v. 改正,消除,治疗
Trojan['trəudʒən] n. 木马病毒
worm[wə:m] n. "蠕虫"程序,蠕虫病毒,蠕虫指令(指计算机病毒)
heuristic[hjuə'ristik] adj. 启发式的,探索的
analyses[ə'næləsi:z] n. 分析,解析,分解,梗概(analysis 的复数形式)
quarantine['kwərənti:n] n. 隔离,检疫

infallibl[in'fæləbl] adj. 绝对可靠的,绝无错误的
cloak[kləuk] v. 隐藏,掩盖,掩饰,伪装
outlet['autlet, -lit] n. (感情、精力等的)发泄途径(或方法、手段),排遣
inadvertent[ˌinəd'və:tənt] adj. 非故意的,出于无心的,由疏忽造成的
infiltrate['infiltreit, in'fil-] v. 使潜入,使渗入,使浸润

 Phrases

virus signature 病毒识别码,病毒特征值
viral exploits 病毒攻击
weed out 从……删除不好的部分,删去
take for granted 理所当然的

 Abbreviations

malware   malicious software   恶意软件

Listening Comprehension: Hacker and Cracker

Listen to the article and answer the following 3 questions based on it. After you hear a question, there will be a break of 15 seconds. During the break, you will decide which one is the best answer among the four choices marked (A), (B), (C) and (D).

Questions
1. Which term was originally a positive title?
   (A) Hacker
   (B) Cracker

（C）Phishers

（D）None of the above

2. Why has the popular definition of hacker been changed?

（A）Due to sensationalized depictions from industrial experts

（B）Due to exaggerated depictions from social critics

（C）Due to sensationalized depictions in modern media

（D）Due to exaggerated depictions from hackers themselves

3. Which of the following behavior(s) is (are) illegitimate?

（A）Tricking others' credit card numbers via computer

（B）Tampering with files in others' computers without permission

（C）Breaking into networks with malicious intent

（D）All of the above

Words

amateur[ˈæmətə] n. 业余爱好者	snoop[snuːp] v. 窥探,偷窃
arcane[ɑːˈkein] adj. 神秘的,晦涩难懂的	legitimate[liˈdʒitimit] adj. 合法的
recondite[riˈkɔndait] adj. 深奥的	resent[riˈzent] v. 憎恶,怨恨
sensationalize[senˈseiʃənˌlaiz] v. 加以渲染,使耸人听闻	phisher[ˈfiʃə] n. 网络钓鱼者
	trick[trik] v. 哄骗,欺诈

Phrases

take into account 考虑
tamper with 篡改,干预,损害

Dictation: Trojan Horses

This article will be played three times. Listen carefully, and fill in the numbered spaces with the appropriate words you have heard.

The name "Trojan horse" comes from a legend told in the *Iliad* about the *siege* of the city of Troy by the Greeks. Legend has it that the Greeks, unable to penetrate the city's ___1___, got the idea to give up the siege and instead gave the city a giant wooden horse as a gift ___2___. The Trojans (the people of the city of Troy) accepted this

Unit 10 Computer Security and Privacy

__seemingly__   3   gift and brought it within the city walls. However, the horse was   4   with soldiers, who came out at **nightfall**, while the town   5   , to open the city gates so that the   6   of the army could enter.

Thus, in the world of computing, a Trojan horse is any program that   7   the user to run it, but **conceals** a harmful or malicious **payload**, and usually opens up   8   to the computer running it by opening a   9   . For this reason, it is sometimes called a Trojan by analogy to the citizens of Troy. The payload may take effect   10   and can lead to many undesirable effects, such as deleting all the user's files, or more commonly it may   11   further harmful software into the user's system to serve the creator's longer-term   12   . Trojan horses known as **droppers** are used to **start off** a worm   13   , by injecting the worm into users' local networks.

Since Trojan horses have a   14   of forms, there is no single method to delete them. The simplest responses involve clearing the   15   Internet file and deleting it   16   . Normally, antivirus software is able to detect and remove the Trojan   17   . If the antivirus cannot find it, booting the computer from   18   media, such as a **live** CD, may allow an antivirus program to find a Trojan and delete it. Updated anti-spyware programs are also efficient against this   19   . Most Trojans also   20   in registries, and processes.

Words

Iliad['iliəd] n. 《伊利亚特》(古希腊描写特洛伊战争的英雄史诗,相传为荷马所作)
siege[si:dʒ] n. 围城,围攻
seemingly['si:miŋli] adv. 貌似,表面上

nightfall['naitfɔ:l] n. 黄昏,傍晚
conceal[kən'si:l] v. 隐藏
payload['peiləud] n. 有效负荷
dropper['drɔpə] n. 落下的人或物
live[laiv] adj. 最新的

Phrases

start off   出发,动身

Unit 11

Software Engineering

Unit 11　Software Engineering

Part 1

Reading and Translating

Section A: How Software Engineering Works

Virtually all countries now depend on complex computer-based systems. National infrastructures and utilities rely on computer-based systems and most electrical products include a computer and controlling software. Industrial manufacturing and distribution is completely computerized, as is the financial system. Therefore, producing and maintaining software cost-effectively is essential for the functioning of national and international economies.

Software engineering is an engineering discipline whose focus is the cost-effective development of high-quality software systems. Software is abstract and intangible. It is not constrained by materials or governed by physical laws or by manufacturing processes. In some ways, this simplifies software engineering as there are no physical limitations on the potential of software. However, this lack of natural constraints means that software can easily become extremely complex and hence very difficult to understand.

The notion of software engineering was first proposed in 1968 at a conference held to discuss what was then called the "software crisis". This software crisis resulted directly from the introduction of new computer hardware based on integrated circuits. Their power made hitherto unrealizable computer applications a feasible proposition. The resulting software was orders of magnitude larger and more complex than previous software systems.

Early experience in building these systems showed that informal software development was not good enough. Major projects were sometimes years late. The software cost much more than predicted, was unreliable, was difficult to maintain and performed poorly. Software development was in crisis. Hardware costs were tumbling whilst software costs were rising rapidly. New techniques and methods were needed to control the complexity inherent in large software systems.

These techniques have become part of software engineering and are now widely used. However, as our ability to produce software has increased, so has the complexity of the software systems that we need. New technologies resulting from the convergence of computers and communication systems and complex graphical user interfaces place new demands on software engineers. As many companies still do not apply software

217

engineering techniques effectively, too many projects still produce software that is unreliable, delivered late and over budget.

We have made tremendous progress since 1968 and that the development of software engineering has markedly improved our software. We have a much better understanding of the activities involved in software development. We have developed effective methods of software specification, design and implementation (Figure 11-1). New notations and tools reduce the effort required to produce large and complex systems.

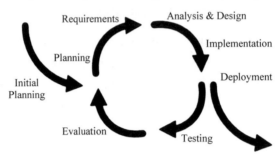

Figure 11-1　Iterative model of software engineering

We know now that there is no single "ideal approach" to software engineering. The wide diversity of different types of systems and organizations that use these systems means that we need a diversity of approaches to software development. However, fundamental notions of process and system organization underlie all of these techniques, and these are the essence of software engineering.

Software engineers can be rightly proud of their achievements. Without complex software we would not have explored space, would not have the Internet and modern telecommunications, and all forms of travel would be more dangerous and expensive. Software engineering has contributed a great deal, and as the discipline matures, its contributions in this century will be even greater.

 Words

virtually['vɜːtʃuəli] *adv.* 事实上,实质上
notion['nəuʃn] *n.* 概念,观念,看法
hitherto[ˌhiðə'tuː] *adv.* 迄今,至今
proposition[ˌprɔpə'ziʃən] *n.* 主张,提议,建议
tumble['tʌmbl] *v.* (价格或数量)暴跌,骤降,使倒下

markedly['mɑːkidli] *adv.* 显著地,明显地
notation[nəu'teiʃn] *n.* 符号
underlie[underlie] *v.* 构成……的基础,位于……之下
essence['esns] *n.* 本质,实质
rightly['raitli] *adv.* 确实地

Unit 11　Software Engineering

 Phrases

result from 由……引起
place on 寄托,把……放在……上
over budget 超过预算

 Exercises

Ⅰ. Read the following statements carefully, and decide whether they are true (T) or false (F) according to the text.

____ 1. The focus of software engineering is the rapid development of complex software systems.
____ 2. The notion of software engineering was first proposed in a paper in 1968.
____ 3. This software crisis resulted directly from the development of computer hardware.
____ 4. New notations and tools contribute to higher efficiency and less workload in producing large and complex software systems.
____ 5. As an engineering discipline, software engineering has matured adequately today.

Ⅱ. Choose the best answer to each of the following questions according to the text.

1. Which of the following descriptions is not the characteristic of software?
   A. Abstract and intangible
   B. Not constrained by materials
   C. Not governed by physical laws or by manufacturing processes
   D. Easy to understand and simple to produce as there are no physical limitations

2. What problem(s) existed widely in informal software development in the early years?
   A. Over schedule
   B. Cost much more than budget
   C. Difficult to maintain
   D. All of the above

3. Which of the following statements is wrong about the techniques in software engineering?
   A. Techniques are needed to control the complexity of the large software systems.

B. Techniques are the essence of software engineering.

C. Techniques are now widely used in software engineering.

D. New technologies bring new challenges to software engineers continually.

Ⅲ. Identify the letter of the choice that best matches the phrase or definition.

a. black-box testing

b. extreme programming (XP)

c. white-box testing

d. class diagram

e. Gantt chart

_____ 1. A widely used agile method of software development that includes practices such as scenario-based requirements, test-first development, and pair programming.

_____ 2. A UML diagram types that shows the object class in a system and their relationships.

_____ 3. An approach to testing where the testers have no access to source code of a system or its components.

_____ 4. An alternative name for a bar chart.

_____ 5. An approach to program testing where the tests are based on knowledge of the structure of the program and its components.

Ⅳ. Fill in the numbered spaces with the words or phrases chosen from the box. Change the forms where necessary.

```
developer    connect    behind    need    involve
collaborate  cycle      begin     use     refer
```

Software Engineering vs. Software Development

The difference between software engineering and software development __1__ with job function. A software engineer may be __2__ with software development, but few software __3__ are engineers.

To explain, software engineering __4__ to the application of engineering principles to create software. Software engineers participate in the software development life cycle through __5__ the client's needs with applicable technology solutions. Thus, they systematically develop processes to provide specific functions. In the end, software engineering means __6__ engineering concepts to develop software.

On the other hand, software developers are the driving creative force __7__ programs. Software developers are responsible for the entire development process. They are the ones who ___8___ with the client to create a theoretical design. They then have computer programmers create the code ___9___ to run the software properly. Computer programmers will test and fix problems together with software developers. Software developers provide project leadership and technical guidance along every stage of the software development life ___10___ .

Ⅴ. **Translate the following passages into Chinese.**

Software Evolution

In software engineering, software evolution is referred to as the process of developing, maintaining and updating software for various reasons. Software changes are inevitable because there are many factors that change during the life cycle of a piece of software. Some of these factors include:

- Requirement changes
- Environment changes
- Errors or security breaches
- New equipment added or removed
- Improvements to the system

For many companies, one of their largest investments in their business is for software and software development. Software is considered a very critical asset and management wants to ensure they employ a team of software engineers who are devoted to ensuring that the software system stays up-to-date with ever evolving changes.

Section B: Testers and Programmers Working Together

Let's look at an example of how a tester and programmer might work on a user story or feature. Patty Programmer and Tammy Tester are working on a user story to calculate the shipping cost of an item, based on weight and destination postal code. Tammy writes a simple test case in a **tabular** format that is supported by their Fit-based test tool (Table 11-1):

Table 11-1 A simple test case

Weight	Destination Postal Code	Cost
5kg	80104	$ 7.25

Meanwhile, Patty writes the code to send the inputs to the shipping cost API and to get the calculated cost. She shows Tammy her unit tests, which all pass. Tammy thinks Patty's tests look ok, and they agree Patty will check in [1] the code.

Next, Patty checks in a **fixture** to automate Tammy's tests. Patty **calls** Tammy **over** to show her that the first simple test is working. Tammy **writes up** more test cases, trying different weights and destinations within the U.S. Those all work fine. Then she tries a

Canadian postal code, and the test dies with an exception. She shows this to Patty, who realizes that the shipping cost calculator API defaults to U.S. postal codes, and requires a country code for postal codes in Canada and Mexico. She hadn't written any unit tests for any other countries yet.

Tammy and Patty pair to revise the inputs to the unit tests. Then Patty pairs with Carl Coder to change the code that calls the API. Now the test looks like this (Table 11-2):

Table 11-2 A test case

Weight	Destination Postal Code	Country Code	Cost
5kg	80104	U.S.	$ 7.25
5kg	T2J 2M7	CA	$ 9.40

This back-and-forth testing and coding process could take all kinds of forms. Patty might write these "story tests" herself, in addition to her unit tests. Or, she and Tammy may decide that they can cover all of Tammy's acceptance tests with unit-level tests. Patty might be in a remote office, using an online collaboration tool to pair with Tammy. Either or both might pair with other team members. They might need help from their database expert to set up the test database. The point is that testing and coding are part of one process, in which all team members participate.

Tammy can keep identifying new test cases until she feels all the risky areas have been covered. She might test with the heaviest possible item, and the most expensive destination. She might test having a large quantity of one item, or many items to the same destination. Some edge cases might be so unlikely she doesn't bother with them. She may not keep all the automated tests in the regression test suite. Some tests might be better done manually, after a UI is available.

Patty has written unit tests with Hawaii as the shipping destination, but Tammy thinks only continental destinations are acceptable. They both go to talk to the product owner about it. This is the Power of Three. When questions arise, having three different viewpoints is an effective way to make sure you get the right solution, and you don't have to rehash the issue later. This helps prevent requirement changes from flying in under the radar and causing unpleasant surprises later.

It's vital that everyone on the development team understands the business, so don't fall into the habit of only having a tester, an analyst or a programmer communicate with the business experts.

The story about how Tammy and Patty work together shows how closely programmers and testers collaborate. As coding and testing proceed, there are many opportunities to transfer skills. Programmers learn new ways of testing. Testers learn more about code design and how the right tests can improve it.

Patty has completed the UI for selecting shipping options and displaying the cost, but hasn't checked it in yet. She calls Tammy over to her workstation and demonstrates how the end user would enter the destination postal code, select the shipping option, and see the cost right away. Tammy tries this out, changing the postal code to see the new cost appear. She notices the text box for the postal code allows the user to enter more characters than should be allowed for a valid code, and Patty changes the html accordingly. Once the UI looks good, Patty checks in the code, and Tammy continues with her exploratory testing.

Tammy is especially concerned with changing the postal code and having the new cost display, as they identified this as a risky area. She finds that if she displays the shipping cost, goes on to the next page of the UI, then comes back to change the postal code, the new estimated cost doesn't display. She asks Patty to come observe this behavior. Patty realizes there is a problem with values being cached, and goes back to her workstation to fix it.

Showing someone a problem real-time is much more effective than filing a bug in a defect tracking system and waiting for someone to have time to look at it later. If the team is distributed and people are in different time zones, it's harder to do work through issues together. The team will have to make adjustments to get this kind of value. One of your teammates is in a time zone 12.5 hours ahead, but works late into his nighttime to overlap with your morning. You work through test results and examples when you're both online.

Show the customers, too. As soon as you have a prototype, some basic navigation, some small testable piece of code, show it to the customer and get their feedback. Feedback, from our customers, from our automated tests, from each other, is our most powerful tool in staying on track and delivering the right business value.

When we divide our work into small, manageable chunks, plan and conduct testing and coding as part of a single development process, and focus on finishing one chunk of valuable functionality at a time, testing doesn't get squeezed to the end, put off to a future iteration, or ignored altogether.

Get your team together today and talk about how you can all—testers, programmers and everyone else involved with delivering the software—work together to integrate coding and testing. Instead of investing in a big requirements document, capture requirements and examples of desired application behavior in executable tests, and write the code that will make those pass. Meet with your business stakeholders to understand their priorities and explain how much work you can realistically take on each iteration. Stop treating coding and testing as separate activities (Figure 11-2).

It won't happen overnight, but gradually your team will get better and better at really finishing each software feature - including all the testing. Your customers will be delighted to get stable, robust software that meets their needs. Your team will benefit from better-designed code that's easier to maintain and contains far fewer bugs. Best of all, testers and programmers alike will enjoy their work much more!

Developer vs Tester

Figure 11-2 Stop treating coding and testing as separate activities

 Words

tabular[ˈtæbjələ(r)] *adj.* 列成表格的
fixture[ˈfikstʃə(r)] *n.* 固定装置
die[dai] *v.* 停止运转
pair[peə(r)] *v.* 使成对,配对
back-and-forth 反复地,来回地
heaviest[ˈheviːst] *adj.* (在数量、程度等方面)超出一般的

arise[əˈraɪz] *v.* 发生,产生,出现
rehash[ˈriːhæʃ] *v.* 事后反复回想(或讨论)
cache[kæʃ] *v.* 隐藏,缓存
alike[əˈlaɪk] *adv.* 同样地

 Phrases

call over 把……叫过来
write up 详细写出
default to 默认为
take forms 采取形式
the point is 问题在于
edge case 边界用例,极端例子
regression test 回归测试
under the radar 避开别人关注的行为,低调处理
try out 试验,尝试
text box 正文框
work through 解决,完成,干完
get squeezed to 陷入,挤到
put off 推迟
best of all 首先,最好的是,最重要的是

Unit 11　Software Engineering

 Abbreviations

UI　User Interface　用户界面

 Notes

[1]　签入(check in)是将本地上的代码更新到服务器上；签出(check out)是将服务器上的代码更新到本地，开始编辑状态。也就是说，签出后本地代码文件就变成可编辑的了，可以修改了，签入后本地代码文件就变成只读的了，不可编辑，这时别人就可以签出，进行修改了。

 Exercises

Ⅰ. **Read the following statements carefully, and decide whether they are true (T) or false (F) according to the text.**

____ 1. Tammy is a Programmer and Patty is a Tester.

____ 2. Patty tries a Canadian postal code, and the test dies with an exception.

____ 3. Carl is a Coder.

____ 4. Patty and Tammy may decide that they can cover all of Tammy's acceptance tests with unit-level tests.

____ 5. As coding and testing proceed, there are not many opportunities to transfer skills.

Ⅱ. **Choose the best answer to each of the following questions according to the text.**

1. Which of the following is wrong about Tammy?
    A. Tammy writes a simple test case in a tabular format that is supported by their Fit-based test tool.
    B. Tammy is a Tester.
    C. Tammy is a Programmer.
    D. All of the above

2. Which of the following is right about Patty?
    A. Patty is a Tester.
    B. Patty is a Programmer.
    C. Patty writes the code to send the outputs to the shipping cost API and to get the calculated cost.
    D. None of the above

3. Which of the following is wrong about programmers and testers?
   (A) Programmers learn new ways of testing.
   (B) Testers learn more about code design and how the right tests can improve it.
   (C) The story about how Tammy and Patty work together shows how closely programmers and testers collaborate.
   (D) None of the above

Ⅲ. **Identify the letter of the choice that best matches the phrase or definition.**
   a. incremental development
   b. sequence diagram
   c. use case
   d. software architecture
   e. state diagram

   ____ 1. A model of the fundamental structure and organization of a software system.
   ____ 2. A specification of one type of interaction with a system.
   ____ 3. A UML diagram type that shows the states of a system and the events that triggers a transition from one state to another.
   ____ 4. A diagram that shows the sequence of interactions required to complete some operation.
   ____ 5. An approach to software development where the software is delivered and deployed in increments.

Ⅳ. **Fill in the blanks with the words or phrases chosen from the box. Change the forms where necessary.**

| document | contrast | include | reliable | analyze |
| disaster | complex | develop | extend | activity |

What is the Difference between Computer Programming and Software Engineering?

Computer programming encompasses a broad set of ___1___ that include planning, coding, testing, and ___2___. Most computer programmers participate to some ___3___ in all of these phases of program development, but focus on the coding process.

Software engineering is a ___4___ process that uses mathematical, engineering, and management techniques to reduce the cost and ___5___ of a computer program while increasing its ___6___ and modifiability. It can be characterized as more formalized and rigorous than computer programming. It is used on large software projects where cost overruns and software errors might have ___7___ consequences.

Some software engineering activities overlap with the systems ___8___ and design activities. To distinguish between the two, remember that systems analysis and design encompass all aspects of an information system, ___9___ hardware, software, people, and procedures. In ___10___, software engineering tends to focus on software development.

Ⅳ. Translate the following passage into Chinese.

Regression Testing

Whenever developers change or modify their software, even a small tweak can have unexpected consequences. Regression testing is testing existing software applications to make sure that a change or addition hasn't broken any existing functionality. Its purpose is to catch bugs that may have been accidentally introduced into a new build or release candidate, and to ensure that previously eradicated bugs continue to stay dead. By re-running testing scenarios that were originally scripted when known problems were first fixed, you can make sure that any new changes to an application haven't resulted in a regression, or caused components that formerly worked to fail. Such tests can be performed manually on small projects, but in most cases repeating a suite of tests each time an update is made is too time-consuming and complicated to consider, so an automated testing tool is typically required.

Part 2

Simulated Writing: Progress Report

1. 进度报告的作用和内容

进度报告在工程学中应用很广。一旦已经有了成功的提案并且已经获得相应的资源来开发某个项目，就需要向客户及时汇报项目的进展情况。这些进展情况通常用进度报告来汇报。进度报告可以是一页的备忘录或是多页的信件、简短报告、正式报告及演示文稿。这样的报告要针对分配项目的人。报告的目标是对已完成的项目部分及未来的工作计划进行公正的评价，并使项目经理或项目资助人能据此决定该项目的未来。然而，无论项目的规模或重要性如何，都会碰到一些阻碍——额外的需求、错误传达的信息、难题、延期或意料之外的支出。进度报告必须说明这些阻碍，并讨论在项目中正在遇到的困难以及所需的进一步的帮助。

进度报告中应包含的内容取决于具体的情况，但是大多数报告都包括以下内容：
(1) 项目的背景。
(2) 自从上次报告以来所取得的成果。
(3) 新出现的问题。
(4) 未来要做的工作。

(5) 评估自己是否将按照预订的进度和预算完成项目。

2. 进度报告的组织形式

进度报告的结构应当取决于项目的原始提议：利用原有的里程碑或时间安排。了解这一点之后，一个更加全面的成分列表可以提供一个更加清晰的结构，具体如下：

1）简介

通常情况下，应当说明这份报告的目的以及目标受众，应当清楚地定义报告所覆盖的时间范围，然后解释该项目、项目目标以及自上次报告以来的项目进展状态。

2）项目描述

在简短的报告中，这部分内容可以包含到简介中。但是如果将其列为一个独立标题，那么熟悉该项目的读者可以跳过这部分内容；对项目不甚了解的读者，需要从中了解一些概要性的细节问题，如项目的目的和范围、起止时间以及参与的各方等。

3）已完成的工作

这一部分应遵循该项目提案进度中所提出任务的进展，这是报告的主体。这部分可以采用项目-任务法、时间法或综合法来进行陈述。

- 项目-任务法：这种方法关注的是任务。已定义的里程碑可以将报告在逻辑上组织成这种结构。如果同时进行多个半独立的任务，同样可以使用这种方法。
- 时间法：这种方法关注的是时间。如果时间表（或最后期限）比里程碑更重要，则使用这种方法。同样，此方法也适用于简单的线性结构的项目。
- 综合法：上述两种方法也可以结合起来使用。例如，在先前的工作中，可将已经完成的部分分成单个任务。即在这些任务中，关注哪些部分已经完成，哪些部分还在进行中，哪些部分尚未进行。

具体的项目将决定选用哪种方法。如果项目中遇到的困难或是所需的变更与时间有关，那么使用时间法会更有利；类似地，如果遇到的问题或是变更与特定的任务相关，那么就使用项目-任务法。此外，该部分还可以附上财务数据概要，可以使用表格或是附录的形式，或作为一个独立的章节。

4）遇到的问题

进度报告没有必要仅为了给客户看。正如开始所提到的，问题是在报告中希望提到的。不必将这些问题隐藏起来；应该解释清楚碰到了什么问题以及这些问题对项目的关键部分（如时间安排、价格或是质量）有何影响。通常情况下，工程师或专家会从此报告中得到帮助，因为我们与客户共享或提醒了客户项目中出现的问题。所以，如果这个问题是过去出现过的，那么可以说明过去是如何解决的。这是一个很小的问题，却能让我们看起来很出色。如果这个问题尚未解决（就在眼前或是将会出现）并且有能力解决，那么应解释希望如何克服它。

5）需求的变更

在这一部分，要记录项目中的变更：增加的里程碑、新的需求或是进度的变更（好的或坏的）。即使这些变化不会影响到项目的最终目标，仍需要告诉项目的出资人这些问题是如何解决的。

注意：如果这些变更是项目中遇到的问题直接引起的，那么前两部分可以合并。这样需要对结构进行一些调整，即第一个问题及它所需要的变更，然后是第二个问题及其需要的变更，以此类推。

6）工作进度

在这一部分，要讨论为了完成项目目标所制定的计划。在多数情况下，进度报告的这一部分写成与提案中"行动规划"部分相同的方式。区别在于，现在应该比那时对进度和成本有了更好的认识。像"已完成的工作"部分一样，这部分根据项目实际情况，可以使用上述提到的3种方法（项目-任务法、时间法或综合法）中的一个。

7）项目总体评估

由于进度报告并不是针对一个已完成的项目，因此结论部分仅需要对该项目目前的进展情况进行专业评价。不现实的乐观或是过度悲观都是不恰当的。不要随便承诺项目将提早完成，因为一个挫折可能会耗费大量时间。同样，如果落后于进度，也不要过度担心，因为在以后的进程中还可以争取到时间。对工程师来说，更重要的是说明一切可能影响最终产品的期望质量的各种因素。请牢记，进度报告的目的是，使项目经理或出资人能够据此做出决策。

3. 范例

TO：Steven Zhang

Departments of Computer Science，Beihang University

FROM：Mark Hu

SUBJECT：Progress on Scheme Debugging Report

DATE：August 3，2020

This memo describes the progress I have made to date on my independent-study project to write a report on debugging in Scheme. In this memo, I review the nature of the project and describe work I have completed, work I am currently engaged in, and work I plan to complete by the end of the project.

As I described in my memo of July 4, this project will result in a technical report whose purpose is to provide readers with practical information on developing and debugging programs in Scheme, supplementary to the material in your textbook, An Introduction to Scheme and its Implementation.

Project Description

The report is aimed at students in computer science（undergraduate and graduate）who have previous programming experience, but are new to Scheme. The information in this report is needed because readers who have developed programs using compilers for other languages may be unfamiliar with the approaches available with an interactive interpreter and debugger.

Project Scope

In my earlier memo, I proposed to cover the following high-level topics：

- Loading the debugging module into the interpreter
- Establishing break levels
- Applying back-trace

- Managing dependencies
- Saving and loading a customized heap image of the Scheme system
- Debugging local definitions
- Debugging native-code procedure calls
- Debugging when using functional programming style
- Program design and implementation strategies
- Using stubbed procedures
- Differences between RScheme and other Scheme systems

In my current outline, these are divided into three major parts, with an addendum for topic 11. The three parts are: (A) basic debugging procedures—topics 1-3, (B) advanced debugging procedures—topics 4-7, and (C) general program development strategies—topics 8-10.

Work Completed

I have completed first drafts of the sections in part A on loading the debugging module, break levels, and apply-back-trace. I intend to make note of additional material for these sections while working on the later sections, if further background information is needed.

Present Work

I am currently working on the sections in part B. Since these sections are highly interrelated, I am working on them roughly in parallel. I am also currently researching information on other Scheme systems for section 11; I have located information on Gambit and DrScheme. I expect the current work to be completed by the end of this week, August 9th.

Future Work

Next, I will draft the sections in part C and the addendum on other Scheme systems. Finally, I will fully revise the entire draft, integrating further material where deficiencies have become evident during work on other sections. The final report will be ready for your review on August 20th.

Conclusion

Thus far, the project is proceeding well. I have not run into any major problems, nor do I anticipate any in the remaining work.

Listening & Speaking

Dialogue: Using Object-Oriented Analysis and Design Method

(*Henry, Mark and Sophie are making a project planning for a library information management system as their course project.*)

Mark: Having gathered the requirements of the system, we can progress further!

Sophie: Yes. The next step is to produce analysis modeling and design implementation specifications.

Henry: Based on our acquaintance with this system through the requirements gathering, I think we can use object-oriented analysis and design method for easier and more obvious mapping from real world entities to system objects.

Mark: It's a good idea. Using object-oriented analysis and design method, we can model the system as a group of interacting objects and more sense for object-oriented languages.

Sophie: With regard to [1] object-modeling techniques, there are a number of different notations for representing various models showing the static structure, dynamic behavior and run-time deployment of these collaborating objects. Which methodologies or tools shall we use?

[1] Replace with:
1. Concerning
2. Regarding
3. Relating to
4. With respect to
5. As regards

Mark: How about [2] UML, by right of its being standardized and general-purpose?

[2] Replace with:
1. What about
2. What do you think of

Sophie: I completely agree with you, Mark.

Henry: Me too. Then we can focus on the tasks in each stage.

Mark: Yes. In the phase of object-oriented analysis, following the written requirements statement and applying object-modeling techniques, we look at the problem domain and analyze the functional requirements for a system with the aim of producing a conceptual model.

Sophie: What kinds of artifact should be created embodying the conceptual model?

Henry: That will typically be presented as a set of use cases, one or more UML class diagrams and a number of interaction diagrams. It may also include some kind of user interface mock-up.

Mark: Next, the output of analysis provides the input for design. Object-oriented design elaborates the analysis models to produce implementation specifications. The concepts in the analysis model are mapped onto implementation classes and interfaces. The result of object-oriented design is a model of the solution domain, a detailed description of how the system is to be built.

Henry: The deliverables of object-oriented design will be in general a set of sequence diagrams and class diagram.

Sophie: So that, do you mean we must perform the analysis completely before beginning the design?

Mark: Not always. In practice, one activity can feed the other in a short feedback cycle through an iterative process, so analysis and design may occur in parallel. Both analysis and design can be performed little by little, and the artifacts can be continuously grown instead of completely developed in one shot.

Henry: In addition, we may use some acknowledged design concepts such as design patterns and application frameworks, as well as some design principles, for example, dependency injection and composite reuse principles to refine our design.

 **Exercises**

Work in a group, and make up a similar conversation by replacing the statements with other expressions on the right side.

Words

acquaintance[əˈkwentəns] n. （对某事物的）了解	mock-up 模型,原型
model[ˈmɔdl] v. 建模	deliverable [diˈlivərəbl] n. 应交付的产品
artifact[ˈɑːtifækt] n. 人工制品	acknowledged [əkˈnɔlidʒid] adj. 公认的,被普遍认可的
embody[imˈbɔdi] v. 具体表现,体现	

Phrases

with regard to 关于,对于
by right of 由于,因为
so that 如此说来,这样的话,那样的话
in one shot 立刻,马上

Abbreviations

UML Unified Modeling Language 统一建模语言

Listening Comprehension: Extreme Programming

Listen to the article and answer the following 3 questions based on it. After you hear a question, there will be a break of 15 seconds. During the break, you will decide which one is the best answer among the four choices marked （A）,（B）,（C）and（D）.

Questions

1. When did the XP's practice and methodology begin to be used?
   （A）1960s
   （B）1980s
   （C）1990s
   （D）2000s

2. What is the main objective of XP?
   （A）Reducing the cost of design change
   （B）Reducing the cost of requirement change
   （C）Reducing the cost of testing change

（D）Reducing the cost of delivery change

3. Which of the following does not accord with the XP's essential value?
   （A）Emphasizing customer involvement
   （B）Promoting team work
   （C）Keeping the design integrated
   （D）Getting feedback by software testing daily

Words

inescapable[ˌinis'keipəbl] adj. 不可避免的，不可忽视的
practitioner[præk'tiʃənə] n. 从业者，实践者

refactoring[ri'fæktəriŋ] n. 重构

Notes

［1］ Smalltalk 被公认为历史上第二个面向对象的程序设计语言，和第一个真正的集成开发环境（IDE）。它对其他众多的程序设计语言如 Objective-C、Actor、Java 和 Ruby 等的产生起到了极大的推动作用。

［2］ 戴姆勒-克莱斯勒集团公司（Daimler Chrysler）成立于 1998 年，是由原德国戴姆勒-奔驰汽车公司与美国克莱斯勒汽车公司合并而成。强强联手让戴姆勒-克莱斯勒集团公司一跃成为当时世界上第二大汽车生产商。2007 年，戴姆勒-克莱斯勒集团公司完成分拆，联手 9 年后，戴姆勒-奔驰与克莱斯勒又各奔东西。

［3］ 美国航天局的水星计划（NASA's Project Mercury）是美国 1958 年开始实施的第一个载人航天计划。鉴于当时与苏联竞争紧迫形势，该计划的基本指导思想是尽可能利用已经掌握的技术和成果，以最快的速度和简单可靠的方式抢先把人送入太空。

Dictation：Unified Modeling Language（UML）

This article will be played three times. Listen carefully, and fill in the numbered spaces with the appropriate words you have heard.

Unified Modeling Language (UML) is a standardized ___1___ modeling language in the field of software engineering. It is a ___2___ language for visualizing, specifying and constructing the ___3___ of a software-intensive system. UML includes a set of graphical ___4___ techniques and offers a standard way to write a system's ___5___ and abstract models, including conceptual things such as business processes and system functions as well as concrete things such as programming language statements, database schemas and ___6___ software components. UML can be used with all processes, throughout the software development life ___7___, and across different ___8___ technologies.

UML 2.0 has 13 types of diagrams divided into three ___9___: Six diagram types represent structure application structure, three represent general types of ___10___, and four represent different aspects of ___11___, representing three different view of a system model: functional requirements view, static structural view and dynamic ___12___ view.

Under the technical ___13___ of the three methodologists, James Rumbaugh, Grady Booch and Ivar Jacobson, who were collectively referred to as the Three Amigos, UML 1.0 specification draft was ___14___ to the Object Management Group (OMG) in January 1997. Today, UML has ___15___ significantly since the first version of UML, ___16___ by the UML 2.0 major revision that was ___17___ by the OMG in 2005.

UML is not a development method by itself; however, it was designed to be ___18___ with the leading object-oriented software development methods of its time (for example Rumbaugh's Object Modeling Technique (OMT), Booch method). Since UML has ___19___, some of these methods have been recast to take ___20___ of the new notations, and new methods have been created based on UML. The best known is IBM Rational Unified Process (RUP). There are many other UML-based methods like Abstraction Method, Dynamic Systems Development Method and others, designed to provide more specific solutions or achieve different objectives.

Words

view[vju:] n. 视图
amigo[əˈmi:gəu] n. 朋友
recast[ˈri:ˈkɑ:st] v. 重铸,改写

Abbreviations

RUP   Rational Unified Process   统一过程模型

Unit 12

Introduction to Artificial Intelligence

Unit 12　Introduction to Artificial Intelligence

Part 1

Reading and Translating

Section A: Benefits and Risks of Artificial Intelligence

From SIRI[1] to self-driving cars, Artificial Intelligence (AI) is progressing rapidly. While science fiction often portrays AI as robots with human-like characteristics, AI can encompass anything from Google's search algorithms to IBM's Watson[2] to autonomous weapons.

Artificial intelligence today is properly known as narrow AI (or weak AI), in that it is designed to perform a narrow task (e.g. only facial recognition or only Internet searches or only driving a car). However, the long-term goal of many researchers is to create general AI (AGI or strong AI). While narrow AI may **outperform** humans at whatever its specific task is, like playing chess or solving equations, AGI would outperform humans at nearly every cognitive task.

In the near term, the goal of keeping AI's impact on society benefits motivates research in many areas, from economics and law to technical topics such as verification, validity, security and control. Whereas it may be little more than a minor **nuisance** if your laptop crashes or gets hacked, it becomes all the more important that an AI system does what you want it to do if it controls your car, your airplane, your **pacemaker**, your automated trading system or your power grid.[3] Another short-term challenge is preventing a devastating arms race in **lethal** autonomous weapons.

In the long term, an important question is what will happen if the **quest** for strong AI succeeds and an AI system becomes better than humans at all cognitive tasks. As pointed out by I.J. Good in 1965, designing smarter AI systems is itself a cognitive task. Such a system could potentially undergo **recursive** self-improvement, triggering an intelligence explosion leaving human **intellect** far behind. By inventing revolutionary new technologies, such super-intelligence might help us eradicate war, disease, and poverty, and so the creation of strong AI might be the biggest event in human history. Some experts have expressed concern, though, that it might also be the last, unless we learn to **align** the goals of the AI **with** ours before it becomes super-intelligent.

There are some who question whether strong AI will ever be achieved, and others who insist that the creation of super-intelligent AI is guaranteed to be beneficial (Figure 12-1). In some artificial intelligent companies, we recognize both of these possibilities, but also recognize the potential for an artificial intelligence system to intentionally or unintentionally cause great harm. We believe research today will help us better prepare for and prevent such potentially negative consequences in the future, thus enjoying the benefits of AI while avoiding pitfalls.

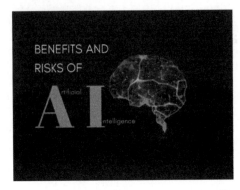

Figure 12-1　Benefits and risks of artificial intelligence

Most researchers agree that a super-intelligent AI is unlikely to exhibit human emotions like love or hate, and that there is no reason to expect AI to become intentionally benevolent or malevolent. Instead, when considering how AI might become a risk, experts think two scenarios most likely:

1. The AI is programmed to do something devastating: Autonomous weapons are artificial intelligence systems that are programmed to kill. In the hands of the wrong person, these weapons could easily cause mass casualties. Moreover, an AI arms race could inadvertently lead to an AI war that also results in mass casualties. To avoid being thwarted by the enemy, these weapons would be designed to be extremely difficult to simply "turn off," so humans could plausibly lose control of such a situation. This risk is one that's present even with narrow AI, but grows as levels of AI intelligence and autonomy increase.

2. The AI is programmed to do something beneficial, but it develops a destructive method for achieving its goal: This can happen whenever we fail to fully align the AI's goals with ours, which is strikingly difficult. If you ask an obedient intelligent car to take you to the airport as fast as possible, it might get you there chased by helicopters and covered in vomit, doing not what you wanted but literally what you asked for. If a super-intelligent system is tasked with an ambitious geo-engineering project, it might wreak havoc with our ecosystem as a side effect, and view human attempts to stop it as a threat to be met.

As these examples illustrate, the concern about advanced AI isn't malevolence but competence. A super-intelligent AI will be extremely good at accomplishing its goals, and if those goals aren't aligned with ours, we have a problem. You're probably not an evil ant-hater who steps on ants out of malice, but if you're in charge of a hydroelectric green energy project and there's an anthill in the region to be flooded, too bad for the ants. A key goal of AI safety research is to never place humanity in the position of those ants.

Stephen Hawking, Elon Musk, Steve Wozniak, Bill Gates, and many other big

Unit 12 Introduction to Artificial Intelligence

names in science and technology have recently expressed concern in the media and via open letters about the risks posed by AI, joined by many leading AI researchers. Why is the subject suddenly in the headlines?

The idea that the quest for strong AI would ultimately succeed was long thought of as science fiction, centuries or more away. However, thanks to recent breakthroughs, many AI milestones, which experts viewed as decades away merely five years ago, have now been reached, making many experts take seriously the possibility of super-intelligence in our lifetime. While some experts still guess that human-level AI is centuries away, some AI researchers guessed that it would happen before 2060. Since it may take decades to complete the required safety research, it is prudent to start it now.

Because AI has the potential to become more intelligent than any human, we have no surefire way of predicting how it will behave. We can't use past technological developments as much of a basis because we've never created anything that has the ability to, wittingly or unwittingly, outsmart us. The best example of what we could face may be our own evolution. People now control the planet, not because we're the strongest, fastest or biggest, but because we're the smartest. If we're no longer the smartest, are we assured to remain in control?

Words

outperform [ˌaʊtpəˈfɔːm] v. （效益上）超过, 胜过
nuisance [ˈnjuːsns] n. 损害, 麻烦事
pacemaker [ˈpeɪsmeɪkə(r)] n. 心脏起搏器
lethal [ˈliːθl] adj. 致命的, 致死的
quest [kwest] n. 追求, 寻找
recursive [rɪˈkɜːsɪv] adj. 循环的
intellect [ˈɪntəlekt] n. 智力, 才智
benevolent [bəˈnevələnt] adj. 仁慈的, 慈善的
malevolent [məˈlevələnt] adj. 恶毒的, 有恶意的
casualty [ˈkæʒuəlti] n. （战争或事故的）伤员, 遇难者, 受害者
thwart [θwɔːt] v. 挫败, 反对
plausible [ˈplɔːzəbl] adj. 振振有词的, 似乎合理的, 似是而非的, 似乎可信的

strikingly [ˈstraɪkɪŋli] adv. 显著地, 突出地
obedient [əˈbiːdiənt] adj. 顺从的, 服从的
cover [ˈkʌvə(r)] v. 行走（一段路程）
vomit [ˈvɒmɪt] n. 呕吐
literally [ˈlɪtərəli] adv. 真正地, 确实地, 简直
task [tɑːsk] v. 派给某人（任务）
pose [pəʊz] v. 造成, 形成
surefire [ˈʃʊəfaɪə] adj. 准不会有错的, 一定成功的
wittingly [ˈwɪtɪŋli] adv. 有意地
unwittingly [ʌnˈwɪtɪŋli] adv. 不经意地
outsmart [aʊtˈsmɑːt] v. 比……更聪明, 用计谋打败

Phrases

in the near term 在短期内
align with 使一致
side effect 副作用，意外的连带后果
step on 踩上……，踏上……
out of malice 出于恶意
think of as 把……看作，被认为是

 Notes

〔1〕　SIRI 是 Speech Interpretation & Recognition Interface 的首字母缩写，原义为语音识别接口，是苹果公司在苹果手机、iPad、iPod Touch、HomePod 等产品上应用的一个语音助手，利用 SIRI 用户可以通过手机读短信、介绍餐厅、询问天气、语音设置闹钟等。

〔2〕　IBM 的沃森（Watson）诞生于世界上最大的科技公司之一的总部，是一款专门用来解决开放式问题回答这一有害问题的计算机。虽然计算机在基于关键字进行闪电式快速搜索方面表现出色，但计算机开发人员长期以来对人工智能的无能为力感到沮丧。为了正确理解上下文识别以及人类交流和语言中的复杂关系，沃森专门设计了一种独特的方法来尝试和解决这个长期存在的问题：开发者可以通过让它玩流行的美国游戏节目《危险边缘》（Jeopardy）来测试它的能力！

〔3〕　**Original**：Whereas it may be little more than a minor nuisance if your laptop crashes or gets hacked, it becomes all the more important that an AI system does what you want it to do if it controls your car, your airplane, your pacemaker, your automated trading system or your power grid.

Translation：如果你的笔记本电脑崩溃或被黑客入侵，那可能只是些小麻烦，但如果 AI 系统控制着你的汽车、飞机、心脏起搏器、自动交易系统或电网，那么它们就会变成大问题。

 Exercises

Ⅰ. **Read the following statements carefully, and decide whether they are true（T）or false（F）according to the text.**

____ 1. The concern about advanced AI isn't malevolence but benevolent.

____ 2. Human-level AI would happen before 2030.

____ 3. Artificial intelligence today is properly known as strong AI.

____ 4. In 1965 Bill Gates point out that designing smarter AI systems is itself a cognitive task.

____ 5. AI（or weak AI）is designed to perform a narrow task like facial recognition.

Unit 12 Introduction to Artificial Intelligence

II. Choose the best answer to each of the following questions according to the text.

1. Which of the following description is not right?
   A. Strong AI would outperform humans at nearly every cognitive task.
   B. Because AI has the potential to become more intelligent than any human, we have no surefire way of predicting how it will behave.
   C. While some experts still guess that human-level AI is centuries away, some AI researchers guessed that it would happen before 2030.
   D. In the long term, an important question is what will happen if the quest for strong AI succeeds and an AI system becomes better than humans at all cognitive tasks.

2. Which of the following is a task performed by weak AI?
   A. Internet searches
   B. Facial recognition
   C. Driving a car
   D. All of the above

3. Which of the following description is right?
   A. AI today can exhibit human emotions like love or hate.
   B. AI today can exhibit human moral characters like benevolent or malevolent.
   C. Strong AI might help us eradicate war, disease, and poverty.
   D. All of the above

III. Identify the letter of the choice that best matches the phrase or definition.
   a. semantic network
   b. artificial neural network
   c. robotics
   d. Turing test
   e. expert systems

   _____ 1. A computer attempts to mimic the actions of the neural networks of the human body.
   _____ 2. The study of robots.
   _____ 3. One measure to determine whether a machine can think like a human by mimicking human conversation.
   _____ 4. A knowledge representation technique that focuses.
   _____ 5. Computer systems that embody the knowledge of human experts.

Ⅳ. Fill in the numbered spaces with the words or phrases chosen from the box. Change the forms where necessary.

> inherent   individual   however   observe   proponent
> exhibit   characteristics   program   debate   resolve

Strong AI versus Weak AI

　　The conjecture that machines can be ___1___ to exhibit intelligent behavior is known as weak AI and is accepted, to varying degrees, by a wide audience today. ___2___ the conjecture that machines can be programmed to possess intelligence and, in fact, consciousness, which is known as strong AI, is widely ___3___. Opponents of strong AI argue that a machine is ___4___ different from a human and thus can never feel love, tell right from wrong, and think about itself in the same way that a human does. However, ___5___ of strong AI argue that the human mind is constructed from small components that ___6___ are not human and are not conscious but, when combined, are. Why, they argue, would the same phenomenon not be possible with machines?

　　The problem in ___7___ the strong AI debate is that such attributes as intelligence and consciousness are internal ___8___ that cannot be identified directly. As Alan Turing pointed out, we credit other humans with intelligence because they behave intelligently—even though we cannot ___9___ their internal mental states. Are we, then, prepared to grant the same latitude to a machine if it ___10___ the external characteristics of consciousness?

Ⅴ. Translate the following passages into Chinese.

Physical Agents

　　A physical agent (robot) is a programmable system that can be used to perform a variety of tasks. Simple robots can be used in manufacturing to do routine jobs such as assembling, welding, or painting. Some organizations use mobile robots that do delivery jobs such as distributing mail or correspondence to different rooms. There are mobile robots that are used underwater for prospecting for oil.

　　A humanoid robot is an autonomous mobile robot that is supposed to behave like a human. Although humanoid robots are prevalent in science fiction, there is still a lot of work to do before such robots will be able to interact properly with their surroundings and learn from events that occur there.

Section B: Deep Learning, Machine Learning, and AI

　　Consider the following definitions to understand deep learning vs. machine learning vs. AI:

Unit 12　Introduction to Artificial Intelligence

(1) Deep learning is a subset of machine learning that's based on artificial neural networks. The learning process is deep because the structure of artificial neural networks consists of multiple input, output, and hidden layers. Each layer contains units that transform the input data into information that the next layer can use for a certain predictive task. Thanks to this structure, a machine can learn through its own data processing.

(2) Machine learning is a subset of artificial intelligence that uses techniques (such as deep learning) that enable machines to use experience to *improve at* tasks. The learning process is based on the following steps:

- Feed data into an algorithm. (In this step you can provide additional information to the model, for example, by performing feature extraction.)
- Use this data to train a model.
- Test and deploy the model.
- Consume the deployed model to do an automated predictive task. (In other words, call and use the deployed model to receive the predictions returned by the model.)

(3) Artificial Intelligence (AI) is a technique that enables computers to mimic human intelligence. It includes machine learning.

It's important to understand the relationship among AI, machine learning, and deep learning (Figure 12-2). Machine learning is a way to achieve artificial intelligence. By using machine learning and deep learning techniques, you can build computer systems and applications that do tasks that are commonly associated with human intelligence. These tasks include image recognition, speech recognition, and language translation.

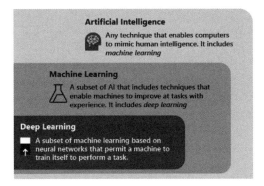

Figure 12-2　The relationship among AI, machine learning, and deep learning

Now that you have the overview of machine learning vs. deep learning, let's compare the two techniques. In machine learning, the algorithm needs to be told how to make an accurate prediction by consuming more information (for example, by performing feature extraction). In deep learning, the algorithm can learn how to make an accurate prediction through its own data processing, thanks to the artificial neural network structure.

Table 12-1 compares the two techniques in more detail.

Table 12-1 Machine learning vs. deep learning

	All machine learning	Only deep learning
Number of data points	Can use small amounts of data to make predictions	Needs to use large amounts of training data to make predictions
Hardware dependencies	Can work on low-end machines. It doesn't need a large amount of computational power	Depends on high-end machines. It inherently does a large number of matrix multiplication operations. A GPU can efficiently optimize these operations
Featurization process	Requires features to be accurately identified and created by users	Learns high-level features from data and creates new features by itself
Learning approach	Divides the learning process into smaller steps. It then combines the results from each step into one output	Moves through the learning process by resolving the problem on an end-to-end basis
Execution time	Takes comparatively little time to train, ranging from a few seconds to a few hours	Usually takes a long time to train because a deep learning algorithm involves many layers
Output	The output is usually a numerical value, like a score or a classification	The output can have multiple formats, like a text, a score or a sound

Because of the artificial neural network structure, deep learning excels at identifying patterns in unstructured data such as images, sound, video, and text. For this reason, deep learning is rapidly transforming many industries, including healthcare, energy, finance, and transportation. These industries are now rethinking traditional business processes.

Named-entity recognition is a deep learning method that takes a piece of text as input and transforms it into a pre-specified class. This new information could be a postal code, a date, a product ID. The information can then be stored in a structured schema to build a list of addresses or serve as a benchmark for an identity validation engine.

Deep learning has been applied in many object detection use cases. Object detection comprises two parts: image classification and then image localization. Image classification identifies the image's objects, such as cars or people. Image localization provides the specific location of these objects.

Object detection is already used in industries such as gaming, retail, tourism, and self-driving cars.

Like image recognition, in image captioning, for a given image, the system must generate a caption that describes the contents of the image. When you can detect and label objects in photographs, the next step is to turn those labels into descriptive sentences.

Usually, image captioning applications use convolutional neural networks to identify objects in an image and then use a recurrent neural network to turn the labels into consistent sentences.

Machine translation takes words or sentences from one language and automatically translates them into another language. Machine translation has been around for a long time, but deep learning achieves impressive results in two specific areas: automatic translation of text (and translation of speech to text) and automatic translation of images.

With the appropriate data transformation, a neural network can understand text, audio, and visual signals. Machine translation can be used to identify snippets of sound in larger audio files and transcribe the spoken word or image as text.

Text analytics based on deep learning methods involves analyzing large quantities of text data (for example, medical documents or expenses receipts), recognizing patterns, and creating organized and concise information out of it.

Companies use deep learning to perform text analysis to detect insider trading and compliance with government regulations. Another common example is insurance fraud: text analytics has often been used to analyze large amounts of documents to recognize the chances of an insurance claim being fraud.

Artificial neural networks are formed by layers of connected nodes. Deep learning models use neural networks that have a large number of layers.

The following sections explore most popular artificial neural network typologies.

The feedforward neural network is the most basic type of artificial neural network. In a feedforward network, information moves in only one direction from input layer to output layer. Feedforward neural networks transform an input by putting it through a series of hidden layers. Every layer is made up of a set of neurons, and each layer is fully connected to all neurons in the layer before. The last fully connected layer (the output layer) represents the generated predictions.

Recurrent neural networks are a widely used artificial neural network. These networks save the output of a layer and feed it back to the input layer to help predict the layer's outcome. Recurrent neural networks have great learning abilities. They're widely used for complex tasks such as time series forecasting, learning handwriting and recognizing language.

A convolutional neural network is a particularly effective artificial neural network, and it presents a unique architecture. Layers are organized in three dimensions: width, height, and depth. The neurons in one layer connect not to all the neurons in the next layer, but only to a small region of the layer's neurons. The final output is reduced to a single vector of probability scores, organized along the depth dimension.

Convolutional neural networks have been used in areas such as video recognition, image recognition and recommender systems.

Words

featurization [fiːtʃəraiˈzeiʃən] n. 特征化，特性化
caption [ˈkæpʃn] n. 标题
convolutional [ˌkɔnvəˈluːʃən(ə)l] adj. 卷积的
recurrent [riˈkʌrənt] adj. 循环的
snippet [ˈsnipit] n. 片段

transcribe [trænˈskraib] v. 改编，转录，抄写
concise [kənˈsais] adj. 简明的，简练的，简洁的
claim [kleim] n. （向公司等）索赔
typology [taiˈpɔlədʒi] n. 分类法，类型学
feedforward [ˈfiːdfɔːwəd] n. 前馈（控制）

 Phrases

improve at 提升，改善
excel at 擅长于，擅长
image captioning 图像标注
insider trading 内线交易

 Abbreviations

GPU Graphics Processing Unit 图形处理器

 Exercises

Ⅰ. Read the following statements carefully, and decide whether they are true (T) or false (F) according to the text.

　　____ 1. AI is a subset of machine learning.
　　____ 2. Machine learning is a subset of deep learning.
　　____ 3. Object detection consists of two parts: video classification and then video localization.
　　____ 4. Recurrent neural networks are widely used for complex tasks such as time series forecasting, learning handwriting and recognizing language.
　　____ 5. Deep learning models use neural networks that have many layers.

Ⅱ. Choose the best answer to each of the following questions according to the text.
　　1. Which of the following is right?
　　　　A. Artificial Intelligence (AI) includes machine learning.

Unit 12 Introduction to Artificial Intelligence

    B. Machine learning is a subset of artificial intelligence.
    C. Deep learning is a subset of machine learning.
    D. All of the above

2. Which of the following belongs to artificial neural network?
    A. Convolutional neural network
    B. Recurrent neural network
    C. Feedforward neural network
    D. All of the above

3. How many kinds of artificial neural networks are mentioned in this text?
    A. One
    B. Two
    C. Three
    D. Four

Ⅲ. Identify the letter of the choice that best matches the phrase or definition.
    a. propositional logic
    b. computer vision
    c. perceptron
    d. AI
    e. deep learning

    ____ 1. A technique that enables computers to mimic human intelligence.
    ____ 2. An artificial neuron similar to a single biological neuron.
    ____ 3. A language made up from a set of sentences that can be used to carry out logical reasoning about the world.
    ____ 4. An area of AI that deals with the perception of objects through the artificial eyes of an agent, such as a camera.
    ____ 5. A subset of machine learning that's based on artificial neural networks.

Ⅳ. Fill in the blanks with the words or phrases chosen from the box. Change the forms where necessary.

think	like	refer	simple	actual
input	comprise	give	depend	connect

Multilayer Perceptron

    A Multi-Layer Perceptron (MLP) is a deep, artificial neural network. A neural network is ___1___ of layers of nodes which activate at various levels ___2___ on the previous layer's nodes. When ___3___ about neural networks, it may be helpful to isolate your thinking to a single node in the network.

MLP ___4___ to a neural network with at least three layers of nodes, an input layer, some number of intermediate layers, and an output layer. Each node in a ___5___ layer is ___6___ to every node in the adjacent layers. The ___7___ layer is just that it is the way the network takes in data. The intermediate layer(s) are the computational machine of the network, and they ___8___ transform the input to the output. The output layer is the way that results are obtained from the neural network. In a ___9___ network where the responses are binary, there would ___10___ be only one node in the output layer, which outputs a probability like in logistic regression.

Ⅴ. **Translate the following passages into Chinese.**

LSTM Networks

Long Short Term Memory networks—usually just called "LSTMs"—are a special kind of RNN, capable of learning long-term dependencies. They were introduced by Hochreiter & Schmidhuber (1997), and were refined and popularized by many people in following work. They work tremendously well on a large variety of problems, and are now widely used.

LSTMs are explicitly designed to avoid the long-term dependency problem. Remembering information for long periods of time is practically their default behavior, not something they struggle to learn!

Part 2

Simulated Writing: Meeting Minutes

1. 简介

会议记录是会议的准确记录的书面材料。会议记录记录会议的决定以及会议中通过决议的行动,更重要的是,它提供了一个用于在下次会议上评估进展的回顾文档。这个过程使通过决议行动的个人执行和非执行的情况一目了然,使其成为一种有用的维持纪律的方法。会议记录还可以告知没有参加会议的人们会上讲了什么。

2. 内容

每次会议前都应该制定一个会议日程,详细列出在会议上应该讨论的问题。会议记录应该包括以下的信息:

(1) 会议的时间、日期以及地点;

(2) 出席会议人员的名单,以及缺席人员的名单;

(3) 以前会议记录中通过的部分,以及起因于这些会议记录的任一问题;

（4）对议事日程中的每一项，记录所讨论的主要观点以及做出的决定；

（5）一致通过的行动的列表；

（6）对于行动中的每一项，要有负责人以及期限列表；

（7）下一次会议的时间、日期以及地点；

（8）会议记录的人员姓名。

3．书写技巧

可以使用许多技巧来书写有效的会议记录：

（1）在会议前分发会议日程（通过电子邮件），这样可以使会议的参与成员有机会来做准备。

（2）在会议议程的最后部分写入"其他事宜"项作为书写最后项的地方。

（3）会议记录应简洁而且突出重点。如果想要记录会议中的每一句话，最好考虑用录音来补充。

（4）当要求某个团队成员去执行某个任务时，就记录一个"行动"标记，这样使得在下次会议时能够很容易地阅读之前的会议记录，并且做上"行动"标记。

（5）不论是在会议过程中书写会议记录（如果会议记录员是一个快速打字员），还是在会议之后马上书写，都要遵循越早完成、准确率越高的原则。

（6）书写记录时要用过去式，所书写的是已经发生过的讨论。从笔记打成会议记录的过程，是在记录一个过去的事件。

4．格式

组织的名称

年月日

时间和地点

出席名单：出席会议的成员姓名

缺席名单：缺席会议的成员姓名

会议进程：

- 会议（时间）由（某个人，通常是主席）宣布开始开会
- 会议记录（之前的会议日期）的修正和认可
- 提出和讨论的焦点问题
- 采取的行动
- 会议中止于（时间）

将来的业务：

这里用来提醒人们以下几项：

- 在下次会议之前将被提交的谈话内容
- 为即将举行的会议提供可能的会议日程
- 团队成员已经承担的任务

会议记录由（姓名）提交

5. 范例

Go 3D Game
Minutes of the 6th Group Meeting

Date: October 9, 2020
Time: 9:30 a.m. - 10:00 a.m.
Duration: 0.5 hour
Venue: Prof. Smith's office
Present: Prof. Smith,
　　　　　Chau Chun Ting (Charles),
　　　　　Chang Kin Fung (Tony)
Minutes recorder: Chang Kin Fung (Tony)
Absent: Lam Sheung Yan (Michael)
　　　　　Au Kwok Wang (Chris)

(1) **Approval of Minutes of the Last Meeting**

Minutes of the last meeting were approved as an accurate record.

(2) **Discussion of Project Development**

- Charles raised the question about the camera: if the camera is above the character at some particular angle, then we are unable to see very far to the front and may not see the enemies.
- Professor Smith said that there was no so-called "good" view angle. If the camera view is that of the character, then we can see the virtual world, but we are unable to see the character. The player may lose his orientation since he has no sense about where the character is.
- Tony asked whether it was a problem for the character to turn around because the scene would change very quickly and thus make the player feel uncomfortable.
- Prof. Smith said that limiting the speed of turnaround could solve the problem. He said that the main point was to make the game interesting and exciting. The view angle was not that important.
- Professor Smith suggested that we should design a map to display the location of the character so that the players can be aware of the progress and the place of the character.

(3) **Meeting Arrangements**

- Professor Smith asked each group to give a simple demo of their GO in the next group meeting.
- For the demo, each group should be able to implement a 3D environment with the character's movements, for instance, forward and backward movements.
- The purpose of the demo is to make sure each group has some basic ideas of how

Unit 12 Introduction to Artificial Intelligence

to implement 3D objects and control them.

(4) Adjournment of Meeting

The meeting was adjourned at 10:00 a.m.

(5) Next Meeting

Date: October 16, 2020

Time: 2:00 p.m.-3:00 p.m.

Place: GO Lab

(6) Actions Agreed Upon

Action list, dated 9 October 2020				
Item no.	Action	By	Deadline	Status
a	Give a simple demo of a 3D sky environment with the character's movements	Charles	Oct.16, 2020	
b	Give a simple demo of a 3D water environment with the character's movements	Tony	Oct.16, 2020	
c	Give a simple demo of a 3D land environment with the character's movements	Patrick	Oct.16, 2020	
d	Give a simple demo of a character	Chris	Oct.16, 2020	

Written by Tony on October 10, 2020.

Part 3

Listening and Speaking

Dialogue: Artificial Intelligence

(*After class, Sophie & Henry are standing by the door, waiting for Mark.*)

Henry: Excuse me, Sophie. As you know Artificial Intelligence today is very hot. May I ask you some questions about AI?

Sophie: Sure. What can I do for you? [1]

Henry: What do you think of Artificial Intelligence?

[1] Replace with:
1. Can I help you?
2. May I help you?

Sophie: Let me see. To my understanding, the term Artificial Intelligence (AI) was **coined** in 1956, but AI has become more popular today thanks to increased data volumes, advanced algorithms, and improvements in computing power and storage.

Henry: Well, could you please[2] talk about AI's history briefly?

[2] Replace with:
1. would you please
2. could you kindly

Sophie: Of course. Early AI research in the 1950s explored topics like problem solving and symbolic methods. In the 1960s, the U.S. Department of Defense took interest in this type of work and began training computers to **mimic** basic human reasoning. For example, the Defense Advanced Research Projects Agency (DARPA) completed street mapping projects in the 1970s. And DARPA produced intelligent personal assistants in 2003, long before Siri①, Alexa② or Cortana③ were **household** names.

Henry: So this means that those work impacted AI today?

Sophie: Absolutely. This early work paved the way for the automation and formal reasoning that we see in computers today, including decision support systems and smart search systems that can be designed to **complement** and **augment** human abilities.

(When they are talking, Mark comes toward them.)

Sophie & Henry: Hi, Mark.

Mark: Hi, Henry and Sophie.

Sophie: You are just on time. Just before Henry was asking me about AI. I heard that you are quite familiar with AI.

Mark: A little bit. To my knowledge, while Hollywood movies and science fiction novels depict AI as human-like robots that take over the world, the current evolution of AI technologies isn't that **scary**—

Unit 12 Introduction to Artificial Intelligence

Mark: or quite that smart. Instead[3], AI has evolved to provide many specific benefits in every industry.

> [3] Replace with:
> 1. On the contrary
> 2. Rather

Henry: You mean specific benefits in every industry?

Mark: Yes. AI automates repetitive learning and discovery through data. But AI is different from hardware-driven, robotic automation. Instead of automating manual tasks, AI performs frequent, high-volume, computerized tasks reliably and without **fatigue**. For this type of automation, human inquiry is still essential to set up the system and ask the right questions.

Sophie: I think AI adds intelligence to existing products. In most cases, AI will not be sold as an individual application. Rather, products you already use will be improved with AI capabilities, much like Siri was added as a feature to a new generation of Apple products. Automation, conversational platforms, bots and smart machines can be combined with large amounts of data to improve many technologies at home and in the workplace, from security intelligence to investment analysis.

Mark: You are right. AI adapts through progressive learning algorithms to let the data do the programming. AI finds structure and regularities in data so that the algorithm acquires a skill: The algorithm becomes a classifier or a predictor. So, just as the algorithm can teach itself how to play chess, it can teach itself what product to recommend next online. And the models adapt when given new data. Back propagation is an AI technique that allows the model to adjust, through training and added data, when the first answer is not quite right.

Henry: Ok, so what else?

Sophie: Well, AI analyzes more and deeper data using neural networks that have many hidden layers. Building a fraud detection system with five hidden layers was almost impossible a few years ago. All that has changed with incredible computer power and big data. You need lots of data to train deep learning models because they learn directly from the data. The more data you can feed them, the more accurate they become.

Mark: Besides, AI gets the most out of data. When algorithms are self-learning, the data itself can become intellectual property. The answers are in the data; you just have to apply AI to get them out. Since the role of the data is now more important than ever before, it can create a competitive advantage. If you have the best data in a competitive industry, even if everyone is applying similar techniques, the best data will win.

Sophie: Indeed, AI achieves incredible accuracy through deep neural networks—which was previously impossible. For example, your interactions with Alexa, Google Search and Google Photos are all based on deep learning—and they keep getting more accurate the more we use them. In the medical field, AI techniques from deep learning, image classification and object recognition can now be used to find cancer on MRIs with the same accuracy as highly trained radiologists.

Henry: Ok, I've got it. Sophie and Mark, thanks for your valuable knowledge.

Sophie & Mark: My pleasure.

 Exercises

Work in a group, and make up a similar conversation by replacing the statements

Unit 12　Introduction to Artificial Intelligence

with other expressions on the right side.

 Words

coin[kɔin] v. 创造（新词，短语），杜撰
mimic[ˈmimik] v. 模仿
household[ˈhaushəuld] adj. 家喻户晓的
complement[ˈkɔmplim(ə)nt] v. 补足，补助
augment[ɔːgˈment] v. 增加，增大

scary[ˈskeəri] adj.（事物）可怕的，引起惊慌的
fatigue[fəˈtiːg] n. 疲劳，疲乏
radiologist[ˌreidiˈɔlədʒist] n. 放射科医生，放射线研究者

 Abbreviations

MRI　Magnetic Resonance Imaging　核磁共振成像

 Notes

① 见本单元 Section A 中的 Notes[1]。

② Alexa 是一家专门发布网站世界排名的网站。Alexa 每天在网上搜集超过 1000GB 的信息，不仅给出多达几十亿的网址链接，而且为其中的每一个网站进行了排名。可以说，Alexa 是当前拥有 URL 数量最庞大、排名信息发布最详尽的网站。

③ 微软小娜（Cortana）是微软公司发布的全球第一款个人智能助理。它"能够了解用户的喜好和习惯"以及"帮助用户进行日程安排、问题回答等"。

Listening Comprehension：Supervised Learning

Listen to the article and answer the following 3 questions based on it. After you hear a question, there will be a break of 15 seconds. During the break, you will decide which one is the best answer among the four choices marked（A），（B），（C）and（D）.

Questions

1. Which of the following is right?
　　（A）Supervised learning is the machine learning task of learning a function that maps an input to an output based on example input-output pairs
　　（B）Supervised learning infers a function from labeled training data consisting of a set of training examples
　　（C）A supervised learning algorithm analyzes the training data and produces an inferred function
　　（D）All of the above

2. Regarding the hand-written digit recognition problem, which of the following is right?

(A) A reasonable data set for this problem is a collection of images of hand-written digits

(B) A reasonable data set for this problem is for each image, what the digit actually is

(C) A set of examples of the form (image, digit) should be considered

(D) All of the above

3. Which of the following can't supervised learning do?

(A) Supervised learning is the machine learning task of learning a function that maps an output to an input based on example output-input pairs

(B) Supervised learning is the machine learning task of learning a function that maps an input to an output based on example input-output pairs

(C) Supervised learning infers a function from labeled training data consisting of a set of training examples

(D) A supervised learning algorithm analyzes the training data and produces an inferred function

 **Words**

map[mæp] v. 映射
entirety[in'taiərəti] n. 全部,完全
outset['autset] n. 开始,开端

Dictation: Unsupervised Learning

This article will be played three times. Listen carefully, and fill in the numbered spaces with the appropriate words you have heard.

Unsupervised learning is a ___1___ of machine learning that learns from test data that has not been ___2___, classified or categorized. Instead of ___3___ to feedback, unsupervised learning identifies **commonalities** in the data and reacts based on the presence or ___4___ of such commonalities in each new piece of data. ___5___ include supervised learning and reinforcement learning.

In the unsupervised ___6___, the training data does not contain any output information at all. We are just given input examples $X_1, X_2, \cdots, X_N$. You may wonder how we could possibly learn anything from mere inputs. Consider the coin ___7___ problem. Suppose that we didn't know the **denomination** of any of the ___8___ in the data set.

We still get similar ___9___ , but they are now ___10___ so all points have the same 'color'. The decision regions in unsupervised learning may be ___11___ to those in supervised learning, but without the labels. However, the correct clustering is less ___12___ now, and even the number of clusters may be ___13___ .

___14___ , this example shows that we can learn something from the inputs by themselves. Unsupervised learning can be ___15___ as the task of *spontaneously* finding ___16___ and structure in input data. For instance, if our task is to ___17___ a set of books into topics, and we only use ___18___ properties of the ___19___ books, we can identify books that have similar ___20___ and put them together in one category, without naming that category.

▸ Words

commonality [kɔmə'næliti] n. 公共，共性	spontaneously [spɔn'teiniəsli] adv. 自发地，自然地
denomination [di,nɔmi'neiʃn] n. 面额	

Glossary

A

a bunch of		大量，许多
a collection of		很多，一批
a smattering of		少数，少量
a whole lot		非常多，多得不能再多了
abbreviate	[əˈbriːvieit]v.	缩写，简写
accelerometer	[əkˌseləˈrɒmitə(r)]n.	加速度计
accommodate	[əˈkɒmədeit]v.	考虑到，顾及
accomplice	[əˈkʌmplis]n.	共犯，帮凶，同谋
accordingly	[əˈkɔːdiŋli]adv.	相应地，因此，依据
acknowledged	[əkˈnɒlidʒid]adj.	公认的，被普遍认可的
acquaintance	[əˈkwentəns]n.	(对某事物的)了解
act as		充当，用作，当作，起……的作用
ad-hoc		特设的，特定目的的
adaptive	[əˈdæptiv]adj.	适应的
add to this		而且，另外
address	[əˈdres]v.	处理(问题)
adhere to		遵守，坚持
advanced	[ədˈvɑːnst]adj.	价格高的，昂贵的
advent	[ˈædvent]n.	(重要事件、人物、发明等的)出现
affordable	[əˈfɔːdəbl]adj.	买得起的，价格实惠的，经济适用的，价格适中的
aggregate	[ˈægrigət，ˈægrigeit]v.	总计，合计
aggressive	[əˈgresiv]adj.	好斗的，挑衅的，富于攻击性的
agility	[əˈdʒiliti]n.	灵敏性，敏捷
algorithm	[ˈælgəriðəm]n.	算法
algorithmic	[ˌælgəˈriðmik]adj.	算法的
align with		使一致
alike	[əˈlaik]adv.	同样地
all over		到处，浑身
all the time		一直
alternative	[ɔːlˈtəːnətiv]n.	二中择一，供替代的选择
amateur	[ˈæmətə]n.	业余爱好者
amigo	[əˈmiːgəu]n.	朋友

among others		其中，包括
analyses	[əˈnæləsiːz] n.	分析，解析，分解，梗概（analysis 的复数形式）
animation	[ˌæniˈmeiʃn] n.	（指电影、录像、电脑游戏的）动画制作；动画片
applet	[eplet] n.	Java 小应用程序（application let）
aptitude	[ˈæptitjuːd] n.	天生的才能，天赋
arcane	[ɑːˈkein] adj.	神秘的，晦涩难懂的
archive	[ˈɑːkaiv] n.	档案，卷宗，案卷
arise	[əˈraz] v.	发生，产生，出现
around	[əˈraund] adv.	大约
arrive	[əˈraiv] v.	（东西）被送来，到达
artifact	[ˈɑːtifækt] n.	人工制品
as per		按照，根据
as sb. put it		正如某人所说的那样
as well as		也，和……一样，不但……而且
as with		如同，和……一样
as-needed		按需的
ask for		请求，寻找
assume	[əˈsjuːm] v.	承担（责任）
at a time		每次，依次，逐一
at the expense of		以……为代价，以牺牲……的利益为代价
at times		有时，间或
augment	[ɔːgˈment] v.	增加，增大
author	[ˈɔːθə(r)] v.	编写
authorization	[ˌɔːθəraiˈzeiʃn, -riˈz-] n.	授权，认可
automated teller machine		自动出纳机，自动柜员机
avenue	[ˈævənjuː] n.	途径，手段

B

back-and-forth		反复地，来回地
backlash	[ˈbæklæʃ] n.	激烈反应
bandwidth-intensive		带宽密集型的
barcode		条形码，条码技术
be associated with		与……有关，与……有关系
be attentive to		注意，留心
be bound to		注定
be characteristic of		具有……特色的

be classified as		被归类为……
be included with		包括在
be poised to do		准备做
be quoted as saying		用……的话说
be riddled with		布满,充满
be set to do		准备做某事
be subject to		受……管制,使服从
be suited for		适合于,适合做
beat out		打败,击败,战胜
behemoth	[biˈhiːməθ]n.	巨头(指规模庞大、实力雄厚的公司或机构)
behind the scenes		在幕后,秘密地
benevolent	[bəˈnevələnt]adj.	仁慈的,慈善的
best of all		首先,最好的是,最重要的是
better off		境况(尤指经济性)较好的,比较富裕
bidding	[ˈbidiŋ]n.	吩咐,投标
big name		成功人士,知名人士
bill	[bil]v.	发账单(要求付款)
bit line		位线,数元线
block	[blɔk]n.	障碍物
boil down to		将……归结为,重点是
bonus	[ˈbəunəs]n.	额外给予的东西,意外获得的东西,赠品
boot	[buːt]v. & n.	引导,引导程序(= bootstrap)
bootstrap	[ˈbuːtstræp]n.	解靴带,引导程序,辅助程序
bot	[bɔt]n.	(能执行特定任务的)网上机器人程序(robot 的缩略)
brand	[brænd]v.	使显得独一无二,标明……与众不同
breakthrough	[ˈbreikθruː]n.	突破,突破性进展
brew	[bruː]v.	煮(咖啡),酿制(啤酒),沏(茶)
brilliant	[ˈbriljənt]adj.	超群的,杰出的
bring forth		提出(建议、证据等)
broadband	[ˈbrɔːdbænd]n.	宽带
buddy	[ˈbʌdi]n.	朋友,同伴,伙伴
build	[bild]n.	构建
bully	[ˈbuli]v.	恐吓,伤害,胁迫
burst	[bəːst]n.	短暂的突然发作,一阵
bus	[bʌs]n.	(电脑的)总线
buzz	[bʌz]n.	时髦的(词语、想法或活动)

Glossary

by right of		由于，因为
by the way		顺便提一句
bystander	[ˈbaistændə(r)] n.	旁观者
bytecode	[ˈbaitkəud] adj.	字节码

C

cable	[ˈkeibl] n.	有线电视（= cable TV）
cache	[kæʃ] v.	隐藏，缓存
cage	[keidʒ] v.	将……放入，将……限制于
call over		把……叫过来
camcorder	[ˈkæmkɔːdə] n.	可携式摄像机
capability	[ˌkeipəˈbiliti] n.	功能，才能
capacitive	[kəˈpæsitiv] adj.	电容性的
capacitor	[kəˈpæsitə(r)] n.	电容器，电容
caption	[ˈkæpʃn] n.	标题
cardboard	[ˈkɑːdbɔːd] n.	硬纸板
cardinal	[ˈkɑːdinl] adj.	最重要的，基本的
casualty	[ˈkæʒuəlti] n.	（战争或事故的）伤员，遇难者，受害者
cater to		满足……的需要
cause	[kɔːz] n.	事业，运动，（奋斗的）目标
cell tower		蜂窝基站，手机基站
cellular	[ˈseljələ(r)] n.	手机，移动电话，蜂窝电话（= cellular telephone）
chain	[tʃein] n.	连锁店或旅馆系列的事物
champion	[ˈtʃæmpjən] v.	捍卫，为……而斗争，声援
change up		加挡，换高速挡
charge	[tʃɑːdʒ] v.	使充电，收费
charge	[tʃɑːdʒ] n.	费用
check-in		签到，住宿登记手续
checkout	[ˈtʃekaut] n.	（在超级市场）对购物的核算付款，结账
checkstand	[ˈtʃekstænd] n.	（超级市场的）点货收款台
checksum	[ˈtʃeksʌm] n.	校验和，检查和
cipher	[ˈsaifə(r)] n.	密码
claim	[kleim] n.	（向公司等）索赔
class	[klɑːs, klæs] n.	类
client	[ˈklaiənt] n.	客户端
client-side		客户端
clip out		剪辑，剪辑出

cloak	[kləuk]v.	隐藏,掩盖,掩饰,伪装
cluster	[ˈklʌstə]n.	集群,簇
co-founder		共同创立者
coat	[kəut]v.	给……涂上(或盖上、裹上)
coaxial	[kəuˈæksəl]adj.	同轴的
cobble together		胡乱拼凑,匆匆制作
coefficient	[ˌkəuiˈfiʃnt]n.	系数
coherent	[kəuˈhiərənt]adj.	一致的,连贯的
cohesion	[kəuˈhiːʒn]n.	内聚
cohesive	[kəuˈhiːsiv]adj.	使内聚的,黏着的
coin	[kɔin]v.	创造(新词,短语),杜撰
columnar	[kəˈlʌmnə]adj.	印(排)成栏的,柱状的
come a long way		取得很大进展
come about		发生,出现
come across		偶然遇见
come equipped with		配备
come into action		起作用,投入战斗
come into being		开始存在
come of age		成熟,发达
come on		(机器或系统)开始工作
come up with		提出(计划、想法等)
comma-delimited		逗号分界
commission	[kəˈmiʃən]n.	佣金,手续费,任命
commonality	[kɔməˈnæliti]n.	公共,共性
commonplace	[ˈkɔmənpleis]adj.	普通的,普遍的
communal	[kəˈmjuːnəl, ˈkɔmjə-]adj.	共有的,共用的
compatibility	[kəmˌpætiˈbiliti]n.	兼容性,适合性
complement	[ˈkɔmplim(ə)nt]v.	补足,补助
compliant	[kəmˈplaiənt]adj.	(与系列规则相)符合的,一致的
composite key		组合键,复合关键字
con	[kɔn]n.	反对,反对的理由
conceal	[kənˈsiːl]v.	隐藏
concede	[kənˈsiːd]v.	承认(某事属实、合乎逻辑等)
concise	[kənˈsais]adj.	简明的,简练的,简洁的
concurrent	[kənˈkʌrənt]adj.	并发的,一致的,同时发生的
concussion	[kənˈkʌʃən]n.	冲击,震荡,脑震荡
configuration	[kənˌfigjuˈreiʃən]n.	配置
configure	[kənˈfigə]v.	(尤指对计算机设备进行)配置,对(设备或软件进行)设定

conquer	[ˈkɔŋkə(r)] v.	攻克,征服
construct	[kənˈstrʌkt] n.	结构体
contemplate	[ˈkɔntəmplet] v.	思考,预期
convergence	[kənˈvɜːdʒəns] n.	一体化,集中,收敛
conviction	[kənˈvikʃn] n.	定罪,证明有罪
convolutional	[ˌkɔnvəˈluːʃən(ə)l] adj.	卷积的
cookie	[ˈkuki] n.	小型文本文件
cookie jar		饼干罐
copious	[ˈkəupiəs] adj.	大量的,充裕的,丰富的
copyright	[kɔpirait] v.	获得……的版权
core	[kɔː] n.	核,核心,芯
corpus	[ˈkɔːpəs] n.	文集,(事物的)主体
correspondence	[ˌkɔrəˈspɔndəns] n.	通信
cost-effective		有成本效益的
cost-prohibitive		成本高昂的
couch	[kautʃ] n.	睡椅,沙发
count	[kaunt] n.	计数,计算
counter-productive		产生相反效果的
counterpart	[ˈkauntəpɑːt] n.	配对物,极相似的人或物
couple	[ˈkʌpl] v.	耦合
cover	[ˈkʌvə(r)] v.	行走(一段路程)
craft	[krɑːft] n.	工艺,手艺
cram	[kræm] v.	填满,塞满
crumble	[ˈkrʌmbl] v.	坍塌,损坏
cryptography	[kripˈtɔgrəfi] n.	密码使用法,密码系统
cure	[kjuə] v.	改正,消除,治疗
custom	[ˈkʌstəm] adj.	定制的,定做的

D

dashboard	[ˈdæʃbɔːd] n.	监控大盘
data mart		数据集市,专用数据栈
daunt	[dɔːnt] v.	沮丧,使气馁
dearly	[ˈdiəli] adv.	高价地,昂贵地
dedicated	[ˈdedikeitid] v.	专用的,专门用途的
deem	[diːm] v.	认为,视为,相信
default to		默认为
deliverable	[diˈlivərəbl] n.	应交付的产品
delve	[delv] v.	挖掘
denomination	[diˌnɔmiˈneiʃn] n.	面额

deploy	[diˈplɔi]v.	部署
depression	[diˈpreʃn]n.	抑郁症,精神忧郁
deserve	[diˈzəːv]v.	值得,应得,该得
desperately	[ˈdespəritli]adv.	不顾一切地,绝望地
diaper	[ˈdaiəpə]n.	尿布
die	[dai]v.	停止运转
diode	[ˈdaiəud]n.	二极管
dip	[dip]n.	(使)下降
discard	[disˈkaːd]v.	丢弃,抛弃
discharge	[disˈtʃaːdʒ]v.	放电
discredit	[disˈkredit]v.	使怀疑,使不可置信
discrete	[diˈskriːt]adj.	离散的,不连续的
disparate	[ˈdispərət]adj.	不同的,不相干的,全异的
disparity	[diˈspærəti]n.	不同,不等
distinguish	[disˈtiŋgwiʃ]v.	使杰出,使著名
distribution	[ˌdistriˈbjuːʃən]n.	(商品的)经销,推销,销售
double	[ˈdʌb(ə)l]v.	加倍
downtime	[ˈdauntaim]n.	停止运行时间
dream of		渴望,梦想
dropper	[ˈdrɔpə]n.	落下的人或物
dub	[dʌb]v.	授予称号

E

edge case		边界用例,极端例子
eh	[ei]int.	(表示惊奇、疑问或没听清楚对方的话)啊,嗯,什么
electrical charge		电荷
electronics	[ilekˈtrɔniks]n.	电子器件,电子学
embody	[imˈbɔdi]v.	具体表现,体现
encode	[inˈkəud]v.	(将文字材料)译成密码,编码
encounter	[ˈinˈkauntə(r)]n.	偶遇
encrypt	[inˈkript]v.	加密,将……译成密码
engaging	[inˈgeidʒiŋ]adj.	有趣的,令人愉快的,迷人的
entirety	[inˈtaiərəti]n.	全部,完全
equate	[iˈkweit]v.	等同,使相等,视为平等
escalate	[ˈeskəleit]v.	逐步增强
essence	[ˈesns]n.	本质,实质
etch	[etʃ]v.	蚀刻,侵蚀
Ethernet	[ˈiːθənet]n.	以太网,以太

ever-changing		千变万化的,常变的
evidentiary	[ˌeviˈdenʃiəri]adj.	作为证据的
exabyte	[igzəˈbait]n.	2^{60} 字节
excel at		擅长于,擅长
executive	[igˈzekjutiv]n.	管理人员,主管业务的人,经理
explicit	[ikˈsplisit]adj.	清楚明白的,易于理解的

F

facilitate	[fəˈsiliteit]v.	(指物体、过程等,不用于指人)使(更)容易,使便利
facility	[fəˈsiliti]n.	工具,便利
fatigue	[fəˈtiːg]n.	疲劳,疲乏
featurization	[fiːtʃəraiˈzeiʃən]n.	特征化,特性化
feedforward	[ˈfiːdfɔːwəd]n.	前馈(控制)
fiber-optic		光导纤维
field	[fiːld]n.	字段,信息组,栏
finalize	[ˈfainəlaiz]v.	把(计划、旅行、项目等)最后定下来
find	[faind]v.	知道,得知,获悉
firmware	[ˈfɜːmweə(r)]n.	(计算机的)固件(就是写入EROM或EEPROM(可编程只读存储器)中的程序)
fit in with		适应,符合,与……一致
fix	[fiks]v.	安排,决定
fixture	[ˈfikstʃə(r)]n.	固定装置
flat	[flæt]adj.	(费率等)一律的,稳定的
flowchart	[fləuˈtʃaːt]n.	流程图
fluid	[ˈfluːid]adj.	变化的,流动的,液体的
folk	[fəuk]adj.	民间的,普通平民的
footage	[ˈfutidʒ]n.	连续镜头,电影胶片
for free		免费的
for short		简称,缩写
forensics	[fəˈrensiks]n.	取证,网络法医学
fraudulent	[ˈfrɔːdjulənt]adj.	欺骗性的,不正的
free up		使解脱出来,使空出来
fridge	[fridʒ]n.	冰箱
from scratch		从头做起,白手起家
fulfill	[fulˈfil]v.	达到(目的),履行(诺言等)
fulfilling	[fulˈfiliŋ]adj.	让人感觉有意义的,令人满足的
function	[ˈfʌŋkʃən]v.	有或起作用

| function | [ˈfʌŋkʃn] n. | 函数 |
| further | [ˈfɜːðə(r)] v. | 促进，增进 |

G

gadget	[ˈgædʒit] n.	小装置，小器具
gateway	[ˈgeitwei] n.	网关
gauge	[geidʒ] v.	判定，估计，估算
gear	[giə] v.	准备好，使适应
genetics	[dʒiˈnetiks] n.	遗传学
geolocation	[dʒiəluˈkeiʃn] n.	地理定位
get caught up		被卷入，卷入到
get on		继续做，开始做
get squeezed to		陷入，挤到
give away		赠送，捐赠
give rise to		引起，导致
go a long way		对……大有帮助
go down		停止，被打败
good	[gud] n.	好东西
grocery	[ˈgrəusəri] n.	杂货店

H

hack	[hæk] v.	非法侵入（他人计算机系统）
hand over		移交，交出
hard-core		铁杆的，骨干的
have to do with		和……有关系
heaviest	[ˈhevist] adj.	（在数量、程度等方面）超出一般的
helmet	[ˈhelmit] n.	钢盔，头盔
heuristic	[hjuəˈristik] adj.	启发式的，探索的
high-end		高端的，价高质优的
high-performing		高效的
hindsight perspective		事后诸葛亮
hit the market		打入市场
hitherto	[ˌhiðəˈtuː] adv.	迄今，至今
home screen		首页，主屏幕
host	[həust] v.	主办，主持（活动）
household	[ˈhaushəuld] adj.	家喻户晓的
hypertext	[ˈhaipətekst] n.	超文本（含有指向其他文本文件链接的文本）

I

ice buildup		冰堆积
icon	[ˈaikɔn]n.	图标，图符
identify	[aiˈdentifai]v.	辨认，识别，认出，确定
Iliad	[ˈiliəd]n.	《伊利亚特》（古希腊描写特洛伊战争的英雄史诗，相传为荷马所作）
image captioning		图像标注
impairment	[imˈpɛəmənt]n.	损伤，损害
impending	[imˈpendiŋ]adj.	即将发生的，迫在眉睫的
implausible	[imˈplɔːzəbl]adj.	似乎不合情理的，不像真实的
improve at		提升，改善
in a nutshell		概括地说，简言之
in brief		简单地说
in competition with		与……竞争
in conjunction with		连同……，与……一起
in lieu of		（以……）替代，作为（……的）替代
in line with		和……一致，符合
in mind		记住，考虑到
in one shot		立刻，马上
in part		在某种程度上，部分地，一半
in question		被提及的，讨论中的，相关的
in regard to		在……方面，就……而论
in sight		在望，迫近
in the near term		在短期内
in this day and age		当今
in transit		在运送途中
inadvertent	[ˌinədˈvəːtənt]adj.	非故意的，出于无心的，由疏忽造成的
incentivize	[inˈsentivaiz]v.	以物质刺激鼓励
incriminate	[inˈkrimineit]v.	使负罪，连累
indelible	[inˈdeləbl]adj.	无法忘记的
inescapable	[ˌinisˈkeipəbl]adj.	不可避免的，不可忽视的
infallible	[inˈfæləbl]adj.	绝对可靠的，绝无错误的
infancy	[ˈinfənsi]n.	初期
infiltrate	[ˈinfiltreit, inˈfil-]v.	使潜入，使渗入，使浸润
infrared	[ˌinfrəˈred]adj.	红外线的
inhibit	[inˈhibit]v.	阻止，阻碍
insider	[inˈsaidə]n.	知情人，了解内幕的人，消息灵通人士
insider trading		内线交易

instance	['instəns]n.	实例,情况,建议
intact	[in'tækt]adj.	完整无缺的,未经触动的,未受损伤的
integrated circuit		集成电路
intellect	['intəlekt]n.	智力,才智
interface	['intəfeis]v.	(使通过界面或接口)接合,连接
interpreter	[in'tə:pritə]n.	解释程序
intrigue	[in'tri:g, 'intri:g]v.	激起……的兴趣,引发……的好奇心
invoke	[in'vəuk]v.	调用
iterate	['itəreit]v.	迭代(数学或计算过程,或一系列指令)

J

jailbreak	['dʒeilbreik]n.	越狱,破解
just about		几乎
just the same		仍然,依然,照样
just-in-time		及时,恰好

K

keep in mind		记住
keep up		保持,继续(做某事)
kernel	['kɜ:n(ə)l]n.	内核
keypunch	['ki:pʌntʃ]n.	键盘穿孔机
knight	[nait]v.	授以爵位

L

laden	['leidn]adj.	载满的,装满的
landline	['lænd‚lain]n.	座机电话
layman	['leimən]n.	外行
layout	['leiaut]n.	布局,布置,设计
legitimate	[li'dʒitimit]adj.	合法的
lethal	['li:θl]adj.	致命的,致死的
leverage	['li:vəridʒ]v.	发挥杠杆作用,施加影响
library	['laibrəri]n.	(程序)库,文件库
light up		照亮,点燃
like never before		前所未有
line of sight		视线,瞄准线
link	[liŋk]n.	链路,链接,关联,关系
LinkRot		出错链接页面
lipstick	['lipstik]n.	口红,唇膏

literally	[ˈlitərəli]*adv.*	真正地,确实地,简直
live	[laiv]*adj.*	最新的
livestock	[ˈlaivstɔk]*n.*	牲畜,家畜
living hell		活地狱,活受罪
lobby	[ˈlɔbi]*n.*	(公寓、旅馆、剧院等公共建筑物的)门厅,门廊,前厅,穿堂,休息室
long gone		已经过去
long-expected		期待已久的
look through		逐一查看,翻阅
look up		查阅(词典或参考书),(在词典、参考书等中)查找
low profile		不引人注目的形象
loyalty	[ˈlɔiəlti]*n.*	忠诚,忠实

M

major	[ˈmeidʒə]*adj.*	较大的,重要的
make up		组成,构成
malevolent	[məˈlevələnt]*adj.*	恶毒的,有恶意的
mandatory	[ˈmændətəri]*adj.*	强迫性的,强制的,义务的
manifesto	[ˌmæniˈfestəu]*n.*	宣言,声明
manipulate	[məˈnipjuleit]*v.*	(熟练地)操作,使用
map	[mæp]*v.*	映射
markedly	[ˈmɑːkidli]*adv.*	显著地,明显地
mascot	[ˈmæskɔt, -kət]*n.*	吉祥物,福神
mass	[mæs]*n.*	民众,大量
mechanics	[miˈkæniks]*n.*	力学
medium	[ˈmiːdiəm]*n.*	介质,媒介
megaphone	[ˈmegəfəun]*n.*	扩音器,传声筒
metadata	[ˈmetəˌdeitə]*n.*	元数据
metallic	[məˈtælik]*adj.*	金属的,金属性的
metamorphose	[ˌmetəˈmɔːfəuz]*v.*	变化,发生质变
mimic	[ˈmimik]*v.*	模仿
misconception	[ˌmiskənˈsepʃən]*n.*	误解,错觉,错误想法
mix	[miks]*n.*	混乱,迷惑
mock-up		模型,原型
model	[ˈmɔdl]*v.*	建模
modularity	[ˌmɔdjuˈlæriti]*n.*	模块性
momentum	[məuˈmentəm]*n.*	势头,动量,动力
morale	[məˈrɑːl]*n.*	士气

multiply	[ˈmʌltiplai] v.	成倍增加, 迅速增加
multitude	[ˈmʌltitjuːd] n.	众多, 大量
mundane	[mʌnˈdein] adj.	单调的, 平凡的
mushroom	[ˈmʌʃrum] v.	快速生长, 迅速增长
myth	[miθ] n.	神话, 虚构的人, 虚构的事

N

nightfall	[ˈnaitfɔːl] n.	黄昏, 傍晚
nightmare	[ˈnaitmeə(r)] n.	难处理之事, 噩梦
norm	[nɔːm] n.	常态, 标准
normalization	[ˌnɔːməlaiˈzeiʃn] n.	规范化, 正常化, 标准化, 正态化
notable	[ˈnəutəbl] adj.	著名的
notation	[nəuˈteiʃn] n.	符号
note	[nəut] n.	便条
note	[nəut] v.	着重提到, 强调, 指出, 表明
notebook computer		笔记本型电脑, 笔记本式计算机, 笔记型电脑
notion	[ˈnəuʃn] n.	概念, 观念, 看法
nuisance	[ˈnjuːsns] n.	损害, 麻烦事

O

obedient	[əˈbiːdiənt] adj.	顺从的, 服从的
obsessive	[əbˈsesiv] adj.	着迷的, 迷恋的, 难以释怀的
offensive	[əˈfensiv] adj.	无礼的, 冒犯的
offload	[ˌɒfˈləud] v.	减轻(负担)
old school		守旧派
on demand		一经要求, 点播
on the off chance		说不定, 看能不能, 希望
on-demand		按需的, 随需应变的
on-premise		部署, 预置
once in a while		偶尔, 间或
opaque	[əuˈpeik] adj.	不透明的, 难懂的
opinionated	[əˈpinjəneitid] adj.	固执己见的, 顽固的
opt for		选择
or else		(表示另外一种可能性)或者
orchestration	[ˌɔːkiˈstreiʃn] n.	和谐的结合
ore	[ɔː(r)] n.	矿石
other than		不同于, 除了
out	[aut] adj.	面市的

out of malice		出于恶意
out of the box		能够满足一定需求的
out there		在那里，存在
outlet	[ˈautlet,-lit]n.	（感情、精力等的）发泄途径（或方法、手段），排遣
outperform	[ˌautpəˈfɔːm]v.	（效益上）超过，胜过
outset	[ˈautset]n.	开始，开端
outside of		在……的外面
outsmart	[ˌautˈsmɑːt]v.	比……更聪明，用计谋打败
outstrip	[ˌautˈstrip]v.	超过，胜过
over	[ˈəuvə(r)]prep.	超过
over budget		超过预算
overhead	[ˌəuvəˈhed, ˈəuvəhed]n.	经常费用，经常开支

P

pacemaker	[ˈpeismeikə(r)]n.	心脏起搏器
packet	[ˈpækit]n.	包，束，分组，小包
packet-switched		包交换
pair	[peə(r)]v.	使成对，配对
pal	[pæl]n.	好友，伙伴
palette	[ˈpælit]n.	调色板，颜料
panacea	[ˌpænəˈsiːə]n.	万灵药，万能之计
paraphernalia	[ˌpærəfəˈneiliə]n.	（尤指某活动所需的）装备
parse	[pɑːz]v.	分解，解析
pay homage to		向……表示敬意
pay-as-you-go		先使用后付费
payload	[ˈpeiləud]n.	有效负荷
per-request		每个请求
perceive	[pəˈsiːv]v.	察觉，发觉，感知
peripheral	[pəˈrifərəl]n.	外围设备，辅助设备（如打印机、扫描仪等）（也作 peripheric）
perk	[pɜːk]n.	（工资之外的）补贴，津贴，额外待遇
perspective	[pəˈspektiv]n.	观点，看法
peruse	[pəˈruːz]v.	细读，研读
petabyte	[ˈpetəbait]n.	2^{50} 字节
phish	[fiʃ]v.	网络钓鱼
phisher	[ˈfiʃə]n.	网络钓鱼者
physics	[ˈfiziks]n.	物理成分，物理现象，物理学
place on		寄托，把……放在……上

plant	[plɑːnt, plænt]v.	安置,置放,插
planted evidence		栽赃,伪造证据
plausible	[ˈplɔːzəbl]adj.	振振有词的,似乎合理的,似是而非的,似乎可信的
playground	[ˈpleigraund]n.	活动场所
plug-in		插件程序
plus	[plʌs]conj.	而且,此外
point	[pɔint]v.	为(某人)指出
point-of-sale		销售点的,售货点的
polyglot persistence		多语言持久性
polymorphic	[ˌpɔliˈmɔrfik]adj.	多态的
pop up		突然出现,冷不防冒出
pornography	[pɔːˈnɔgrəfi]n.	淫秽作品,色情书刊(或音像制品等)
port	[pɔːt]n.	端口
portable	[ˈpɔːtəbl]adj.	便携式的,易携带或移动的
portal	[ˈpɔtl]n.	壮观的大门,门户网站
pose	[pəuz]v.	造成,形成
posit	[ˈpɔzit]v.	认为……为实
post	[pəust]v.	张贴
power outlet		电源(引)出口,电源插座
power user		高级用户,超级用户
practitioner	[prækˈtiʃənə]n.	从业者,实践者
predecessor	[ˈpriːdisesə]n.	前任,(被取代的)原有事物
prevalence	[ˈprevələns]n.	流行,卓越
pricey	[ˈpraisi]adj.	高价的,过分昂贵的
primary key		主键,主(关)键(字)
prior to		在……之前,居先
pro	[prəu]n.	赞成的论点
proactive	[ˌprəuˈæktiv]adj.	主动的,先发制人的
probe	[prəub]v.	探查,查明
profile	[ˈprəufail]n.	简介,传略
prominent	[ˈprɔminənt]adj.	著名的
prompt	[prɔmpt]adj.	迅速的,及时的
proponent	[prəˈpəunənt]n.	支持者,倡导者
proposition	[ˌprɔpəˈziʃən]n.	主张,提议,建议
proprietary	[prəˈpraiətri]adj.	专有的
protect against		保护,保卫
protocol	[ˈprəutəkɔl]n.	(数据传递的)协议
prototype	[ˈprəutətaip]n.	原型,标准,模范

provided	[prəˈvaidid]conj.		如果，假如
provision	[prəˈviʒn]v.		为……提供所需物品
proximity	[prɔkˈsimiti]n.		邻近，接近
publicize	[ˈpʌblisaiz]v.		宣传，公布，引人注意
put off			推迟

Q

quantum	[ˈkwɔntəm]n.		量子，量子论
quarantine	[ˈkwɔrənti:n]n.		隔离，检疫
quaternary	[kwəˈtɜ:nəri]adj.		四进制的
qubit			量子比特
quest	[kwest]n.		追求，寻找

R

rack up			积累，击倒，获胜
radiologist	[ˌreidiˈɔlədʒist]n.		放射科医生，放射线研究者
rate	[reit]v.		评估，给……估价
ratify	[ˈrætifai]v.		批准，认可
recast	[ˈri:kɑ:st]v.		重铸，改写
recondite	[riˈkɔndait]adj.		深奥的
recurrent	[riˈkʌrənt]adj.		循环的
recursive	[riˈkɜ:siv]adj.		循环的
redundancy	[riˈdʌndənsi]n.		冗余，冗余度，过多，过剩，冗长
refactoring	[riˈfæktəriŋ]n.		重构
refer to			指的是，参考，涉及
reference model			参考模型
referral	[riˈfɜ:rəl]n.		推荐，引荐来源(指给某个网站带来了流量的其他网站)
regardless	[riˈgɑ:dləs]adv.		不管怎样，无论如何
regression test			回归测试
rehash	[ˈri:hæʃ]v.		事后反复回想(或讨论)
reimburse	[ˌri:imˈbɜ:s]v.		偿还，向……付还，报销(所花的费用)
remote control			遥控，远程控制，遥控装置
render	[ˈrendə]v.		着色，致使，提出
repeating group			重复组
repository	[riˈpɔzitəri]n.		仓库
resent	[riˈzent]v.		憎恶，怨恨
reside	[riˈzaid]v.		居住
resistive	[riˈzistiv]adj.		抗(耐、防)……的，电阻的

273

respective	[ris'pektiv]*adj.*	各自的,分别的
responsive	[ri'spɔnsiv]*adj.*	反应迅速的,积极响应的
restock	[ˌriː'stɔk]*v.*	补充(货源)
result from		由……引起
retouch	[ˌriː'tʌtʃ, 'riːtʌtʃ]*v.*	修描(底片等)
reveal	[ri'viːl]*v.*	显示,透露,揭露
review	[ri'vjuː]*n.*	评论
revolve around		以……为中心
rewire	[riː'waiə]*v.*	重接电线
right up until		一直到
rightly	['raitli]*adv.*	确实地
rigidity	[ri'dʒidəti]*n.*	严格
ring up		把(售货金额)记入现金收入记录机,给……打电话
roam	[rəum]*v.*	漫游
route	[ruːt]*v.*	按某路线发送,给……规定路线(次序,程序)
rug	[rʌg]*n.*	小地毯,垫子
run out of		用光,用完

S

saturated	['sætʃəreitid]*adj.*	饱和的,充满的
scale	[skeil]*n.*	磅秤
scale down		缩小
scale up		增加
scaled-down		缩小比例的
scam	[skæm]*n.*	阴谋,诡计,(尤指)欺诈,骗局
scary	['skeəri]*adj.*	(事物)可怕的,引起惊慌的
schema	['skiːmə]*n.*	模式
scheme	[skiːm]*n.*	方案,计划,设计图
scour	['skauə(r)]*v.*	(彻底地)搜寻,搜查
scramble	['skræmbl]*v.*	把……搅乱,使混杂
script	[skript]*n.*	脚本
scrupulous	['skruːpjələs]*adj.*	仔细的,细致的
sedentary	['sedntri]*adj.*	需要久坐的,惯于久坐不动的
seemingly	['siːmiŋli]*adv.*	貌似,表面上
selfie	['selfi]*n.*	自拍照(尤指那些自拍后上传到社交网站的照片)
semantic	[si'mæntik]*adj.*	语义的

sensationalize	[senˈseiʃənˌlaiz]v.	加以渲染,使耸人听闻
serve as		充当,担任,为
session	[ˈseʃn]n.	会话,会议
shed light on		阐明,解释
sheer	[ʃiə]adj.	绝对的,完全的,透明的
shortcut	[ˈʃɔːtkʌt]n.	快捷方式,捷径
shortened form		简称,简写
side effect		副作用,意外的连带后果
siege	[siːdʒ]n.	围城,围攻
sift through		筛选,通过
sign up		注册
signify	[ˈsignifai]v.	表示,说明
slate	[sleit]n.	石板,板岩
slingshot	[ˈsliŋʃɔt]n.	弹弓
smooth	[smuːð]adj.	顺利的,光滑的,平稳的
snail	[sneil]n.	蜗牛,行动迟缓的人或物
snap	[snæp]v.	给……拍快照,快摄(照片)
sniff	[snif]v.	嗅
snippet	[ˈsnipit]n.	片断
snoop	[snuːp]v.	窥探,偷窃
snowplow	[ˈsnəuplau]n.	雪犁,扫雪机,犁雪机(等于 snowplough)
so that		如此说来,这样的话,那样的话
social aspect		社会要素,社会层面
solace	[ˈsɔləs]n.	慰藉,给以安慰的人(或事物)
soldering iron		烙铁,焊铁
solid-state		固态的
sophistication	[səˌfistiˈkeiʃn]n.	(技术、产品等的)复杂性,精密性,尖端性
spacer	[ˈspeisə]n.	垫片,隔圈,隔离物,衬垫
spawn	[spɔːn]v.	大量产生,造成,引发,引起
spearhead	[ˈspiəˌhed]v.	当……的先锋,带头
specs	[speks]n.	说明,规格(spec 的名词复数),规范
spike	[spaik]n.	猛增
spin up		启动
spit out		吐出……,愤怒地说
split a check		付账的时候几个人分账单
spoilage	[ˈspɔilidʒ]n.	(食物的)变质,腐败
spontaneously	[spɔnˈteiniəsli]adv.	自发地,自然地

spoof	[spu:f] v.	欺骗
spot	[spɒt] v.	发现,准确地定出……的位置
sprint	[sprint] n.	冲刺
spur	[spɜː(r)] v.	促进,加速
staging area		临时数据交换区
stalwart	[ˈstɔːlwət] adj.	健壮的,强壮的
stamp	[stæmp] n.	印章,戳记
stand for		代表
stand-alone		(计算机)独立的
staple	[ˈsteipl] n.	主要产品,日常必需品
start of		出发,动身
start-up		启动,新成立的企业,创业者
starter	[ˈstɑːtə(r)] n.	起始者,初学者
stem from		出自,来源于,发生于
step on		踩上……,踏上……
stick around		呆在原处(等待)
stock options		职工优先认股权,在指定时期内定价定额购股权(stock option 的名词复数),购股选择权
storefront	[ˈstɔːfrʌnt] n.	网上店铺,虚拟店面
stream	[striːm] v.	流,流动
strikingly	[ˈstraikiŋli] adv.	显著地,突出地
stuffed	[stʌft] adj.	充满的,饱的
subscriber	[səbˈskraibə] n.	订户,签署者,捐献者
subscription	[səbˈskripʃən] n.	(报刊等的)订阅费
successor	[səkˈsesə] n.	后继者,后续的事物
succumb to		屈服于,屈从于
superposition	[ˌsjuːpəpəˈziʃən] n.	重叠
surefire	[ʃuəˈfaiə] adj.	准不会有错的,一定成功的
survey	[sɜːˈvei, ˈsɜːvei, sə-] n.	民意调查,民意测验,抽样调查
synchronize	[ˈsiŋkrənaiz] v.	同步,同时发生
synonymous	[siˈnɒniməs] adj.	同义的

T

Tablet PC		平板电脑,平板型计算机
tabular	[ˈtæbjələ(r)] adj.	列成表格的
tailor	[ˈteilə] v.	(为某一特定目的而)剪裁,制作
take advantage of		利用
take for granted		理所当然的

take forms		采取形式
take into account		考虑
take the form of		表现为……的形式,采取……的形状
take turn		轮流
tamper with		篡改,干预,损害
tap into		利用,开发
tap-to-call		点击呼叫
task	[tɑːsk] v.	派给某人(任务)
tell	[tel] v.	辨别,断定
teller	[ˈtelə(r)] n.	(银行的)出纳,出纳员
terabit	[ˈterəbit] n.	兆兆位,万亿比特
text box		正文框
textbook	[ˈtekstbuk] adj.	经典的,合乎规范的
thanks to		幸亏,多亏,由于
the point is		问题在于
thermostat	[ˈθɜːməstæt] n.	温度自动调节器,恒温器
think of as		把……看作,被认为是
throughout	[θruːˈaut] prep.	遍及
thwart	[θwɔːt] v.	挫败,反对
tile	[tail] n.	平铺
time-critical		时间敏感的,时序要求严格的
time-to-value		价值转换
tinker with		胡乱地修补,鼓捣
to this end		为此
token ring		令牌环
transcribe	[trænˈskraib] v.	改编,转录,抄写
transitive	[ˈtrænsətiv] adj.	传递的,过渡的,可传递的
travel	[ˈtrævl] v.	传送,移动,旅行
trick	[trik] v.	哄骗,欺诈
Trojan	[ˈtrəudʒən] n.	木马病毒
try out		试验,尝试
tsunami	[tsuˈnɑːmi] n.	海啸
tumble	[ˈtʌmbl] v.	(价格或数量)暴跌,骤降,使倒下
tune	[tjuːn] v.	(使)协调
twisted-pair		双绞线
typology	[taiˈpɔlədʒi] n.	分类法,类型学

U

ubiquity	[juːˈbkwəti] n.	无所不在,随处可见

Ultrabook		超薄笔记本电脑
uncontested	[ˌʌnkənˈtestid]adj.	无争议的，无人反对的
uncrackable	[ʌnˈkrækəbl]adj.	不可破解的
under the radar		避开别人关注的行为，低调处理
under wraps		保密，秘而不宣（常指待日后宣布）
underlie	[ˌundərˈlie]v.	构成……的基础，位于……之下
underlying	[ʌndəˈlaiiŋ]adj.	基础的，根本的，在下面的
unprecedented	[ʌnˈpresidentid]adj.	前所未有的，空前的，没有先例的
unveil	[ʌnˈveil]v.	公布
unwittingly	[ʌnˈwitiŋli]adv.	不经意地
up front		在前面
up to date		拥有（或包含）最新信息的
up with		比得上，接近
up-front		预付的
user profile		（在网络或布告牌环境下的）用户简介
utility	[juːˈtiləti]n.	（用于帮助查故障的）工具，实用程序（＝utility program），公用事业，公用事业公司

V

vandalism	[ˈvændəlizəm]n.	故意破坏公共财物的行为，恣意毁坏他人财产的行为
vein	[vein]n.	矿脉，特色，风格
velocity	[viˈlɔsiti]n.	速率，迅速，周转率
veracity	[vəˈræsəti]n.	精确性，诚实
vertices	[ˈvɜːtisiːz]n.	（三角形或锥形的）角顶，顶点，至高点（vertex 的复数）
via	[ˈvaiə]prep.	经由，经过，取道
view	[vjuː]n.	视图
viral	[ˈvairəl]adj.	病毒的，病毒性的，病毒引起的
viral exploits		病毒攻击
virtually	[ˈvɜːtʃuəli]adv.	事实上，实质上
virus signature		病毒识别码，病毒特征值
vitality	[vaiˈtæləti]n.	生命力，活力，热情
vomit	[ˈvɔmit]n.	呕吐

W

wafer	[ˈweifə(r)]n.	薄片，圆片，晶片
walk-out		退席

wear	['wɛə] n.	磨损, 损耗, 损耗量
Web crawler		网络爬虫, 爬网程序
weed out		从……删除不好的部分, 删去
well-defined		定义明确的, 清晰的
whopping	['wɔpiŋ] adj.	巨大的, 很大的
wipe out		摧毁, 毁灭
wire	['waiə] v.	将……联入(计算机网络)
wiretap	['waiətæp] n.	窃听装置, 窃听
with... in mind		把……放在心上, 以……为目的
with regard to		关于, 对于
without you knowing		在不了解你的情况下
wittingly	['witiŋli] adv.	有意地
word line		字线
word-of-mouth		口头的, 口述的
work as		充当, 担任
work out		完成, 得到(解决方法)
work through		解决, 完成, 干完
work-in-progress		半成品(价值), 在制品(完成部分生产程序)
worm	[wə:m] n.	"蠕虫"程序, 蠕虫病毒, 蠕虫指令(指电脑病毒)
wreak havoc		给……造成混乱(或破坏)
write up		详细写出

Y

yard	[ja:d] n.	院子
zoom in		拉近, 放大

Abbreviations

A

API	Application Programming Interface	应用程序接口
ASCII	American Standard Code for Information Interchange	美国信息交换标准代码

C

CAD	Computer Aided Design	计算机辅助设计
CSS	Cascading Style Sheets	级联样式表

D

DVD	Digital Video Dis	数字化视频光盘

E

EBCDIC	Extended Binary-Coded Decimal Interchange Code	扩充的二进制编码的十进制交换码
EDVAC	Electronic Discrete Variable Automatic Computer	离散变量自动电子计算机

F

FTP	File Transfer Protocol	文件传输协议

G

Gig	Gigabyte	千兆字节（GB）
GIMP	GNU Image Manipulation Program	GNU 图像处理程序
GPS	Global Positioning System	全球定位系统
GPU	Graphics Processing Unit	图形处理器

H

HD	High Definition	高分辨率
HTML	Hypertext Markup Language	超文本标记语言

I

IEEE	Institute of Electrical and Electronic Engineers	电器和电子工程师学会
IMP	Interface Message Processor	接口报文处理器

INWG	International Network Working Group	国际互联网工作组
IP	Internet Protocol	互联网协议
ISO	International Organization for Standardization	国际标准化组织
ISP	Internet Service Provider	因特网服务商

L

| LAN | Local Area Network | 局域网,局部区域网,局域网路 |
| WAN | Wide Area Network | 广域网 |

M

malware	malicious software	恶意软件
MAN	Metropolitan Area Network	城域网
MRI	Magnetic Resonance Imaging	核磁共振成像

N

| NFC | Near Field Communication | 近场通信 |

O

| OSI | Open Systems Interconnection | 开放系统互连 |

P

| PIN | Personal Identification Number | 个人识别密码 |

Q

| QR | Quick Response | 快速反应(QR code 是二维码的一种) |

R

RAM	Random Access Memory	随机存取存储器
RFID	Radio Frequency Identification	无线射频识别
ROM	Read Only Memory	只读存储器
RUP	Rational Unified Process	统一过程模型

S

SMS	Short Message Service	短信服务
SSD	Solid State Drive	固态硬盘
SSL	Secure Sockets Layer	安全套接层

T

TCP	Transmission Control Protocol	传输控制协议

U

UI	User Interface	用户界面
UML	Unified Modeling Language	统一建模语言
UPC	Universal Product Code	商品通用条码（扫描后可结账、盘存货物等）
URL	Uniform Resource Locator	统一资源定位器

V

vs.	versus	相对照，相对立

W

W3C	World Wide Web Consortium	万维网联合会

Answers

Unit 1

Part 1 Reading and Translating

Section A

Ⅰ. 1. F   2. F   3. F   4. T   5. T
Ⅱ. 1. B   2. D   3. D
Ⅲ. 1. e   2. b   3. d   4. c   5. a
Ⅳ.
1. sent   2. enforcement   3. stored   4. owns   5. officials
6. sought   7. notified   8. continuous 9. viewing   10. secretly

Ⅴ. 云计算

随着对于计算资源需求的日益增加，很多公司也许会发现利用外界的计算资源比自己内部构建新的计算能力更加经济。云计算作为一种前沿科技，就提供了这样灵活而又丰富的在线计算功能。它是一项因特网的服务，旨在为广大计算机用户提供计算需求。例如，身处（美国）加州的某个雇员在白天可以使用（法国）巴黎的某个办公室（晚上关门）中的网络系统。当一家公司使用这种计算资源的时候，他们会基于所消耗的计算时间和其他资源支付一定的费用，就如同消费者基于他们使用多少度电而向公用公司（如电力公司）支付费用一样。云计算可允许某家公司多样化其网络和服务器的基础设施。某些云计算服务会根据对网站的服务需求的增加而自动给公司的网站添加更多的网络和服务器的功能。网络和服务器的功能可以在世界各地都被复制，以便一台服务器的故障并不会影响到公司的运营。

Section B

Ⅰ. 1. F   2. F   3. F   4. F   5. T
Ⅱ. 1. C   2. D   3. C
Ⅲ. 1. e   2. d   3. c   4. a   5. b
Ⅳ.
1. brought   2. efficiency   3. developing   4. accessible   5. implanted
6. Agricultural 7. disadvantage 8. higher   9. exporting   10. Awareness

Ⅴ. 物联网(IoT)将如何影响我们的日常生活？

物联网(IoT)将如何影响我们日常生活的几乎每一个方面是一个有趣的话题。我们已经看到带有嵌入式互联网连接的技术，在如汽车、建筑物中出现了，而这更多的是为了开发设备之间、设备与用户之间的对话功能。虽然现在大多数物联网的应用主要集中在信息和娱乐上，但我们可以大胆地预测物联网将带来安全领域的重大突破，因为借助物联网，汽车可以变得更加聪明，通过与其他汽车和周围环境的不断的对话，它们不但能够避免交通拥堵，而且能够避免交通事故。

Part 3 Listening and Speaking

Listening Comprehension

1.（B）   2.（C）   3.（B）

Original
Quantum Computer

Silicon electronics are a staple of the computing industry, but researchers are now exploring other techniques to deliver powerful computers. Where a classical computer obeys the well understood laws of classical physics, a quantum computer is a device that harnesses physical phenomenon unique to quantum mechanics to realize a fundamentally new mode of information processing. In a quantum computer data is not processed by electrons passing through transistors, as is the case in today's computers, but by caged atoms known as qubits.

A bit is a simple unit of information that is classically represented by a "1" or a "0" in a conventional electronic computer. In a quantum computer, the fundamental unit of information is not binary but rather more quaternary in nature. A qubit can exist not only in a state corresponding to the logical state 0 or 1 as in a classical bit, but also in states corresponding to a blend or superposition of these classical states. In other words, a qubit can exist as 0, 1, or simultaneously as both 0 and 1, with a numerical coefficient representing the probability for each state.

If large-scale quantum computers can be built, they will be able to solve certain problems much faster than any of our current classical computers, particularly for solving problems with a large amount of data or variables such as searching vast databases, creating uncrackable ciphers or simulating the atomic structures of substances.

Although quantum computing is still in its infancy, experiments have been carried out in which quantum computational operations were executed on a very small number of qubits. Both practical and theoretical research continues with interest and support by many national government and military funding agencies. Professor Artur Ekert of the University of Oxford, best known as one of the inventors of quantum cryptography, believes that quantum computing will eventually *come of age*.

Dictation

1. 20th century   2. citizen   3. mathematical   4. early development   5. career
6. stored   7. memory   8. operate   9. electronic   10. calculation
11. specific   12. manner   13. control unit   14. calculating unit   15. finding
16. a piece of data   17. accordingly   18. advancement   19. architecture   20. majority

Unit 2

Part 1   Reading and Translating

Section A

Ⅰ. 1. F   2. F   3. T   4. T   5. F
Ⅱ. 1. C   2. B   3. D
Ⅲ. 1. c   2. a   3. b   4. e   5. d
Ⅳ.
1. credited   2. influential   3. awarded   4. lifetime   5. microchip
6. recognized   7. miniature   8. developed   9. patented   10. legacy

Ⅴ. 为何智能手机需要使用双核处理器？

双核处理器可以赋予智能手机更强的性能,同时提高了电池续航能力。之所以出现这种局面,是因为智能手机在运行不同任务时有着迥异的性能需求,例如,写短信和玩 3D 游戏比起来就是如此。

在具有当今先进芯片制造工艺(如 28 纳米,1 纳米等于十亿分之一米)的前提下,为实现性能和供电的收放自如,使用多个较小的核要优于使用一个较大的单片核。有了双核处理器,智能手机可以在运行短信这样的任务时关闭一个核(以节省电力),而在需要最强性能的时候将两个核都打开。

Answers

Section B

Ⅰ. 1. F   2. F   3. F   4. T   5. F
Ⅱ. 1. C   2. D   3. D
Ⅲ. 1. d   2. c   3. e   4. b   5. a
Ⅳ.
1. located   2. built   3. Bankers   4. Shorter   5. paying
6. Says   7. computing   8. central   9. announced   10. Instead

Ⅴ. 缓存

将计算机中的内存设置与它们的功能相比照是有益处的。寄存器被用来存储手头上立即执行的数据；主存用于存储在不久远的将来可能会被用到的数据；而海量存储器则被用来存储在不远的将来都不太可能会被用到的数据。许多机器都被设计成具有额外的内存级别，称为缓存。缓存是位于CPU之内的一小块快速内存(也许只有几百KB)。在这个特殊的内存空间里，机器尝试着去复制主存感兴趣的部分。通过这种设置，以往在寄存器和主存之间传输的很多数据被转变成了在寄存器和缓存之间进行传输。这种做法的结果就是CPU可以更快地执行指令，因为它无须再被与主存的通信延迟所拖累。

Part 3   Listening and Speaking

Listening Comprehension

1.（B）   2.（D）   3.（C）

Original

Moore's Law

In 1965, Gordon Moore, the co-founder of Intel observed that the number of transistors per square inch on chips had doubled every two years since the integrated circuit was invented. He then made a now-famous prediction—that this doubling trend would continue for at least 10 more years. Here we are, close to 50 years later, and transistor density still doubles about every 18 months. Due to technological breakthroughs, Moore's Law has been maintained for far longer than the original prediction and most experts, including Moore himself, expect the doubling trend to continue for at least another decade. In fact, Intel states that the mission of its technology development team is to continue to break barriers to Moore's Law.

Interestingly, other computer components also follow Moore's. Law, For example, storage capacity doubles approximately every 20 months, and chip speed doubles about every 24 months. Consequently, the term Moore's Law has been expanded and is now used to describe the amount of time it takes components to double in capacity or speed. Many experts predict that, eventually, a physical limit to the number of transistors that can be crammed onto a chip will end Moore's Law for current CPU technology. But new technology is being developed all the time and so the end of Moore's Law is not yet in sight.

Dictation

1. monitor   2. jet   3. maintenance   4. had   5. reset
6. determined   7. infrastructure   8. magnetic   9. measure   10. traffic
11. portable   12. highways   13. aviation   14. alert   15. forces
16. drones   17. fault   18. major   19. crucial   20. activate

Unit 3

Part 1 Reading and Translating

Section A

Ⅰ. 1. F   2. F   3. T   4. T   5. F
Ⅱ. 1. C   2. C   3. D
Ⅲ. 1. b   2. d   3. e   4. c   5. a
Ⅳ.
1. introduced   2. free   3. offshoot   4. performed   5. programmed
6. reason   7. features   8. market   9. licensing   10. source

Ⅴ. 学校应该如何处理互联网抄袭？

某位高中教师挂掉了28个借助互联网抄袭或复制素材的学生。迫于家长的压力，学校董事会改判这些学生通过该课程，并且该教师也因此辞职。文字处理软件和互联网的存在使得抄袭变得空前容易。学生们可以访问CheatHouse.com或Research Papers Online这样的学期论文网站，抄袭各类主题的完整论文。据某次调查显示，参与调查者有半数认为从长远来看，抄袭"并无大碍或可能并无大碍"，并且有60%表示自己曾经有过抄袭行为。有抄袭行为的学生将此归咎于同侪压力，同学竞争，某些作业属于"没事找事"，以及互联网上充斥着（对抄袭）的放任态度。也有一些反抄袭工具可供老师们使用，其中包含若干基于互联网的服务，比如Turnitin，该工具可以将可疑论文与网上找到的论文进行对比，并生成一份Originality Report（原创度报告），标记出那些可能是复制而来的文本。不过，一些老师不愿调查学生是否诚实创作，而这可能会毁掉学生的学术生涯。

Section B

Ⅰ. 1. F   2. F   3. F   4. F   5. T
Ⅱ. 1. C   2. A   3. D
Ⅲ. 1. e   2. d   3. a   4. b   5. c
Ⅳ.
1. projects   2. marketed   3. dimensionality   4. sensory   5. recently
6. technologies   7. being   8. feelings   9. found   10. imagined

Ⅴ. 跨平台软件

典型的应用程序必须依赖于操作系统来执行其任务。它可能需要窗口管理器的服务与计算机用户通信，或者它可能使用文件管理器检索海量存储数据。可惜的是，不同的操作系统强行规定了以不同的方式对这些服务的请求。因此，对于通过不同的机器设计和不同的操作系统的网络和因特网传输和执行的程序，它们必须是不依赖于特定操作系统和机器的。术语"跨平台"就是用来反映这一附加级别的独立性的。也就是说，跨平台软件是独立于操作系统设计和机器硬件设计的，因此它在网络中是可执行的。

Part 3 Listening and Speaking

Listening Comprehension

1.（B）   2.（B）   3.（D）

Original

Integrated Development Environment（IDE）

Abbreviated as IDE, Integrated Development Environment is a programming environment integrated into a software application that provides comprehensive facilities to computer programmers for software development. An IDE normally consists of a source code editor，a compiler and/or interpreter，build automation tools，and usually a debugger.

The aim of IDE is to abstract the **configuration necessary** to piece together command line utilities in a **cohesive** unit, which theoretically reduces the time to learn a language, and increases developer productivity. For example, code can be compiled while being written, providing instant feedback on syntax errors.

IDEs initially became necessary when doing development in front of a console or terminal. Early languages did not have one, since they were prepared using flowcharts, coding forms, and keypunches before being submitted to a compiler. Dartmouth BASIC was the first language to be created with an IDE. Its IDE was command-based, and therefore did not look much like the menu-driven, graphical IDEs of today. However, it seamlessly integrated editing, file management, compilation, debugging and execution in the manner **characteristic** of a modern IDE.

Microsoft Visual Studio, Delphi, JBuilder, Eclipse, and NetBeans are all well-known examples of IDEs in the world today.

Dictation

1. primarily	2. selection	3. suite	4. free	5. instead of
6. editing	7. commercial	8. require	9. benefits	10. stability
11. risks	12. lack	13. compatibility	14. acceptance	15. feel
16. gathering	17. recent	18. view	19. innovation	20. popularity

Unit 4

Part 1 Reading and Translating

Section A

Ⅰ. 1. T   2. T   3. F   4. F   5. F
Ⅱ. 1. D   2. D   3. C
Ⅲ. 1. b   2. c   3. d   4. e   5. a
Ⅳ.
1. While   2. typically   3. versions   4. specifically   5. However
6. run   7. designed   8. cameras   9. considering   10. used

Ⅴ. 微软的任务管理器

可以通过执行一个叫作任务管理器的实用程序(同时按住 Ctrl、Alt 和 Delete 键)来监视 Windows 操作系统中的一些内部活动。例如,通过选择任务管理器窗口中的进程标签,可以浏览进程表。以下是一个可以做的实验:在启动任何应用程序前看一下进程表。(用户也许会惊讶进程表中已经有如此多的进程。这是操作系统维持基本功能的必要进程)之后打开一个程序,并确认进程表中出现了这个程序对应的进程。还可以查看进程被分配了多少内存。

Section B

Ⅰ. 1. F   2. T   3. F   4. F   5. F
Ⅱ. 1. C   2. D   3. D
Ⅲ. 1. b   2. a   3. e   4. c   5. d
Ⅳ.
1. separates   2. hinder   3. Supporters   4. developers   5. programmers
6. known   7. variants   8. creative   9. viruses   10. closed

Ⅴ. 多核操作系统

传统的分时/多任务系统给人一种计算机可以同时运行多个进程的假象,然而它们只是通过在人们无法察觉的速度下快速地切换任务。现代系统延续了这一做法,但最新的多核 CPU 确实能够同时运行两个、四个或更多的进程。与一组单核的计算机一起工作不同，多核计算机包含多个独立的处理器（在这种情况下称为核）来共享计算机的外围设备、内存，以及其他资源。对于多核操作系统，这意味着调度程序必须考虑每个核上执行哪些进程。在不同核上运行不同的进程时，解决多进程之间的竞争变得更具有挑战性，因为当一个进程需要进入一个关键的区域时，停止所有核上的中断会显得十分低效。于是计算机科学目前有很多活跃的研究领域是关于如何更好地建立适应多核世界的操作系统机制的。

Part 3　Listening and Speaking

Listening Comprehension

1．（B）　　　　2．（A）　　　　3．（C）

Original

Android

Android is a Linux-based operating system developed by the Open Handset Alliance, a group that includes Google and more than 30 technology and mobile companies. The most widely used mobile operating system in the world, Android was built from the ground **up with** current mobile device capability **in mind**, which enables developers to create mobile applications that take full advantage of all the features a mobile device has to offer. It is an open platform, so anyone can download and use Android, although hardware manufacturers must **adhere to** certain specifications in order to be called "Android compatible." A variety of manufacturers produce devices that run the Android operating system, adding their own interface elements and bundled software. As a result, an Android smartphone manufactured by Samsung may have different user interface features from one manufactured by Google.

Features unique to recent versions of the Android operating system include the following:

* Google Play app store provides access to apps, songs, books, and movies.
* Google Drive provides access to email, contacts, calendar, photos, files, and more.
* Face recognition or fingerprint scanner can unlock the device.
* Share contacts and other information by touching two devices together (using NFC technology).
* Speech output assists users with vision impairments.
* Voice recognition capability enables users to speak instructions.
* Built-in heart rate monitor works with phone apps.

Dictation

1．based　　　　2．version　　　　3．kernel　　　　4．offered　　　　5．copied
6．eventually　　7．release　　　　8．Instead　　　　9．freely　　　　10．modify
11．known　　　12．popular　　　13．creation　　　14．penguin　　　15．Silicon Valley
16．merged　　　17．wealthy　　　18．donated　　　19．grateful　　　20．maintains

Unit 5

Part 1　Reading and Translating

Section A

Ⅰ．1．T　　　　2．F　　　　3．F　　　　4．F　　　　5．F
Ⅱ．1．D　　　　2．C　　　　3．D
Ⅲ．1．e　　　　2．b　　　　3．c　　　　4．a　　　　5．d
Ⅳ．
　　1．founded　　　2．seniors　　　3．programming　　　4．acquired　　　5．creating

| | 6. required | 7. described | 8. fully | 9. reusable | 10. texting |

Ⅴ．可编程的智能手机

用于手持、移动和嵌入式设备的软件通常由在其他环境下所使用的相同的通用编程语言开发出来。随着智能手机有了更大的键盘和额外的许可，有些应用程序甚至可以使用智能手机自身来开发。然而，在大多数情况下，智能手机软件一般会在台式计算机上使用专门的软件系统进行开发，这个专门的软件系统能够提供编辑、翻译和测试智能手机软件的工具。简单的应用程序通常用 Java、C++ 和 C# 进行编写。但是，编写更复杂的应用程序或核心系统软件可能需要并发和事件驱动编程的额外支持。

Section B

Ⅰ． 1. T　　2. T　　3. T　　4. F　　5. F
Ⅱ． 1. B　　2. C　　3. D
Ⅲ． 1. e　　2. a　　3. c　　4. d　　5. b
Ⅳ．
1. tasked　　2. making　　3. looks　　4. applied　　5. plumbing
6. submitted　　7. changes　　8. goes　　9. losing　　10. done

Ⅴ．编程语言的文化

正如自然语言一样，不同的编程语言的用户往往也会显现出文化的差异，他们时常会仔细考虑其观点的价值。有时候这些差异值得注意，例如，正如当涉及到不同的编程范式的时候。但在另一些时候，这些差异却又有些微妙了。举个例子来说，过程和函数的主题是不同的，但 C 语言开发者却将二者都看作是函数。这是因为 C 语言程序中的过程往往被看作没有返回值的函数。另外一个类似的例子是 C++ 语言的开发者将对象内的过程看作成员函数，然而对应的通用术语却是方法。这种差异可以追踪到这样一个事实，即 C++ 语言是作为 C 语言的延伸发展而来的。另一个文化差异就是，用 Ada 语言编写的程序通常是用保留字（或者大写，或者黑体）进行排版的——这是一种 C、C++、C#、FORTRAN 或 Java 等语言的用户没有广泛实施的传统。

Part 3　Listening and Speaking

Listening Comprehension

1.（A）　　2.（D）　　3.（B）

Original

Writing the Code

So far, the skills we have learned helped us to understand the customers and users' problem and to devise a high-level solution for it. Now, we must focus on implementing the solution as software. That is, we must write the programs that implement the design. This task can be daunting, for several reasons.

First, the designers may not have addressed all of the characteristics of the platform and programming environment; structures and relationships that are easy to describe with charts and tables are not always straightforward to write as code.

Second, we must write our code in a way that is understandable not only to us when we revisit for testing, but also to others as the system evolves over time. In the real world, most software is developed by teams, and a variety of jobs are required to generate a quality product. Even when writing the code itself, many people are usually involved, and a great deal of cooperation and coordination is required. Thus, it is very important for others to be able to understand not only what you have written, but also why you have written it and how it **fits in with** their work. To be a truly excellent programmer, you must know that programming is communicating with other programmers first and communicating with the computer second.

Third, we must take advantage of the characteristics of the design's organization, the data's structure, and the programming language's constructs while still creating code that is easily reusable. The most critical standard is the need for a direct correspondence between the program design components and the program code components. The entire design process is of little value if the design's modularity is not carried forward into the code. Design characteristics, such as low coupling, high cohesion, and well-defined interfaces, should also be program characteristics, so that the algorithms, functions, interfaces, and data structures can be traced easily from design to code and back again. In case of requirements changing, they are made first to the high-level design and then are traced through lower design levels to the code that must be modified.

Although much of coding is an individual endeavor, all of coding must be done with your team in mind. Your use of information hiding allows you to reveal only the essential information about your components so that your colleagues can invoke them or reuse them. Your use of standards enhances communication among team members. And your use of common design techniques and strategies makes your code easier to test, maintain, and reuse. No matter which programming language to be used, and no matter how the code to be worked out, you should keep some of the software engineering practices above in mind as you write your code.

Dictation

1. fast-paced	2. Market	3. evolve	4. emerge	5. enough
6. business	7. Initially	8. lightweight	9. people-centric	10. Alliance
11. statement	12. interactions	13. documentation	14. customer	15. responding
16. prior	17. Extreme	18. Adaptive	19. Feature	20. Dynamic

Unit 6

Part 1 Reading and Translating

Section A

Ⅰ. 1. F   2. F   3. F   4. T   5. F

Ⅱ. 1. B   2. C   3. A

Ⅲ. 1. a   2. e   3. d   4. b   5. c

Ⅳ.
1. complexity   2. subscriptions   3. inventories   4. analysis   5. approximately
6. launched   7. called   8. tracking   9. consisting   10. libraries

Ⅴ. 个人计算机的数据库系统

个人计算机被广泛应用在各种从基础到复杂的应用程序中。在基础的"数据库"应用中，如存储圣诞贺卡列表或维护保龄球联赛的数据记录，电子表格系统常常可以代替数据库软件，因为这类应用仅仅需要存储、打印和排序数据的功能。不过在 PC 市场中，会有一些真正意义上的数据库系统，微软公司的 Access 就是其中之一。这是一个完整的关系数据库系统，以及图表和报表生成软件。它提供了一个极好的例子，即在本文中所呈现的原则是如何构成当前市场上流行产品的支柱的。

Section B

Ⅰ. 1. F   2. F   3. T   4. T   5. T

Ⅱ. 1. D   2. D   3. B

Ⅲ. 1. d   2. e   3. c   4. b   5. a

Ⅳ.
1. designed   2. inconsistencies   3. pinpoint   4. competitive   5. targeting

6. mined   7. buying   8. concerned   9. costs   10. changes

Ⅴ．分布式数据库

随着网络功能的发展，数据库系统已发展到包括分布式数据库，分布式数据库一般是指将数据分布在多台机器上。例如，一家国际公司可能会在本地站点存储和维护本地雇员记录，但经由网络可将那些记录连接，以创建一个单独的分布式数据库。

分布式数据库可以包含碎片式和/或被复制的数据。第一种情况以稍前的雇员记录的例子举例证明，数据库中的不同片段被存储在不同的位置。在第二种情况下，相同的数据库成分的副本被存储在不同的位置。这样的副本可以提高信息检索的效率。这两种情况都产生了在更传统的集中式数据库中没有出现的问题——如何掩盖数据库的分布式特性，使其充当一个连贯的系统？或者说如何保证数据库副本部分之间的更新保持同步。所以，分布式数据库是当前的研究领域。

Part 3　Listening and Speaking

Listening Comprehension

1.（B）　　　　2.（C）　　　　3.（A）

Original

Data Mining

　　Data mining, or knowledge discovery, is the computer-assisted process of analyzing enormous sets of data and then extracting it into useful information. Data mining tools predict behaviors and future trends, supporting to make proactive, knowledge-driven decisions.

　　Data mining derives its name from the similarities between searching for valuable information in a large database and mining a mountain for a vein of valuable ore. Both processes require either sifting through an immense amount of material, or intelligently probing it to find where the value resides.

　　Data mining is primarily used today by companies with a strong consumer focus. Data mining can help spot sales trends, develop smarter marketing campaigns, and accurately predict customer loyalty. For example, one grocery chain in the U.S. used the data mining capacity of Oracle software to analyze local buying patterns. They discovered that when men bought diapers on Thursdays and Saturdays, they also tended to buy beer. Further analysis showed that these shoppers typically did their weekly grocery shopping on Saturdays. On Thursdays, however, they only bought a few items. The retailer concluded that they purchased the beer for the upcoming weekend. Using this newly discovered information, the grocery chain could move the beer display closer to the diaper display and make sure beer and diapers were sold at full price on Thursdays to increase revenue.

　　Although data mining is a relatively new term, the technology is not. For many years, businesses have used powerful computers to sift through volumes of data such as supermarket scanner data to produce market research reports. In recent years, data mining has also been widely used in a wide range of industries, such as genetics, medicine, education, and electrical power engineering.

Dictation

1. universally   2. date back   3. real-life   4. collection   5. central
6. distributed   7. access   8. facilitate   9. definition   10. transform
11. architectural   12. operational   13. decision support   14. address   15. high costs
16. databases   17. enterprise   18. present   19. trends   20. accomplish

Unit 7

Part 1　Reading and Translating

Section A

Ⅰ. 1. F　　2. F　　3. T　　4. F　　5. F
Ⅱ. 1. A　　2. D　　3. C
Ⅲ. 1. c　　2. a　　3. e　　4. b　　5. d
Ⅳ.
1. governing　　2. connected　　3. properly　　4. receiving　　5. built
6. called　　7. transmission　　8. used　　9. carries　　10. broken

Ⅴ. 以太网

以太网是使用总线拓扑结构实现局域网的一组标准。它的名字起源于最初的以太网设计,其中机器是通过同轴电缆(称为以太)连接。作为最初是在 20 世纪 70 年代开发,现在由 IEEE 标准化为 IEEE 802 标准族的一部分,以太网是个人计算机联网最常用的方法之一。事实上,以太网控制器已经成为了目前零售市场上个人计算机的标准组件。

今天实际上有多个版本的以太网,反映了技术的进步和更高的传输速率。然而所有以太网家族都有着一些共同特点,其中有数据打包进行传输的格式,使用曼彻斯特编码(一种用 0 表示一个下行信号,用 1 表示一个上升的信号的方法)进行实际的位传输,并利用 CSMA / CD 进行控制传送。

Section B

Ⅰ. 1. F　　2. T　　3. F　　4. T　　5. F
Ⅱ. 1. D　　2. B　　3. C
Ⅲ. 1. b　　2. d　　3. c　　4. a　　5. e
Ⅳ.
1. enables　　2. watching　　3. called　　4. embedded　　5. detects
6. determines　　7. turn　　8. directs　　9. provides　　10. referred

Ⅴ. 虚拟专用网络

虚拟专用网络(VPN)是一个通过公共网络(通常是互联网)传输的专有的、安全的网络,以允许验证用户专有性、安全访问公司的网络。例如,VPN 可以允许在外旅行的员工,商业伙伴,或者是在另一个子办公网点或是有公共无线网络连接的员工安全地通过互联网访问公司的网络。一个称作隧道的流程会被用于在互联网中传输信息,一些特殊的加密技术也会被用于保护数据,以使得其即便在传输过程中被截获也无法被理解。本质上,VPN 允许一个组织提供安全的远程连接以接入公司网络,而无需使用者在物理上到达公司的内部网络覆盖区域。

Part 3　Listening and Speaking

Listening Comprehension

1. (B)　　2. (D)　　3. (B)

Original

IPv6

Internet Protocol Version 6 is a new version of Internet Layer protocol for packet-switched internetworks which is designed to be an evolutionary step from IPv4.

IPv4 provides an addressing capability of about 4 billion addresses, which was deemed sufficient in the design stages of the early Internet when the explosive growth and world-wide distribution of networks were not anticipated. An escalating demand for IP addresses acted as the driving force behind the development of the large address space offered by the IPv6. According to industry estimates, in the wireless domain, more than a billion mobile phones, PDAs, and other wireless devices will require Internet access, and each will need its own unique IP address.

Consisting of 128 bits as compared to 32 bits in IPv4, IPv6 has a very large address space, which allows more flexibility in allocating addresses and routing traffic. It is now possible to support 2^{128} unique IP addresses. With this large address-space scheme, IPv6 has the capability to provide unique addresses to each and every device or node attached to the Internet, and eliminates the need to use techniques such as network address translation to avoid **running out of** the available address space.

Dictation

1. interface
2. protocol
3. routing
4. wireless
5. Technically
6. gateway
7. model
8. packets
9. forwards
10. output
11. configuration
12. traffic
13. unwanted
14. fundamentally
15. functionality
16. switching
17. initially
18. protection
19. firewall
20. directly

Unit 8

Part 1   Reading and Translating

Section A

Ⅰ. 1. F   2. F   3. T   4. T   5. T

Ⅱ. 1. C   2. B   3. B

Ⅲ. 1. e   2. d   3. a   4. b   5. c

Ⅳ.
1. common
2. online
3. activities
4. designate
5. confirmation
6. posts
7. celebrities
8. followers
9. contacts
10. professionally

Ⅴ. 在线社交网络

在线社交网络,也称为社交网站,是一些鼓励在线社区成员与其他注册用户分享其兴趣、想法、故事、照片、音乐和视频的站点。大多数社交网络包括聊天室、新闻组及其他的交流服务。流行的社交网站包括 LinkedIn 和 Facebook 等等,其中 Facebook 号称具有超过 25 亿的活跃用户。在一些社交网络站中,如 Second Life,用户可使用虚构的身份和其他用户在角色扮演类型的环境中进行互动。

媒体共享网站是一种特定类型的在线社交网络,它能够让会员共享如照片、音乐和视频等媒体。Flickr、Fotki 和 Webshots 都是十分流行的照片分享社区,PixelFish 和 YouTube 是十分流行的视频共享社区。

Section B

Ⅰ. 1. F   2. T   3. F   4. F   5. T

Ⅱ. 1. C   2. D   3. D

Ⅲ. 1. d   2. c   3. e   4. a   5. b

Ⅳ.
1. tremendously
2. using
3. resulting
4. called
5. faster
6. allowing
7. equally
8. associated
9. upgrading
10. designed

Ⅴ. Internet2

既然互联网已经从一个研究项目转向为一个家庭的商品,那么研究机构就继续进行一个名为 Internet2 的项目。Internet2 是一个纯粹的学术项目,涉及众多与工业界和政府共同合作的大学。其目标是研究在互联网应用中如何满足高带宽通信的需求,如昂贵的最先进设备(如望远镜和医疗诊断设备)的远程访问和控制。目前研究的一个例子是由机器人手实施的远程外科手术，机器人手可以模仿经由视频查看病人的远程外科医生的手。可以访问 http://www.internet2.org 了解更多关于 Internet2 的信息。

Part 3　Listening and Speaking

Listening Comprehension

1．(C)　　　　2．(B)　　　　3．(A)

Original

How a World-Shaking Technology Came About: Tim Berners-Lee Invents the World Wide Web

The son of British mathematicians employed on the team that built the early computer Manchester Mark I, Tim Berners-Lee was born in London and graduated from Oxford University's Queen's College, where he built a computer with a *soldering iron*.

In 1980, while an independent contractor at the Switzerland-based European Organization for Nuclear Research (CERN), Berners-Lee proposed a project based on the concept of hypertext (text with links, or references to other text), to facilitate sharing and updating information among researchers. With other researchers, he built a prototype system named Enquire.

After leaving CERN he took ideas similar to those used in Enquire to create what he then called the WorldWideWeb, for which he designed and built the first browser. The first Website, which appeared as http://info.cern.ch/ (still in operation under that name) and went online August 6, 1991, provided an explanation about what we now call the World Wide Web and how one could own a browser, set up a Web server, and so on.

In 1994 Berners-Lee founded the World Wide Web Consortium (W3C) at the Massachusetts Institute of Technology. It comprised various companies willing to create standards and recommendations to improve the quality of the Internet. It was not until 2000 and 2001 that popular browsers began to support this standard.

For his pioneering work, Berners-Lee was knighted by Queen Elizabeth II in 2004. In 2009 he was elected to the United States National Academy of Sciences in Washington, D.C.

Dictation

1. consist	2. operate	3. mixture	4. order	5. fetch
6. spider	7. automated	8. optimize	9. query	10. considerable
11. source	12. cache	13. holds	14. updated	15. terms
16. satisfying	17. returned	18. since	19. relevance	20. beyond

Unit 9

Part 1　Reading and Translating

Section A

Ⅰ．1．F　　　2．T　　　3．F　　　4．T　　　5．F

Ⅱ．1．C　　　2．D　　　3．D

Ⅲ．1．b　　　2．c　　　3．e　　　4．d　　　5．a

Ⅳ．
1．fighting　　2．willing　　3．making　　4．proudly　　5．comparing
6．simplify　　7．using　　8．found　　9．visited　　10．successful

Ⅴ. 在线使用我的信用卡安全吗？

网上购物者情有可原地担心，在电子商务交易过程中提供的个人信息和信用卡号码可能被劫持和被不当使用。许多购物者担心黑客可能使用数据包嗅探器截获在互联网中传输的信用卡号码信息。

为了保护你的信用卡的数据不被嗅探器非法获取，你应该只通过安全连接进行电子交易。安全连接会对你的计算机和网站之间传输的数据进行加密。即使黑客可以捕获包含支付数据的数据包，你的加密的信用卡号码实际上对于非法的意图是没用的。创建安全连接的技术包括 SSL/TLS 和 HTTPS 等。

Section B

Ⅰ. 1. F   2. F   3. F   4. F   5. T
Ⅱ. 1. C   2. C   3. D
Ⅲ. 1. a   2. e   3. b   4. c   5. d
Ⅳ.
1. converging   2. popularity   3. availability   4. significantly   5. ticketing
6. stored   7. purchasing   8. delivered   9. based   10. custom

Ⅴ. 社交工具对于当今网站有什么样的影响？

随着基于互联网企业数量的迅速增长，社交工具不过是另一种销售渠道。随着客户充分利用自己的网上影响力，直接从企业得到响应，社交渠道正在充当实时的客户服务平台。快速理会客户的企业可以利用这一趋势，来打造品牌的真实性和客户忠诚度。同样，疏于将社交工具纳入到业务中的企业，比起更注重社交的有能力的竞争者会冒着失去客户的风险。

因此，社交工具通过鼓励和激励企业透明度赋予消费者权力。因为这些社交渠道的不断成熟，保持透明度将成为企业战略日益重要的组成部分。今天为客户服务的交互是正确的，而且这将对今后更多公司的做法也是正确的。

Part 3   Listening and Speaking

Listening Comprehension

1.（B）   2.（D）   3.（C）

Original

Social Commerce

Social commerce—the use of social networking sites (such as Facebook, Twitter, and Pinterest) and other social media to promote online sales—is huge. At perhaps the simplest level, posts by individuals about buying products or Liking Facebook pages may influence their friends' purchases both online and offline. You can also buy gifts within Facebook for your friends and you can use a service such as SellPin to sell products on Pinterest. Businesses can create custom Amazon Pages and use Amazon Posts to put content on their Amazon and Facebook pages simultaneously, as well as place ads on social networking sites to generate traffic to their Web site or social media pages. Facebook also allows ads to be targeted to specific individuals, such as individuals in a specific geographical area who like cycling. To help determine relevant ads for each person, individual ads can be hidden by the user (and then different targeted ads appear in their place). A new feature is the ability to include downloadable apps in Facebook ads.

A more recent social commerce option includes offering goods and services for sale within social networking sites. Dubbed F-commerce and F-stores, the number of businesses and individuals selling real goods and real services inside Facebook is increasing. Products can either be sold directly within Facebook or the Facebook page can contain a link that brings the visitor to the appropriate Web page to purchase that item when the link is clicked.

Another impact of social media on ecommerce is the **social aspect**. In addition to the word-of-mouth effect, businesses can also harness social networking information located in an individual's social networking profile or Facebook page. And the use of social media monitoring companies and tools to analyze social media activity related to a particular business is a fast-growing market.

Dictation

1. individuals	2. mobile commerce	3. conjunction	4. movie	5. via
6. displayed	7. venue	8. purchased	9. loan	10. banking
11. emerging	12. typically	13. tablet	14. field	15. vendors
16. counter-free	17. personnel	18. checkout	19. due	20. guests

Unit 10

Part 1   Reading and Translating

Section A

Ⅰ. 1. T   2. T   3. F   4. T   5. T
Ⅱ. 1. C   2. D   3. D
Ⅲ. 1. e   2. c   3. a   4. b   5. d
Ⅳ.
　1. called   2. discovering   3. disclosing   4. properly   5. adopter
　6. submitting   7. paying   8. affecting   9. vulnerabilities   10. depending

Ⅴ. 为什么有些网站允许我使用 email 地址作为用户名？

　　没有两个用户可以拥有相同的 email 地址，也就是说，你的 email 地址是独一无二的。这意味着你可以使用你的某一个网站的 email 地址和密码，来验证另外一个网站你的身份。例如，Facebook、Google 和 Twitter 是 3 个能够为其他应用程序提供身份验证服务的流行网站。通过使用其中某个网站的 email 地址访问这些网站之外的其他网站，不必创建或记住单独的用户名和密码，就可访问各种网站。

Section B

Ⅰ. 1. F   2. T   3. F   4. T   5. T
Ⅱ. 1. C   2. D   3. D
Ⅲ. 1. a   2. b   3. d   4. c   5. e
Ⅳ.
　1. Taking   2. teaches   3. anonymous   4. deficient   5. helping
　6. gained   7. hacking   8. knowing   9. stopping   10. acquired

Ⅴ. 生物识别设备究竟有多火？

　　生物识别设备在安全领域最近获得了很大的成功，因为它们可以提供一种几乎万无一失的身份识别和验证方法。例如，一些食品杂货店、零售店和加油站使用的生物识别付款，其中客户的指纹可以被指纹读取器读取，而指纹读取器可被连接到支付方式如支票账户或信用卡。在这种情况下，用户不需要记住自己的用户名和密码。拥有的东西可能会丢失、复制或者被盗。相反，个人特征是唯一的，不会被遗忘或丢失。

　　生物识别设备的确不完美。如果你割破了手指，那么指纹识别器可能会识别不出你是一个合法用户。手形阅读器可能会传播细菌。抑或是在紧张的情况下，你的签名可能不会与文件上的相匹配。当你喉咙痛时，语音识别系统可能也会识别不出你。另外，很多人不是很喜欢使用虹膜扫描仪的这种想法。

Part 3   Listening and Speaking

Listening Comprehension

　1.（A）   2.（C）   3.（D）

Original

Hacker and Cracker

When you think of computer security, it's a good bet that some of your thinking drifts to hackers and crackers. These are both security threats that you have to **take into account**. But do you know the difference?

Originally, the term "hacker" described any amateur computer programmer intensely interested in the arcane and recondite workings of any computer operating system, and discovers ways to make software run more efficiently. In a broader sense, hacker describes anyone who writes computer programs, modifies computer hardware, or tinkers with computers or electronic devices for fun. Hackers might discover holes within systems and "hack" on a problem until they find a solution, and always keep trying to make their equipment work in new, more efficient ways. Hackers constantly seek further knowledge, freely share what they have discovered, and never intentionally damage data.

Due to sensationalized depictions in films and other modern media, the popular definition of hacker has changed to describe a person who maliciously breaks into computer networks with the intent to snoop, steal data, or **tamper with** files.

Legitimate hackers resent the association of the term hacker with criminal activity. They use the term "cracker" to describe someone who breaks into networks or otherwise violates the system integrity of remote machines with malicious intent. "Phishers" are similar to crackers. A phisher tries to trick users into giving sensitive information such as government ID numbers, credit card numbers or account passwords.

Dictation

1. defenses	2. offering	3. harmless	4. filled	5. slept
6. rest	7. invites	8. access	9. backdoor	10. immediately
11. install	12. goals	13. outbreak	14. variety	15. temporary
16. manually	17. automatically	18. alternate	19. threat	20. hide

Unit 11

Part 1 Reading and Translating

Section A

Ⅰ. 1. F   2. F   3. T   4. T   5. F
Ⅱ. 1. D   2. D   3. B
Ⅲ. 1. b   2. d   3. a   4. e   5. c
Ⅳ.
1. begins   2. involved   3. developers   4. refers   5. connecting
6. using   7. behind   8. collaborate   9. needed   10. cycle

Ⅴ. 软件演化

在软件工程领域,软件演化是指基于各种原因的软件开发、软件维护以及软件更新的过程。软件改变是不可避免的,因为在一个软件的生命周期中有许多因素会发生改变。这些因素包括:

- 需求的变更
- 环境的变化
- 错误或安全漏洞
- 添加了新设备或删除了旧设备

• 系统的改进

对于很多公司,它们最大的业务投资之一就是软件和软件开发。软件被视作是非常关键的资产,因此管理者希望确保他们所雇佣的软件工程师团队能够致力于确保软件系统通过不断演化来保持最新。

Section B

Ⅰ. 1. F　　　2. F　　　3. T　　　4. T　　　5. F

Ⅱ. 1. C　　　2. B　　　3. D

Ⅲ. 1. d　　　2. c　　　3. e　　　4. b　　　5. a

Ⅳ.
1. activities　　2. documenting　　3. extent　　4. development　　5. complexity
6. reliability　　7. disastrous　　8. analysis　　9. including　　10. contrast

Ⅴ. 回归测试

每当开发人员更改或修改他们的软件时,即使很小的调整也可能产生意想不到的后果。回归测试是测试现有的软件应用程序,以确保所做的更改或添加未破坏任何现有的功能。其目的是捕获可能意外引入到新的构建版或候选发布版中的错误,并确保先前已消除的错误仍然被消除。通过重新运行最初解决已知问题时编写的测试方案,可以确保对应用程序的任何新的更改都不会导致性能下降或导致以前正常工作的组件失效。此类测试可以在小型项目上手动执行,但是在大多数情况下,每次进行更新时都重复进行一整套测试非常耗时且复杂,因此通常需要使用自动化测试工具。

Part 3　Listening and Speaking

Listening Comprehension

1.（A）　　　2.（B）　　　3.（C）

Original

Extreme Programming

Extreme Programming（XP）is a form of agile software development methodologies and one of the best-known iterative processes. In XP, the phases are carried out in extremely small or "continuous" steps compared to the older, "batch" processes. Four basic activities are performed within the software development process: coding, testing, listening and designing.

The main aim of XP is to reduce the cost of change. Proponents of XP in general regard ongoing changes to requirements as a natural, inescapable and desirable aspect of software development projects; they believe that adaptability to changing requirements at any point during the project life is a more realistic and better approach than attempting to define all requirements at the beginning of a project and then expending effort to control changes to the requirements.

XP is successful because it emphasizes customer involvement and promotes team work, improving a software project in four essential ways: communication, simplicity, feedback and courage. XP programmers communicate with their customers and fellow programmers; they keep their design simple and clean; they get feedback by testing their software starting enday the; they deliver the system to the customers as early as possible and implement changes as suggested. With this foundation XP programmers are able to courageously respond to changing requirements and technology.

Extreme Programming was created by Kent Beck, a prominent Smalltalk[1] practitioner, during his work on a project at DaimlerChrysler[2] since 1996. And a book on the method, Extreme Programming Explained, was written by him and published in 1999.

Although XP itself is relatively new, many of its practices have been around for some time. For example, the "practice of test-first development, planning and writing tests before each micro-increment" was used as early as NASA's Project Mercury[3], in the early 1960. Refactoring, modularity, bottom-up and incremental design were described by Leo Brodie in his book published in 1984.

Dictation

1. general-purpose 2. graphical 3. artifacts 4. notation 5. blueprints
6. reusable 7. cycle 8. implementation 9. categories 10. behavior
11. interactions 12. behavior 13. leadership 14. proposed 15. matured
16. followed 17. adopted 18. compatible 19. evolved 20. advantage

Unit 12

Part 1 Reading and Translating

Section A

Ⅰ. 1. F 2. F 3. F 4. F 5. T
Ⅱ. 1. C 2. D 3. C 4. a 5. e
Ⅲ. 1. b 2. c 3. d 4. a 5. e
Ⅳ.
1. programmed 2. However 3. debated 4. inherently 5. proponents
6. individually 7. resolving 8. characteristics 9. observe 10. exhibits

Ⅴ. 物理智能体

物理智能体（机器人）是一个用来完成各项任务的可编程系统。简单的机器人可以用在制造行业，从事一些日常的工作，如装配、焊接或油漆。有些组织使用移动机器人去做一些日常的分发工作，如分发邮件或信件到不同的房间。移动机器人可以在水下探测石油。

人型机器人是一种自治的移动机器人，它模仿人类的行为。虽然人型机器人只在科幻小说中流行，但是要使这种机器人能合理地与周围环境交互并从环境里发生的事件中学习，这里面还有很多工作要做。

Section B

Ⅰ. 1. F 2. F 3. F 4. T 5. T
Ⅱ. 1. D 2. D 3. C 4. b 5. e
Ⅲ. 1. d 2. c 3. a 4. b 5. e
Ⅳ.
1. comprised 2. depending 3. thinking 4. refers 5. given
6. connected 7. input 8. actually 9. simple 10. likely

Ⅴ. LSTM 网络

长短期记忆网络通常被称为"LSTM"，是一种特殊的 RNN，它能够学习长期依赖关系。它由 Hochreiter & Schmidhuber（1997）提出，并在随后的工作中被许多人改进和推广。它们在各种各样的问题上表现得非常好，因此现在被广泛使用。

LSTM 是为了避免长期依赖性问题而专门设计的。记住长期信息实际上是这种模型的默认行为，而无须专门学习。

Part 3 Listening and Speaking

Listening Comprehension

1.（D） 2.（D） 3.（A）

Original
Supervised Learning

Supervised learning is the machine learning task of learning a function that maps an input to an output based on example input-output pairs. It infers a function from labeled training data consisting of a set of training examples. In supervised learning, each example is a pair consisting of an input object (typically a vector) and a desired output value (also called the supervisory signal). A supervised learning algorithm analyzes the training data and produces an inferred function, which can be used for mapping new examples. An optimal scenario will allow for the algorithm to correctly determine the class labels for unseen instances. This requires the learning algorithm to generalize from the training data to unseen situations in a "reasonable" way.

When the training data contains explicit examples of what the correct output should be for given inputs, then we are within the supervised learning setting that we have covered so far. Consider the hand-written digit recognition problem. A reasonable data set for this problem is a collection of images of hand-written digits, and for each image, what the digit actually is. We thus have a set of examples of the form (image, digit).

The learning is supervised in the sense that some 'supervisor' has taken the trouble to look at each input, in this case an image, and determine the correct output, in this case one of the ten categories {0, 1, 2, 3, 4, 5, 6, 7, 8, 9}.

While we are on the subject of variations, there is more than one way that a data set can be presented to the learning process. Data sets are typically created and presented to us in their entirety at the outset of the learning process.

Dictation

1. branch
2. labeled
3. responding
4. absence
5. Alternatives
6. setting
7. classification
8. coins
9. clusters
10. unlabeled
11. identical
12. obvious
13. ambiguous
14. Nonetheless
15. viewed
16. patterns
17. categorize
18. general
19. various
20. properties

Bibliography

[1] Misty E. Verrmaat, Susan L. Sebok, Steven M. Freund, Jennifer T. Campbell, Mark Frydenberg. Discovering Computers: Tools, Apps, Devices, and the Impact of Technology[M]. Cengage Learning, 2016.

[2] Misty E. Verrmaat, Susan L. Sebok, Steven M. Freund, Jennifer T. Campbell, Mark Frydenberg. Discovering Computers: Technology in a World of Computers, Mobile Devices, and the Internet, Enhanced[M]. Cengage Learning, 2015.

[3] George Beekman, Ben Beekman. Digital Planet: Tomorrow's Technology and You[M]. 10th ed. Pearson Education Limited, 2014.

[4] Deborah Morley, Charles S. Parker. Understanding Computers: Today and Tomorrow[M]. 15th ed. Cengage Learning, 2015.

[5] Gary B. Shelly, Misty E. Verrmaat, Jeffrey J. Quasney, Susan L. Sebok, Steven M. Freund. Discovering Computers, Complete: Your Interactive Guide to the Digital World[M]. Cengage Learning, 2012.

[6] June Jamrich Parsons, Dan Oja. New Perspectives on Computer Concepts, 2014, Comprehensive[M]. Cengage Learning, 2014.

[7] Kenneth C Laudon, Carol Guercio Traver. E-commerce 2014: Business. Technology. Society[M]. 9th ed. Pearson Education, 2014.

[8] Roger S. Pressman. Software Engineering: A Practitioner's Approach[M]. 6th edition. New York, NY: McGraw-Hill, 2005.

[9] Ian Sommerville. Software Engineering[M]. 8th edition. Addison Wesley, 2005.

[10] Timothy J. O'Leary, Linda I. O'Leary. Computing Essentials 2014 Complete Edition[M]. New York, NY: McGraw-Hill, 2014.

[11] Misty E. Vermaat. Discovering Computers 2014[M]. 1st ed. Cengage Learning, 2014.

[12] J. Glenn Brookshear. Computer Science: An Overview[M]. 11th ed. Cengage Learning, 2012.

[13] Brian K. Williams, Stacey C. Sawyer. Using Information Technology[M]. 11th ed. New York, NY: McGraw-Hill, 2015.

[14] June Jamrich Parsons. New Perspectives on Computer Concepts, 2016, Comprehensive[M]. Cengage Learning, 2016.

[15] Nell Dale, John Lewis. Computer Science Illuminated[M]. 5th ed. Jones & Bartlett Learning, 2013.

[16] Jeff Butterfield. Illustrated Course Guide: Written Communication—Soft Skills for a Digital Workplace[M]. Cengage Learning, 2010.

[17] Timothy J. O'Leary, Linda I. O'Leary. Daniel A. O'Leary. Computing Essentials 2015 Complete Edition[M]. New York, NY: McGraw-Hill, 2015.

[18] John M. Lannon, Laura J. Gurak. 科技交流：职场沟通、调研分析与文档写作[M]. 王朔中, 译. 13版. 北京：清华大学出版社, 2016.

[19] 吕云翔. 软件工程专业英语[M]. 北京：清华大学出版社, 2014.

[20] 吕云翔. 计算机英语实用教程[M]. 北京：清华大学出版社, 2015.

[21] 吕云翔. 计算机英语教程[M]. 2版. 北京：人民邮电出版社, 2016.

[22] 吕云翔. 大学实用计算机英语教程[M]. 2版. 北京：机械工业出版社, 2016.

[23] 吕云翔. 计算机专业英语[M]. 北京：电子工业出版社, 2018.

[24] Misty E. Vermaat, Susan, L. Setbok, Steven M. Freund, Jennifer T. Campbell, Mark Frydenberg.

Discovering Computers 2017 Enhanced Edition: Tools, Apps, Devices, and the Impact of Technology[M]. Cengage Learning, 2017.

[25] Deborah Morley, Charles S. Parker. Understanding Computers: Today and Tomorrow, 16th Edition[M]. Cengage Learning, 2017.

[26] Timothy J. O'Leary, Daniel O'Leary, Linda I. O'Leary. Computing Essentials 2017 Complete Edition: Making IT Work for You[M]. New York, NY: McGraw-Hill, 2017.

[27] June Jamrich Parsons. New Perspectives on Computer Concepts 2016, Comprehensive[M]. Cengage Learning, 2017.

[28] June Jamrich Parsons. New Perspectives on Computer Concepts 2018, Comprehensive[M]. Cengage Learning, 2018.

[29] Timothy J. O'Leary, Daniel O'Leary, Linda I. O'Leary. Computing Essentials 2021 Complete Edition: Making IT Work for You[M]. New York, NY: McGraw-Hill, 2020.

图书资源支持

感谢您一直以来对清华版图书的支持和爱护。为了配合本书的使用,本书提供配套的资源,有需求的读者请扫描下方的"书圈"微信公众号二维码,在图书专区下载,也可以拨打电话或发送电子邮件咨询。

如果您在使用本书的过程中遇到了什么问题,或者有相关图书出版计划,也请您发邮件告诉我们,以便我们更好地为您服务。

我们的联系方式:

地　　址:北京市海淀区双清路学研大厦 A 座 714

邮　　编:100084

电　　话:010-83470236　010-83470237

客服邮箱:2301891038@qq.com

QQ:2301891038(请写明您的单位和姓名)

资源下载: 关注公众号"书圈"下载配套资源。

书　圈

获取最新书目

观看课程直播